ORDINAL MEASUREMENT
IN THE BEHAVIORAL SCIENCES

ORDINAL MEASUREMENT
IN THE BEHAVIORAL SCIENCES

Norman Cliff
University of Southern California

John A. Keats
University of Newcastle

2003

LAWRENCE ERLBAUM ASSOCIATES, PUBLISHERS
Mahwah, New Jersey   London

Lawrence Erlbaum Associates, Inc., Publishers
10 Industrial Avenue
Mahwah, New Jersey 07430

Cover design by Kathryn Houghtaling Lacey

Library of Congress Cataloging-in-Publication Data

Copyright information for this volume can be obtained by contacting
the Library of Congress.

ISBN: 0-8058-2093-0

Printed in the United States of America
10   9   8   7   6   5   4   3   2   1

Contents

Preface

This book is motivated to a large extent by our dissatisfaction with current practices in behavioral measurement. Most of the basic data consists of dichotomous responses, and much of the rest is made of responses on short scales. Neither type of data furnishes information that can inherently be considered more than ordinal. The dominant contemporary treatment of this data is to derive from it scores on interval-scale latent variables through the application of one or another"model" that is presumed to explain the data. We feel that, in the majority of instances, the application of these models is inappropriate: The models either do not fit the data, or are even inherently self-contradictory.

Application of these models then can lead to unwarranted inferences by users concerning the status of the derived variables, although in many instances little use is ever made of their presumed interval-scale properties. These methods are also difficult to apply, particularly in small-sample contexts such as classroom or research measurement unless additional assumptions that are even more unrealistic are made.

What we try to do in this book is to provide alternatives to these methods, alternatives that stay much closer to the original data. Thus, our approach can be looked on as a turn to simple empiricism in psychological measurement. However, our empiricism is based on ordinal rather than interval scale concepts, and so we feel it is more realistic than current approaches or older ones such as classical test theory. Behavioral data is inherently noisy, so we emphasize providing summary scores and also information on the relative amount of noise there is in the data, rather than imposing a parametric model on it.

The largest segment of the book is devoted to methods for analyzing test responses, but we also provide extensive discussions of ordinal approaches to analyzing data that are judgments of stimuli.

Methods for treating psychological data in ways consistent with its ordinal nature have received much less attention than model-fitting approaches have. One of our hopes in publishing this book, which presents much of the material that is currently available in widely scattered sources, is to stimulate additional developments of this nature. Some new developments of this nature are also included.

The book reflects important facets of our long-term research interests. Cliff published a number of papers on these topics over the years, and the publication of his book on ordinal statistics, *Ordinal Methods for Behavioral Data Analysis* (1996), reinforced the idea of a need to increase the availability of ordinal measurement methods. The interest of Keats in applying an ordinal approach to test theory dates to the 1950s and he has extended these developments in subsequent decades, including his (1972) *Introduction to Quantitative Psychology*. Another area that uses ordering is the unfolding technique, in which Keats was a pioneer. Ordinal test theory and the unfolding methods are applicable to cross-cultural studies, a neglected focus in measurement, and this is another important topic here.

A wide spectrum of persons who are concerned with psychological measurement should find this book relevant. It should find a place in courses on psychological measurement from upper undergraduate level to graduate seminars, because it takes measurement in a different but important direction. We have made a considerable effort to keep the mathematics to a minimum, and what remains is at a low technical level. Inevitably in a quantitative field there are a number of formulas, but our intent was to make them useful and show their interrelationships in a simple, informal manner. Professionals whose research involves measurement will find that the book provides useful and simple methods as well as stimulating thought about measurement's real issues.

The book is very much a collaborative effort, but primary responsibility for its content was divided between authors on the basis of interests and previous research. Keats was the main author of chapters 1, 3, 4, 5, 9, 10, and Appendix A; Cliff was primarily responsible for the remaining chapters, 2, 6, 7, and 8. However, the book is the outcome of much exchanging of drafts, comments, and suggestions, so it is overall a mutual creation.

We wish to thank a number of people for contributing to the development of the ideas. Over the years, many of Cliff's students have participated in the developments and discussions included here. Among them most recently are Drs. John Caruso of the University of Montana, Lei Chang of Hongkong University, Du Feng of Texas Tech University, Jeffrey Long of the University of Minnesota; earlier students were Drs. Linda M. Collins, Robert F. Cudeck, Rex M. Green, Jerard F. Kehoe, Douglas J. McCormick, Thomas J. Reynolds, and Judith M. Zatkin. Drs. Don Munro and Mark Chorlton, as well as Scott Brown, of the University of Newcastle, who worked on the writing and testing of the computer program used and listed in Appendix A and used it in the analysis of data reported in chapter 10, are also thanked for their help. However, the responsibility for the final result, including any errors, omissions, and misinterpretations, rests with us.

Our wives, Rosemary Cliff and Daphne Keats have been highly supportive of this effort, as well as helpful in many ways, and we are very grateful to them.

Norman Cliff
John A. Keats

Chapter 1

The Purpose of Psychological Assessment

The aim of this book is to provide the reader with a background of ordinal theory which can be used to assess psychological tests and psychological and psychophysical scales and to assist with the interpretation of data obtained by means of these instruments and methods. The need for such a book at this time arises in part from the fact that university courses in psychology and education often contain very little such background and theory relating to tests and scales. Recently, however, there has been a resurgence of interest in testing and a concern that people using tests should be adequately trained to do so. This concern has been expressed by the International Test Commission (1998, 2000). There is a felt need for more courses and relevant books in this field of ordinal measurement in the behavioral sciences.

Current books on this topic often perpetuate ideas that led to the rejection of the classical test theories (CTT) of the 1950s, which came to paradoxical conclusions. Other current books are pitched at such a high mathematical level as to be inaccessible to most behavioral scientists. It is not unreasonable to argue that the field has been overintellectualized in that many of the representations are based on matrix algebra, latent trait theory, and maximum likelihood methods which are not needed to assess psychological and educational tests and to develop their applications. Moreover, they tend to lend an aura of exactitude to score numbers that do not justify such confidence. We consider this issue again in the next chapter.

NEW MYTHS AND OLD RULES

Some texts written by proponents of item response theory (IRT) contain comparisons of that theory with CTT. As an example we can consider Embretsen's chapter 1 (Embretson, 1999) in Embretsen and Hershberger (1999). Although it is not our view that CTT is without flaws, our methods do overlap with it to a certain extent, so it will be useful to go over Embretson's (1999) "rules." In her presentation, "Old Rules," which purportedly characterize CTT, and "New Rules," which purportedly characterize IRT, are compared. We believe that these "rules" erroneously characterize CTT, IRT, or both, leaving the reader with an inappropriate idea of the state of knowledge in the area.

"Old Rule 1. The standard error of measurement applies to all scores in a particular population" (Embretson, 1999, p. 11). Embretson characterized this as descriptive of CTT. However, it was long known among experts in CTT that this was not the case (Keats, 1957; Keats & Lord, 1962). Methods for estimating individual standard errors were beyond the capabilities of routine computing application at that time and the methods were never implemented when computing facilities improved. It is true that the "constant standard error" myth was perpetuated in many measurement texts (e.g., McDonald, 1999, pp. 68 and 130) and in the manuals of some test publishers.

The old rule is contrasted with: "New Rule 1. The standard error of measurement differs between persons with different response patterns but generalizes across populations" (Embretsen, 1999, p. 11). However, the sense in which IRT provides a quantity that corresponds to the "standard error of measurement" of CTT is not clear; what is apparently intended in this "New Rule" is some sort of average discrepancy between estimated true score and actual true score, rather than a specific quantity like CTT's standard error of estimate. Although this "Rule" is true in IRT under ideal conditions, it holds with several caveats. One is that the error of measurement depends on the model fitted. The assertion "generalizes across populations" will often be false because the relations among items will differ in different populations. This is a particularly sensitive issue when the populations are from different cultures, including different ethnic groups. Empirical investigations of issues like this are extremely rare in IRT in comparison to the confidence with which the conclusions are stated. In a more technical vein, IRT does not usually provide a literal "standard error of measurement" in the same sense one would normally expect, accuracy of measurement being defined in other ways.

The mischaracterization continues. "Old Rule 2. Longer tests are more reliable than shorter tests. New Rule 2. Shorter tests can be more reliable than longer tests" (Embretsen, 1999, p. 12). Although a specific form of the

"Old Rule" (the Spearman–Brown formula) was part of CTT, it was to be applied under very specific circumstances. An accurate statement of the Old Rule would have included the proviso "other things being equal." The methods of item analysis under CTT, and even informal versions of it, could well lead to an improvement of reliability with a shorter test, so New Rule 2 is not new. However, the usual fact is that if items are constructed reasonably carefully, Old Rule 2 applies as a general finding under IRT as well as CTT. Incidentally, one weakness of IRT is that there is no provision for estimating the increase in accuracy of measurement from adding more than one item.

There is a third dubious comparison. "Old Rule 3. Comparing test scores across multiple forms depends on test parallelism or equating. New Rule 3. Comparing test scores is optimal when test difficulty levels vary between persons" (Embretsen, 1999, p. 13). This is one case where the Old Rule is an accurate description of CTT. The New Rule 3 is an accurate description of IRT, provided it is modified to include the requirement that the items at different difficulty levels have more-or-less equal discriminating power. Embretsen's arguments in favor of this New Rule neglect to consider the necessity of extensively pretesting items to determine their difficulty and discriminating power before they can be used in actual measurement. It is very possible that "savings" to the examinee under IRT in terms of number of items taken are largely illusory if the number of testings required to estimate item parameters are included. It is also true that estimates of accuracy of measurement with computer adaptive testing have rarely been tested in a manner that satisfies ordinary tenets of the scientific method, which would require comparison of truly independent measurements.

"Old Rule 4. Unbiased estimates of item properties depend on representative samples from the target population" (Embretson, 1999, p. 13). This is true of CTT. However, "New Rule 4. Unbiased estimates of item properties may be obtained from unrepresentative samples" (Embretson, 1999, p. 13) is true of IRT, but in a more limited sense than might be inferred from the statement and discussion. For "New Rule 4" to apply, two things must be true: The IRT model must fit the data and the same model must fit two or more sets of data. Where the former is not the case, such as when the items are multidimensional, it is very doubtful that unbiased and comparable estimates of item parameters would be obtained. When the latter is not true, as when there are cultural differences between the groups, including ethnic, gender, age, or educational differences, the statement will not necessarily apply.

In this section, the problems of dealing with various aspects of testing have been noted. These problems would have justified the production of a book concerned with them. In addition to the book by Embretson and Herschberger (1999) dealing with rules of measurement there is a book by McDonald (1999) on Test Theory, which is commented on in a later chapter.

Whereas the applications of tests and scales are once again being widely understood, the relationships between these theories and those of psychophysical scaling are not being so widely appreciated. Initially psychophysical scaling was developed to explore possible relationships between physical measurement and the perceived psychological intensity of stimuli measured on a physical dimension (i.e., between the perceived weight of an object and its actual physical weight as measured by a balance). It was hoped to define a psychophysical function relating the physical measure to the psychological intensity. This endeavor was more closely linked to purely experimental psychology than to a concern to tackle psychological problems using quantitative methods.

The currently dominant test theories, loosely grouped under the label of item response theory or IRT, depend on untestable assumptions as shown later, and in the absence of testable assumptions rely on goodness of fit to data for their justification. This reliance is not scientifically justifiable because many different theoretical formulations can account for the same set of data.

THIS BOOK'S MOTIVATION

The theoretical background and its application presented in this book do not suffer from these defects. The theoretical background presented depends on testable assumptions at each stage and includes optimal ways of estimating the underlying order of persons being assessed by the instruments. The theory requires only elementary algebra with few extensions to understand it. Furthermore, the ordinal theory applies to data from items that order the subjects into any number of ordered categories. A particularly important application of the theory is to assess the suitability of tests or other instruments for each of two or more different cultures.

Another reason for producing this book lies in the fact that the most scientifically defensible theory of measurement in the behavioral sciences, the Luce and Tukey (1964) conjoint measurement theory, has not received the attention in the literature that it deserves (see Cliff, 1991). The reasons for the neglect of this theory by experimental psychologists and by those concerned with individual differences in behavior are obscure. The theory itself is based, in testing applications, on consistent conjoint ordering of both persons and stimuli or items, and so is linked with ordinal measurement. Interval scaling requires a further axiom, the cancellation axiom, as noted by Harrington (1985). However, this axiom has seldom been examined empirically, and is sometimes overlooked by writers who assume that the conjoint ordering of persons and items is sufficient to define interval scales. Jensen (1980) is one such person (see Harrington, 1985). Although McDonald (1999) discussed interval scaling, he does not refer to conjoint measurement and the cancellation axiom in relation to test theory.

A further point we should make here is that the ordinal methods we describe in later chapters can be applied in small samples such as with classroom tests or research instruments whereas IRT cannot, except in a very limited form. Also, Many CTT and OTT formulas apply to total scores on heterogeneous (multifactor) tests, whereas IRT can be applied there in only a limited way. These points are discussed in more detail later.

SOME HISTORICAL BACKGROUND OF TESTING

The method of presentation in the balance of this chapter is to some extent historical because this approach shows the stages at which certain important ideas were first put forward and the reasons why some of these ideas were later rejected while others persisted despite theoretical and practical objections. The history cited is selective and readers interested in this aspect should consult Thorndike and Lohman's (1990) *A Century of Ability Testing* for further details.

Social Changes and Their Effects on Test Development

One purpose of this chapter is to link the development of tests to certain social changes that took place since the 1850s. The early reasons for developing tests are presented with a description of how these reasons led to certain types of tests and methods for their construction. Many of these reasons were based on the need to solve certain social problems, a need which still exists today. However, the way in which testing contributes to the solution of these problems has changed considerably over the years, and, of course, research results have changed the perception of these problems and their treatment.

Over the early period of test development, the discipline of experimental psychology itself was being established by Wundt (1902) following the work of Weber and Fechner (see Fechner, trans. 1965) among others. Within 20 years workers from this laboratory, such as J. McK. Cattell (1890) were studying individual differences in response times and sensitivity to various kinds of physical stimulation. In the other direction, Binet also published on psychophysical methods applied to weight perception in addition to his pioneering work on psychological testing (Binet & Simon, 1916).

Mental Age and IQ

Another purpose of the chapter is to acquaint the reader with the various types of tests and scales that have been developed and marketed over the years. In a course based on this book, copies of some of these tests should be available to students.

The assessment of people on a variety of variables has a long history but it increased dramatically in the 20th century. The main reason for this increase lies in the aggregation of large numbers of people into larger towns and cities from smaller villages and rural centers, which was brought about by the industrial revolution. During this time there was also a rapid increase in population.

This aggregation in western countries drew attention to the need for institutions to supervise children and to take care of the mentally retarded and the mentally ill. The aggregation of children into large population units also led to exploitation of child labor and to the development of delinquent gangs so well described by Dickens in his *Oliver Twist* and elsewhere. In the mid-19th century, the arguments for establishing compulsory schooling were based in part on these two social problems of child labor exploitation and child delinquency, as is shown by the Hansard reports of the House of Commons debates at the time. The role of schools as child-minding centers justified their establishment; their role as educational agencies came later. Problems associated with the developmentally delayed and the physically and mentally handicapped, which could be handled at the village level, were also greatly accentuated by urbanization.

In recent decades, the developing countries of Africa, Asia, and elsewhere have experienced urbanization, which has led to the same sorts of problems of child delinquency and exploitation as well as the caring for the developmentally delayed and the physically handicapped such as the blind and deaf. Although some of these countries are developing universal education, they have not yet managed to provide services needed by handicapped children. The assessment of children before the introduction of compulsory education was restricted to private schools usually conducted by religious bodies. With compulsory education came the assessment of almost all children on the subjects taught in schools. One need for assessment arose with the recognition of the fact that not all children of the age of admission to schooling could benefit from the type of education provided. The test to identify such children was developed in France by Binet and Simon (1916) in the early 20th century. This was one of the first psychological tests based on empirical data and statistical analysis.

Binet developed the concept of mental age, which was later extended to the ratio IQ by Stern (1914). The test was administered on an individual basis and the children had to respond to the questions in their own words and actions.

A creative answer test of this kind requires the tester to be very familiar with answers to be judged as correct. This test became widely used in translation in United States, England, and Australia and led to the development of a large number of intelligence tests for children including the maze test for children and adults constructed in Australia by Porteus (1915). The task was to identify children who could and could not benefit from the type of education provided.

While these tests were being developed, a quite different type of test was being used to assess performance in skills such as reading and arithmetic. Although some of these tests were also creative answer tests, others were multiple choice with the subject having to choose from a number of alternatives, only one of which was correct. The need for such tests seems to have been first appreciated by Kirkpatrick (1900) who wrote:

> It is desirable to have tests of such a nature that they can be taken by children as well as adults, that they shall be such that all persons tested will have about equal opportunity for the exercise of the ability tested, and that in the interest of economy of time, the tests so far as possible shall be so planned that they can be given to a whole class or school at once, instead of to each individual separately. (pp. 279–280)

Kelly (1903) elaborated on this proposal by calling for "norms in terms of which a child can readily be classed for pedagogical purposes" (p. 371). Later, Kelly (1914) suggested the use of standard scores, which were calculated as the difference between a score and the mean score for the appropriate standardization group divided by the standard deviation of scores for that group. To avoid decimals and negative numbers the standard scores were multiplied by 10 or 15, and were increased by 50 or 100 to produce positive numbers. This method is in very wide use today but has problems. For example, the number obtained does not give a precise indication of the position a person would have relative to the standardization group. Scores from tests can be skewed in either direction and display other forms of non-normality.

Figure 1.1 presents examples of test score distributions for the same test at different ages smoothed by the hypogeometric distribution (Keats, 1964). These examples show the extent of this skewness. To overcome this problem the norms were sometimes supplemented by percentile ranks (i.e., the percentage of the standardization group gaining a particular score or less). Otis (1917) suggested that standard scores could have percentile ranks built into them by means of the normal distribution with a mean of 100 and a standard deviation of 15.

Such scores were sometimes called IQs. The parameters 15 and 100 arose from the fact that the Binet IQ tended to have these parameters at various age levels, and this choice would make the two IQs more comparable. This comparability led to confusion. The Otis approach is the one used today as the basis of the deviation IQ used in such tests as the Wechsler Adult Intelligence Scale (WAIS; Wechsler, 1997).

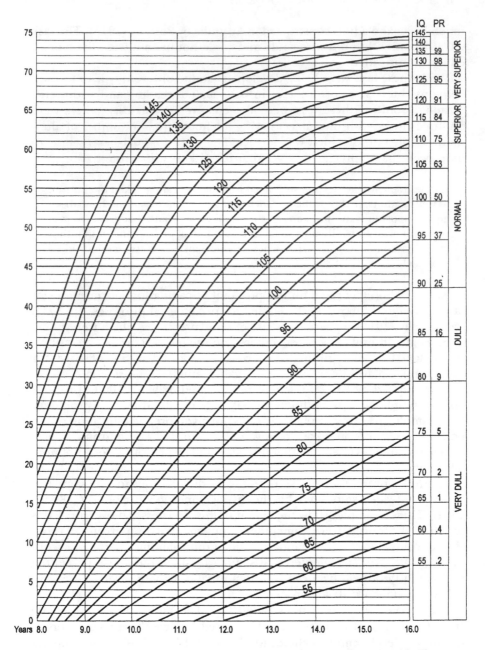

FIG. 1.1. Raw scores (y axis) and IQs (curves) as a function of age (x axis). The spacing of the curves at different ages shows that the IQ scores have different, and non-normal, distributions at different ages.

8

Derived in this way, the IQ is essentially an ordinal measure. However, there are problems with this approach when used to combine subtests to form a total IQ in the way used by Wechsler (1939). These problems are discussed in chapter 3 and a more efficient method for combining scores from subtests is given (see pp. 62–63, 71–72).

As noted by a number of writers, the extremely common use of the normal curve was based on a mutual misunderstanding between researchers and mathematical statisticians. The researchers believed that statisticians had *proved* that all distributions of measures of natural phenomena must conform to the normal curve. On the other hand, the statisticians believed that empirical scientists had *found* that the distributions of most if not all measures of natural phenomena did in fact conform to the normal distribution. Actually, there is no mathematical proof or empirical evidence in support of normal distribution, but the effects of this absence of proof are noted in later chapters. The statisticians were doubtless also influenced by the fact that the normal distribution has some very satisfying statistical properties.

Educational Testing

Tests are extensively used by teachers today to monitor the progress of their students and, in particular, to detect those who are having difficulties in some subject areas and so need remedial instruction. In some cases the results of these tests may indicate the need for further testing. For example, children who are poor readers may be given special tests to determine whether or not they are dyslexic or whether or not they are able to think operationally at a particular level according to Piaget's tasks (Piaget, 1947; Keats, 1985). These formal assessments of school performance may be made relative to the particular class or school or relative to a representative sample from a population.

On a larger scale, tests such as the Scholastic Aptitude Tests (SAT) are also used to select students who are more likely to succeed in college or university. Although scores that order performance in a particular subject are readily obtained, the problem of combining these across subjects when not all students attempt all subjects has not been solved in a satisfactory way. Another problem with these selection tests arises from the need to create a new test yearly and make scores on each new version equivalent.

Thus, the field of educational testing was developed to help solve practical problems. Is this child likely to benefit from the type of education universally provided? Or, more recently, what type of education will be most appropriate for this child? Is this child doing much better or worse in one subject than she or he is doing in another? Is it necessary to provide some remedial teaching for this child in a particular subject? Should this student be admitted to this type of secondary school rather than some other type? Should this student be admitted to a particular university faculty? The solutions to these problems would require ordering rather than measuring procedures.

Military and Industrial Testing

Although it seems reasonable to use written tests to select for higher education, it seems less obvious that they will be useful for selecting applicants for training in the skilled trades. The fact that they can be effective for this broader purpose was shown in their use for selecting personnel for various aspects of military training during World War I. This practice was opposed in France by psychiatrists despite Binet's advice and the army testing activity in Germany and the United States. Thus the need for tests became more evident because of large-scale warfare and its need for assessment of adults.

In World War II a situation arose in Australia rather similar to that in France in World War I. The Army Medical Corps in Australia successfully objected to the rejection of volunteers on the basis of psychological tests after the Medical Corps had pronounced them to be fit for service. However, the Psychology Corps had the responsibility for allocating recruits for various types of training. It therefore allocated all recruits shown by the tests to be mentally unfit for service to the Medical Corps. It did not take long for the Medical Corps to remove its objection to the rejection of volunteers on the basis of psychological tests (D. W. McElwain, personal communication, 1962).

Psychological tests would not have been used so widely if they had not been shown to be valid in a variety of situations. The military situation is one that enables checks to be carried out on the situational validity and economic advantages of testing. The United States Army Air Force admitted 1,000 recruits for training without applying the standards it usually used for admission, which were based on group testing. The results after training showed clearly the economic advantages of testing. Many validity studies have confirmed this finding in other areas. Although the economic advantages of testing are important, the human benefit of preventing the needless training and subsequent disappointment of those who are shown to be unsuited for the type of occupation being considered is also as great or even greater.

That the success of psychological tests in practice had led to a certain complacency was noted by Tomkins (1952) and confirmed by Buros (1977). Tomkins observed that because tests had been so successful, psychologists had stopped doing research that might improve them. Buros (1977) reported that "except for the tremendous advances in electronic scoring, analysis and reporting of test results, we don't have much to show for fifty years of work [from 1927 to 1977]" (p. 10). This statement is a little extreme when it is appreciated that the Likert (1932) method of constructing attitude scales by using three or more ordered categories (polytomous items) was first suggested in 1932. It is shown in the following chapters that there were improvements that could have been made, but for various reasons, including perhaps that suggested by Tomkins, they were not.

In the field of vocational guidance, selection, and promotion, psychological tests have become widely used. The need for validating special tests for particular vocations became apparent. These were not only cognitive tests but tests of vocational interest and preference and other personality tests. This field is growing rapidly these days. The adaptation of such tests for use in developing countries is a matter for concern and is discussed later.

Identifying Abnormality

Apart from the problems that arose from aggregating children into larger population groups in the 19th century, there were also problems with regard to the mentally retarded referred to earlier and the mentally ill. In the smaller villages it was quite possible to look after the small number of people of these types by community support. However, when they were aggregated into the larger towns and cities it was not possible to provide the individual attention required to keep such people safe and well in the community. Large institutes sometimes called asylums were established to provide them minimal food and protection. The question of classifying such people into groups had to be solved.

With the crude classification used in the 19th century all who, for whatever reason, did not learn to speak were placed in the category labeled "idiots" or even "gibbering idiots". Such people were treated in a most inhumane manner, with a minimum of attention to proper feeding and cleanliness. The category called *idiots* included those who were profoundly deaf but at that time there was no means of testing to identify them or to assess their ability if they were deaf. There was a great deal of unfortunate suffering. Others in the asylums would have been psychotic and others again would have been profoundly mentally retarded, but there were no bases for separating these groups. Thus, there was a great need for both psychophysical and psychological tests to help diagnose people from these groups.

The category above the *idiots* was referred to as the "imbeciles." These people were able to speak and understand speech but did not seem to be able to learn to read. They were put into separate institutions and given simple manual work to do in return for food, clothing, and accommodation. Again there was a problem of diagnosis and a need for special training and education. The categories of *idiots*, *imbeciles*, and *normals* correspond in some respects to Piaget's (1947) sensorimotor, semiotic functions, and operational thinking.

Today psychological tests are used to assist in the diagnosis of all such groups and to monitor the effects of various kinds of treatment on them. With today's diagnostic assessment techniques and medical treatments many who formerly would have been kept in institutions and away from the community are now being treated within the community with much greater effectiveness and humanity, as well as with greater economy. In some ways this is a return to the pre-Industrial Revolution days when people with intellectual and behavioral problems were cared for in small communities.

The difference lies in the greater knowledge of diagnosis and treatment of behavioral problems available. Psychological testing has contributed greatly to developing these tools. Some of the clinical psychological tests used with special groups are personality tests, which have a similar rationale to that of the cognitive tests. Their administration may appear to be relatively simple but their interpretation is usually complex and requires special training and experience. Projective tests such as the Rorschach Test and the Thematic Apperception Test are quite different and do not fall within the scope of the theory presented here.

Decision Methods

In a large number of situations in which psychological tests are used, be they educational, vocational, or clinical, the final evaluation is in terms of the assignment of individuals to one of a set of ordered categories. For example, children below a certain single or composite score will receive different schooling from those above that score; adults above a certain score will be admitted to some kind of technical or university education, those below that score will not. There is a cut-off score for making such important decisions.

If there is a single score shown to be valid for making this kind of decision in a particular situation, then the evaluation is clear. However, it must be appreciated that such a cut-off score does have a fuzzy edge because no psychological test is entirely free from assessment error. Decisions about persons whose scores are close to the cut-off score must be considered carefully in terms of both test characteristics and social and other factors, which may have affected their responding one way or the other. The possible long-term effects of a particular decision have to be taken into account.

Another type of situation arises when it is desired to establish cut-off scores based on two or more test results. The practice over many decades has been to use one of two approaches, although the rationale for these is not commonly specified. One approach is to add the scores to obtain a composite score, which can then be used to establish a single cut-off score.

The component parts of the composite can be equally weighted, or some parts may be regarded as more important and so given a greater weight.

A second approach involves establishing a cut-off score for each of the tests separately and requiring a person to satisfy all of these before continuing to a further stage (e.g., admission to a certain type of training). This is referred to as the multiple cut-off procedure. Another example is the university entrance requirement applying in many Australian states, which included passes at a certain level in English and Latin as well as passes in a specified number of other subjects. As pointed out by Lord (1962), there is no complete justification for either approach. When the test scores are almost perfectly correlated, both single and multiple cut-offs will produce essentially the same results; when there is zero correlation between the scores, multiple cut-off points must be used to produce the best allocation.

Definition of Cut-Off Lines. However, most sets of scores from psychological tests fall between these two extremes, they are significantly positively correlated, but almost never coming close to being perfectly correlated. In the same article, Lord showed how for two tests a hyperbola could be defined to establish a boundary that would produce the best allocation for tests with a given level of correlation. Figure 1.2 presents a two-variable case with an optimum curved cut-off line for positive correlations between the variables. Again, it must be emphasized that all such cut-off lines have fuzzy edges and people with scores close to them should receive careful consideration.

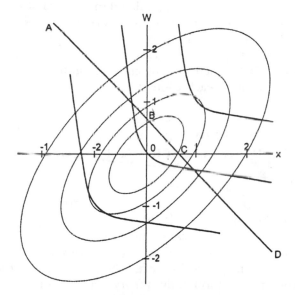

FIG. 1.2. Simple (straight) and optimum (curved) cutoff lines for selection.

Although there was a great impetus to the development of psychological tests arising from the socioeconomic effects of industrialization and from the needs of the armed forces during war time, the reasons for using psychological testing have persisted and increased in number. Their use has grown with increased prosperity in the developed countries. Furthermore, a much wider range of tests to cover different circumstances has been developed (e.g., tests to detect neurological damage). One outcome of this increase in testing was the formation of the International Test Commission (ITC) in Montreal, in 1978.

TESTING IN DEVELOPING COUNTRIES

In most developing countries there has been a great increase in urbanization in recent years, and this, in turn, has led to the kinds of problems of aggregation and of acquiring new skills that occurred previously elsewhere during the Industrial Revolution. The recognition of these problems has led to greater interest in psychological and educational testing in those countries. The task of translating and adapting existing tests from developed countries for use in developing countries noted on page 61, raises further problems, which are part of the general problem of cross-cultural assessment. The alternative solution of constructing tests within the developing countries needs to be considered. These problems will be discussed in chapter 5 in terms of recently formulated International Test Commission (ITC) guidelines for adapting tests for different cultures and the ordinal test theory (OTT) developed in chapters 4 to 6. Chapter 2 describes the various types of psychological tests and assessments used in research and practice. The types of assessments will be classified in terms of the types of responses required within each content area.

THE EVOLUTION OF PHYSICAL
AND PSYCHOLOGICAL MEASUREMENT THEORY

During World War I a professor of physics, Professor Campbell, became aware that although physics was sometimes referred to as the science of measurement there was no undergraduate text setting out the theory of measurement from the physical scientists' point of view. In 1917 he published a book called *Physics: The Elements* (see Campbell, 1957) and this text was widely used in the physical sciences when teaching the theory of measurement. The simplest form of this theory assumed it was possible to carry out two distinct kinds of operations. The first of these was an ordering operation, which enabled the scientist to compare two objects with regard to an attribute and decide which of the two had more of that attribute. This operation had to be transitive so that if for three objects A was greater than B and B greater than C, then A was greater than C. If these conditions were satisfied, then the objects could be arranged on an ordinal scale. The second condition was that sets of objects could be combined with respect to the attribute in such a way that the combinations could also be compared and ordered. This pair of requirements has been refined and elaborated over the years in psychology, as noted briefly before, and we refer in later chapters to those developments and discuss their relevance to testing and other aspects of psychological measurement.

THE DEVELOPMENT OF TEST THEORY
AND PRACTICE

Up until the 1960s test theory and practice were working closely together. For example, the concepts of test reliability and validity and the effects of shortening or lengthening tests among others were rooted in test theory. The dominant test theory was based on the theory of measurement error used in the physical sciences, which treated any quantitative empirical measure as consisting of the true measure plus or minus an error term. This definition was taken up in psychology and came to be referred to as "weak true score theory" (Gulliksen, 1950). However, physical measurement assumed operations and conditions that could not be applied in psychology and certain inconsistencies and paradoxes became evident in the 1960s. In the early 1960s a "strong true score theory" was proposed by Keats and Lord (1962) and developed by Keats (1964) and Lord (1965). Although these theories corrected one or more of the errors of simple true score theory they are too complicated and computationally too difficult for applied use. Computers were not widely available. At the same time, Rasch (1960) and Luce and Tukey (1964) were developing conjoint measurement, which described practical operations and set down conditions for measurement in psychology in general and psychological testing in particular. By means of some highly dubious assumptions the Rasch formulation was generalized to what is now called Item Response Theory (Lord & Novick, 1968). The various versions of this "theory" are subject to many of these assumptions.

The axioms of conjoint measurement draw attention to the difference between simple ordering of persons and conjoint ordering, which involves the ordering of both persons and items or stimuli. Conjoint ordering must be examined to test for the homogeneity of the items. Items measuring a single dimension, should be ordered in the same way by both high and low scorers. Conjoint ordering is an important consideration in studies of differences in performance in different cultures; see chapters 5 and 10.

Although tests of cognitive performance are the ones most commonly used, other tests or scales directed toward the measurement of attitudes and preferences or values have also been developed and their use is increasing. This work was given great impetus from the article by Likert (1932) who argued that the procedures used in the cognitive area at that time could be used to prepare attitude scales of various kinds. The scales usually consisted of multiple-choice items involving a common set of ordered categories, such as strongly agree, agree, neither agree nor disagree, disagree, and strongly disagree. These categories were scored in terms of arbitrary integers such as +2, +1, 0, −1, and −2 or a variation of this.

Other types of response alternatives were also used to indicate the frequency with which a person behaved in a certain way. For example, never, seldom, sometimes, often, and very often could be used to obtain a report of a person's attending church or drinking alcohol. These self-report items required studies to discover the extent to which they were valid indicators of people's actual behavior on the one hand or simply an expression of a person's desire to present himself or herself in a socially desirable way. In a surprising number of studies, such self-reporting has been found to be acceptably accurate.

MATHEMATICAL MODELS IN TESTING

Necessity of Such Models

As most of us go through the educational system we are repeatedly tested, usually with paper and pencil tests although sometimes now they are administered via computer. Many of these tests are constructed by our own teachers, but many others are developed by central educational agencies or by commercial companies. When we take tests, numbers are assigned to our performance. Where do these numbers come from? What justification do they have? Are they numbers that have the same properties as other numbers such as the amount of money in our pocket or purse, or the temperature on a thermometer, or the distance from the earth to the sun? In this section we briefly review the history of numerical practices in the assignment of test numbers and indicate why we, the authors, are dissatisfied with most of what is currently done.

A fundamental idea in assigning numbers meaningfully is that in order for numbers, such as test scores, to be assigned to events such as actual test responses, there must be a quantitative model or a minitheory that connects them. The model can be simple or complex, empirically testable or untestable, but it must be there.

Simple Measurement Theory

Through the 1960s, much of testing was based on what we have referred to earlier as "Classical Test Theory," and here will call "simple measurement theory." It skips over testing as a physical process and just concerns itself with the numbers that result, calling them scores. On a multi-item test where answers were scored right or wrong, the score would be the number of items correctly answered or some adjustment of that score such as a "correction for guessing" that subtracts a fraction of the wrong answers from the rights. In other situations it could be the numerical translation of the letter grade assigned by a teacher or a grade to an essay. Simple measurement theory then makes some assumptions about those numbers and sets out to examine the properties of the scores in various ways.

It is not our purpose to denigrate this approach. It has been highly useful and the scientific quality of many areas of behavioral science would be improved if it were more widely applied in a sophisticated way. However, it has a number of deficiencies. For one thing, it rests on assumptions that are often untestable and often falsified when they can be tested. It also assumes properties for the score numbers that they clearly do not justify.

Thus, we feel strongly that it is preferable to base test practice on some alternative. We summarize some simple measurement theory below. *True score plus error theory,* as developed by such early psychologists as Spearman (1904) and others through about 1950 when the definitive book by Gulliksen (1950) appeared, assumed that a score, wherever it came from, consisted of two parts, a "true score" that was determined by the actual trait that the test measured (which might not be the same as what it was intended to measure; that did not matter at this stage) plus an error score that was like the random error that occurs in any physical measurement. This was expressed in a formula for x_i the score of some person i on a measure:

$$x_i - t_i + e_i \qquad (1.1)$$

The utility of this formulation lies in some assumptions that were then made. One assumption was that true score and error had a correlation of zero, $r_{te} = 0$. Another set of assumptions was that if there was another score variable y_i that was "parallel" to the first in the sense that it measured the same underlying variable, and only that variable, and had the same mean and variance, then (a) the true scores on the two variables would be perfectly correlated; (b) the error scores on the two components would correlate zero; and (c) the error score on one of the variables would correlate zero with the true score underlying the other.

This simple system has a number of useful implications that we might refer to later. Its drawbacks are numerous, however. The first is that it leads us to treat the test numbers as if they had all the same properties as hard numbers that come from physical measurement. A second is a little more technical; this is that it is required to assume that the magnitude of the error scores is the same for all levels of true score whereas it seems clear empirically that this is not the case (see Keats, 1957). A third drawback is that the statistical assumptions that are required to make full use of it can rarely be satisfied. For these and other reasons people interested in a statistical theory to underlie test practice turned to other ideas, mostly in the 1960s.

Axiomatic Measurement Theory

A theoretical development that is important to the basis of mental measurements was the development of highly formal mathematical systems that described the conditions that were necessary if a set of measurements were to provide a scale or scales having certain properties. We do not go into them in any detail here—a bit more will be included in a later chapter—but some specifics are relevant here because of what they say about certain aspects of the statistical theories that are the basis of most modern tests.

The part of axiomatic measurement theory that we describe is called "conjoint measurement theory." It was developed by Luce and Tukey (1964) and extended by various other researchers, and we provide a somewhat simplified version of it that is made specific to the testing context. The theory describes the conditions that are necessary if a set of observations can provide interval scales. ("Interval scale" means that score differences in different parts of the continuum that are equal have the same meaning. We consider this in more detail in the next chapter.) The theory shows that in order for this to happen, we need two sets, such as a set of persons and a set of test items, and a variable that is observed on each combination of a person and an item (hence the term *conjoint*), such as the probability that the person gets the item correct.

The theorems proved in conjoint measurement theory (CMT) say that for interval scales to exist, presumably here of person ability and item difficulty, some conditions have to be satisfied. The one that is relevant to us involves consistency of order. This is that for every person, the items increase in difficulty in the same way. That is, for every pair of persons A and B, there is a perfect rank order correlation between their probabilities of responding correctly across items; if Item X is easier than Item Y for A, Item X is also the easier one for B.

The same must be true for items. If A has a better chance of passing Item X than B does, then A has also a better chance of passing Item Y than B does. It may seem like common sense that this would be true, but generally there are exceptions to this regularity, and in fact the major current statistical theory of test response (IRT) assumes that such exceptions do occur.

It should be noted that even though consistency of ordering is a necessary condition for interval scaling it is not sufficient. This is an aspect of conjoint measurement theory that is often ignored (see Harrington, 1985). However, the additional condition referred to as cancellation has no relevance to ordinal test theory and so need not be dealt with here. This is an advantage that ordinal test theory has over item response theory treated next. Readers interested should refer to Harrington (1985). However, to our knowledge, there has been no empirical check on the cancellation condition on any set of data.

Item Response Theory

Most modern treatments of the statistical basis for mental tests concentrate on what is called item response theory (IRT). We do not do that in this book because we feel that there are obvious flaws in IRT. An important flaw is that the usual versions of IRT conflict with the consistency of ordering aspect of conjoint measurement theory (CMT), that was described earlier; therefore, it cannot provide the interval scales of ability and item difficulty that it purports to.

There are a number of variations on item response theories, in general they are based on the following idea. This is that there is an underlying or latent scale of an ability or personality trait and that the probability of responding positively to the item (i.e., getting it correct or agreeing with it) varies in a simple way across the latent scale. For an ability item, the probability will increase as we go from persons of low ability to those of high. Various mathematical functions have been proposed for what this smooth curve should be, and some years ago it was suggested that the "logistic" function would be a good choice. Here is its formula, Formula 1.1:

$$p_{ij} = e^{(x_i - a_j)} = \text{Exp } (x_i - a_j) \tag{1.2}$$

In the formula, p_{ij} is the probability that Person i answers item j correctly, and it states that this probability depends on the easiness of the item, a_j, and the ability of the person, x_i and the constant e is the base of naperian logs, 2.71828. . . and we can also write $\text{Exp}(x)$ instead of e^x.

The nature of the formula is illustrated in Fig. 1.3 where p_{ij} is plotted against x for several values of a_j, and we can see that the probability starts near zero when the ability is low, increases slowly at first, then more rapidly near the point where a_j and x_i are nearly equal, and then more slowly again, approaching 1.0 as the difference between the ability and easiness parameters becomes more positive. The different curves in the figure correspond to items having different a_j values, but notice that they all have the same shape, differing only in where they are located.

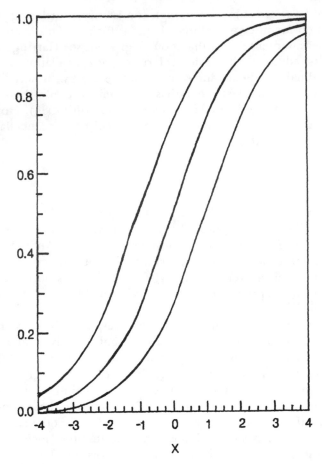

FIG. 1.3.   Logistic or Rasch-model item response curves. The probability of correct response (*y* axis) as a function of ability (*x* axis) for three items ranging in difficulty from easy (leftmost) to hard.

This is an elegant theory, and it is often called the Rasch Model after the Danish statistician who was instrumental in its development (Rasch, 1960). Note that the curves do not cross, and this means that the joint set of items and persons would not violate the independence axiom of CMT, so interval scales of each are possible. However, the trouble with this model is that it seldom fits the data except in cases of very similar items applied to a homogeneous population. In more typical cases it appears that, while the curves have the same general form, some increase more sharply than others. Those increasing sharply are said to be more "discriminating," because they differentiate better between persons low and high on the underlying trait.

Figure 1.4 illustrates this principle, and it is easily incorporated into the model of Formula 1.1 by introducing an item parameter, b_j, that multiplies the exponent to produce the following formula:

$$p_{ij} = \text{Exp } (b_j\{a_i - y_j\}) \qquad (1.3)$$

However, we can see that in Fig. 1.4 curves that have different discrimination parameters will cross. This means that, for two items of equal easiness, a person of low ability will have a better chance of getting the less discriminating item correct, whereas a person of high ability will have a better

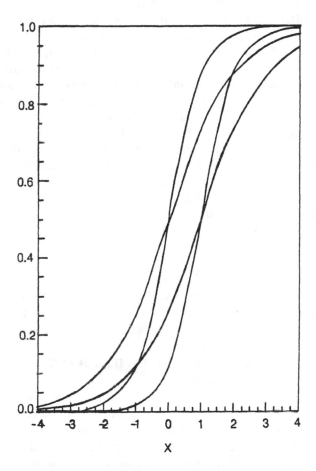

FIG. 1.4. Logistic IRT curves illustrating differential item discrimination. The two curves that rise steeply have higher discrimination values, b_j, than the other two, causing curves to cross.

chance on the more discriminating item. Thus the items cannot be ordered in such a way that the probability of getting them correct increases in the same order for all persons. This is a violation of the independence principle that must be satisfied if we are to achieve interval scales for items and persons. To us, this clearly means that scores derived via IRT models do not have interval–scale status any more than simple raw scores do.

Before leaving, for the time being, the topic of IRT models, we should point out that the model in the last formula is not the one generally applied to data from tests of the familiar multiple choice format. The reason is that for those items the probability of getting the item correct is not zero even for persons of very low ability because they, along with others, can guess among the alternatives and sometimes they will guess correctly. At first thought it might seem that the formula could be adjusted by introducing a constant of $1/k$ where k is the number of alternatives. This sometimes works but more often does not because the incorrect alternatives, called "distractors" in the testing terminology, are not equally attractive to those that do not know the correct answer. In taking multiple-choice tests we have all had the experience of being able to eliminate one or more alternatives as being highly unlikely to be correct. On the other hand, some writers of test items are clever at using sly distractors that look good to those who do not know the correct answer, so they tend to choose that one rather than guessing at random. For these reasons, and probably others that we do not understand, items tend to differ in their probability of correct guessing. This means that a third parameter, c_j, the guessing parameter, must be introduced into the formula:

$$p_{ij} = \text{Exp}(b_j\{a_j - y_i\}) + c_j. \tag{1.4}$$

However, this formula assumes that the guessing parameter is constant across ability, which Keats and Munro (1992) have shown to be untrue.

ORDINAL CONCEPTS AS A BASIS FOR MEASUREMENT

We base this book on the belief that is more scientifically and practically legitimate to base almost all psychological measurement on concepts resting on *order* than it is to assume that scores and other measures have the status of equal-interval scales. This is for several reasons. One is that, as outlined earlier, it is misleading to assume that the relative sizes of score differences have anything like the properties of relative sizes of physical differences. A second reason is that it turns out in practice that order is often the main information that is of interest. The fact that Jane scored five points higher than Fred whereas Fred scored only one point higher than Deborah is less important than that Jane scored higher than Fred who scored higher than Deborah. Most standardized tests report "percentile scores," that is, the percentage of examinees scoring below an individual. This is usually a more meaningful piece of information than that a given score was 540 on a scale from 200 to 800. The latter information requires a good bit of additional information in order to be interpreted correctly, and is open to substantial misinterpretation. Thus we believe that treating tests as providing ordinal information is more legitimate than doing otherwise, but it also provides the information that is of greatest use.

Some of the scales prepared to study attitudes, preferences, and so forth, require the subject to give ordinal responses such as to rank occupations or activities in the order of their preference. Typical of such scales are the Rokeach Scale of Values and the Rothwell–Miller Interest Inventory. The existence of such scales as these emphasizes the main point to be developed in this book, namely that all measures obtained of attitudes, values, etc. are ordinal in nature and should be treated in ordinal statistical terms. An ordinal test theory should be able to deal with cognitive ability tests with two or more ordered categories as well as attitude scales and personality tests with two or more ordered categories and it is the main aim of this book to present such a theory.

ANTITEST ARGUMENTS

Before we leave the question of the importance of psychological and educational testing, it must be noted that there are scholars and practitioners who raise arguments against the use of tests. The antitest movement claims that it is the absolute quality of the person's performance that is the important consideration rather than the comparison of a person's performance with that of a group of persons. However, it is difficult to assess the quality of a performance without relating it to that of persons of a relevant category (e.g., the same gender, age, and culture).

Furthermore, qualitative evaluation by different assessors can lead to inconsistencies. The process by which current ways of selecting apprentices for training in industries in the Newcastle area of Australia were developed provides a case study of these problems of qualitative evaluation and how psychological tests can be used for ameliorating these problems without removing the role of qualitative evaluation. The process involved the ordering of the applicants by means of tests but leaving the final selection to the industries using interviews (Pfister, 1985).

Other opponents of testing raise questions of cultural or ethnic bias. If one minority group obtains a lower average score than the majority group, it is argued that the test is biased against the minority group. For this purpose minority groups may be defined in terms of social class, culture, age, or even gender. In some cases, care is taken that the items included do not show differences between the sexes. Mean differences, however, may be a sign that what is a good scale for one group is not a good scale for another. Thus Black versus White differences in the United States may be due to a possibility that the test constructed for White subjects is not a proper scale for Blacks or it is not measuring the same dimension as the scale for Whites. A method of studying these alternatives is described in the chapters that follow.

Apart from the unfairness claimed if tests show bias, the effect is increased if people become labeled in terms of their performance on a particular occasion. This may be prevented by ensuring confidentiality of records and placing the control of the information strictly in the hands of the person tested. Much of the antitest attitude arises from the activities of the testers themselves rather than the tests. Some users stress the genetic component of a person's performance and seem to exaggerate its role. This strengthens the notion, for example, that a person's IQ is a constant for his or her life, which in turn leads to labeling. When this is generalized to racial differences in IQ being genetic as was suggested by Jensen (1980), the implications become very serious and have led to violent reactions. The antitest movement increased as a result of this tension.

However, at the present time there is a decrease in the antitest movement as people realize that many of the objections arise from poor test practice and can be removed by proper choice of tests and adequate training of testers. The International Test Commission is attempting to establish international standards for test users and the qualifications they should have if they are to have access to certain categories of psychological tests.

SUMMARY

In this chapter an attempt has been made to indicate the need for and purpose of this book and a general indication of its content. The need for a mathematical model or minitheory was stressed and possible examples given. Examples of the kinds of tests to be covered by the theory presented in later chapters are also given. The reader should become familiar with such tests by consulting Buros (1995 or later) and books such as Shaw and Wright (1967) and some specialized books published more recently. Although the presentation is partly historical it is not intended to be a full history of psychological testing and interested readers should consult such references as Thorndike and Lohman (1990).

In the next chapter the question is raised as to what makes a variable a scale and what kinds of scale can be distinguished at a theoretical level are discussed. The relevance of these considerations to the theory of psychological tests and scales in particular is noted.

Chapter 2

What Makes a Variable a Scale?

SCALES AND VARIABLES

The main aim of this book is to suggest how best to translate simple data such as judgments of stimuli or responses to test items into meaningful scores for things or people. Much of it concerns how to evaluate the consistency of such responses in order to reach at least a tentative conclusion concerning (a) How internally consistent the responses are, including whether any measurement is taking place at all, or (b) one method or system of measurement is better than another.

Before going into details on any of those topics, we need to set the stage by considering in a rather general way the nature of scientific variables and what makes one variable better for scientific purposes than another. Because not all things that are called variables have any scientific status, we will typically use the term *scale* here to refer to a variable that has a reasonable degree of scientific status.

We have frequently argued that many, perhaps most, variables used in behavioral research and its applications have only ordinal scale justification (Cliff, 1991, 1992, 1993, 1996). It can be argued even further that they often do not justify even that status because the characteristics necessary to define an order have not been demonstrated for them. One purpose of this book is to attempt to explicate what the characteristics are that data should display if an ordinal variable is to be defined on the basis of them. Then it attempts to pull together, and in some cases extend, the methods for deriving ordinal scales from data, including evaluating the consistency of the data and, consequently, the accuracy that may be assumed for the resulting scales.

25

As a preliminary to that discussion, the present chapter attempts to establish the nature of scientific scales, including what is, and should be, meant by operational definitions. Then, in the context of a satisfactory specification of what operational definitions are, it goes on to define what is best meant by measurement in the behavioral sciences.

THE NATURE OF SCIENTIFIC SCALES

As stated earlier, the term *scale* is used here to represent a variable that is well-defined scientifically. That means that it is valid for scientific purposes. Not every set of distinctions that can be made between entities or abstractions is a scale in this sense, so it is desirable to lay some groundwork in the form of a philosophy of science. Actually, this might better be called a *strategy* of science, because it tries to describe how to define scales that will work in a science and its applications.

We begin by examining the various meanings of "operationism," because that is what behavioral scientists generally think of as the basis for scientific scales. It is argued that much of what has been termed operationism is either internally flawed or inconsistent with the actual practice of successful science. Then, a refined and realistic version of operationism is formulated that is based on what actually goes on in an effective scientific field.

Operationism

What makes something a scale in a science? What *is* such a scale when it achieves that status? These are questions that have been pondered over and over by philosophers and by scientists. The answers to these questions have been of particular concern in behavioral science because of the frequent accusation by others, or suspicion on our own part, that we have no scales in the sense that that term is understood in other sciences. Trying to propose answers that are consistent with procedures that are effective in other sciences has occupied behavioral scientists from Bergman and Spence (1944) to Stevens (1951) to Krantz, Luce, Suppes, and Tversky (1971) to Michell (1990) and beyond.

An attempt at defining scientific scales that has been important in the history of psychology was operationism. Its psychological manifestation (e.g., Bergman & Spence, 1944) was adopted (some would say bowdlerized) from British philosophers (as represented by Smith, 1950). This original British version was an inclusive one: A scientific variable was the set of *all* the operations that were used to define it. Thus, "length" would be all the ways of measuring length from putting rods end to end to measuring the time that a laser beam takes to be reflected back from a mirror.

Bergman and Spence, on the other hand, promoted the idea of an equivalence between the conceptual variable and a single operation to define it. Theirs was an exclusionary definition. For them, the variable "drive" was equivalent to the number of hours of food deprivation, and they meant the equivalence in a very strong sense. One could speak of hours of deprivation when referring to drive, just as one could speak of drive when referring to hours of deprivation. Still a third kind of operationism is represented by the oft-quoted statement by Boring (1945) "Intelligence is what the tests test." This will be seen to be quite different from the other two although it is often cited as if it were equivalent to Bergman and Spence's. We think that none of these three will stand up as a description of how any specific scientific scale is defined (specified or described might be better terms) by good scientists in their work.

The Importance of Operational Definitions

Let us first consider why the use of operational definitions, free of any philosophical trappings, is important in science. Operational definitions—one could perhaps better substitute a term like *empirical specifications* or *procedural descriptions*—constitute the fundamental way in which scientists communicate about their research. In describing our research for technically competent peers, we use on the one hand abstract theoretical terms, whether they be distance, weak nuclear force, DNA transcription, fluid intelligence, or social class, to let others know what the research is about at the level of ideas. But then, on the other hand, we have to let them know specifically how the research was carried out in the real world in terms of concrete, palpable objects, no matter how esoteric those might be.

This concreteness serves several functions. First, it helps the peer in a general cognitive way to orient our research into her[1] own understanding, no matter what language or background she might have. Second, because science is a social process, operating by means of a consensus among peers rather than by authoritative dominance, it tells her how to repeat the research if doubt arises in her mind or if she is so intrigued that she wants to see for herself. Third, it provides a basis for the evaluative process that is so important to the cumulative nature of science. How good are the operations used here as definitions of these variables? Are they known to be unconfounded? How accurate have they been previously shown to be? Are they the latest and best or obsolete versions? Answers to these questions are important to how much value the viewer of the research will place on it.

---

[1]Rather than repeatedly using the stylistically awkward dual gender pronouns—her/his, him/her, and the like—we use only a single gender in a given context, switching genders from context to context in what is intended to be a balanced way.

Finally, in what is perhaps a summary of these other reasons, empirically described procedures serve to ensure that research is tied to the real world of everyday existence, avoiding the temptation to waft it into the realm of pure abstraction. For all these reasons, operational definitions, or empirical descriptions, of variables are central to the scientific enterprise.

Defects in Definitions

The Bergman and Spence (1944) definition is clearly defective in the context of a science that is to be practiced effectively. In any particular instance, the definition is not inclusive enough. If Drive is *equivalent* to hours of deprivation in the rat, then any scientific relations obtained using this definition of Drive apply only in that context. If one wants to know what relations would obtain with Drive operationally defined instead as proximity of a male rat to a female in estrus, one cannot assume that this operational definition is equivalent to the first, but instead has to start from scratch in elucidating its relations, because this, being a different set of operations, must not be Drive but something else, $Drive_2$, perhaps, and so on for all alternative operations. We end up with a different $Drive_1$ for every set of operations, each potentially with its own properties.

But surely Bergman and Spence (1944) did not mean that the interpretation of the constructs they operationally defined should be confined to a narrow definition like "hours of food deprivation in the rat." They intended, as applications of Spence's work bear out, that what was learned empirically about "hours of deprivation" would apply to everything else that was like it in providing motivation for behavior, including abstract human needs. But that was not what they said. They said, "hours of deprivation equals Drive," and were using "equals" in its symmetric sense.

If these authors intended to imply that $Drive_2$ was the same as Drive, then this was not made clear, and this interpretation will have its own problems. Literal, perhaps overliteral, interpretation of their position led investigators to the belief that one could, in the manner of the Lewis Carroll's Humpty Dumpty, define a variable however one wanted. Drive was whatever the investigator operationally defined it, with consequent weakening of this potentially powerful concept. The Bergman and Spence interpretation may have helped lead Stevens (1951) to feel that his infamous definition of measurement as the assignment of numbers according to rule, any rule, was consistent with this kind of narrow operationism.

What is missing from Bergman and Spence's kind of operationism is any concern for how we know what is Drive and what it is not. To a working scientist, a reasonable description of Drive is that it is a variable that enters into certain kinds of relationships with certain other variables. Included in the definition is a specification of what the relationships are, preferably in a mathematical formula, and what the other variables are. The theoretical variable Drive can have various real-world counterparts that are empirically describable, and they all enter into identical, or at least highly similar, empirical relationships with certain other empirical variables. This is what characterizes well-defined scientific scales such as length. Some candidate counterparts of Drive may turn out not to have the right relationships. These are then discarded as not being examples of Drive. Variables that are examples of Drive are variables that are shown to have specific relations with other variables.

It is important, as Smith (1950) implied, that there be numerous different operational definitions of a variable, all of which enter into the same relations with the other variables. If a theoretical variable had only a single empirical counterpart, it would be of little interest or utility. This is an aspect of what has been called in psychology the convergent validation of a variable. Scales are never measured in the abstract. They are measured in the context of their relations with other scales. Two sets of observables are alternative operational definitions of the same scale if they enter into the same relations with other scales, not just because someone says they are the same. Learning to recognize a scale in its various forms can be not only useful and interesting but painful and humbling to the scientist or practitioner. However, the more variables that can be found that behave in the way that is expected of definitions of a construct, the more powerful the construct is, but also the more confidence we have in the individual operational definitions.

It is also important to show that some empirical definition of a scale is distinct from other scales, in fact, that it is as pure as possible, unconfounded by the influence of others. Scientists abandon, quickly or slowly, empirical definitions of theoretical scales that turn out to be confounded with other variables. The demonstration that a new scale or phenomenon exists must take place in such a way as to show that it is not some old scale in a new guise. This is discriminant validation of the scale. Ideally, the social process of science operates in such a way as to ensure the effectiveness of the differentiating of scales from each other.

Michell (1990) correctly pointed out that some operational definitions are more equal than others. That is, some operational definitions are "better" than others. In mature sciences, this seems to mean that they enter into relations in a closer or a more reliable way. There is even a constant search for measurement methods that are better in this sense.

Moreover, an operational definition can be better than another in one context, but worse in another. Temperature is an obvious example. There are different operational definitions of temperature for different ranges of temperature. One works well, that is, enters into the expected relations with other scales, over a range, but then breaks down, that is, no longer enters into relations in the expected way, over others. Similarly, one cannot use the millimeter marks on a meter stick to measure distance in either the micron or the light-year range. Alternative operational definitions of a scale should be available for different contexts, but there should be equating procedures that connect the various definitions.

So a scale is defined operationally not as a single kind of operation à la Bergman and Spence (1944) but in terms of a, preferably large, collection of alternative sets of operations, as Smith (1950) suggested. These can be equated to each other, either directly or in terms of having equivalent relations with other variables. However, even Smith's definition is not sufficient, as Michell (1990) pointed out. First, it does not recognize that some operational definitions are better, to a scientist, than others. Furthermore, it limits the definition of a scale to those operational definitions that are currently in use. One of the thrills of science is demonstrating a new operational definition for a scale. The fun, and payoff in other ways to the scientist, is in going outside the current definition of things and finding something that unexpectedly does behave like the scale, to the delight, amazement, envy, or chagrin of peers. So a scientific scale should include in its definition potential as well as current operational definitions.

Generality of Scales

But surely, a scientific scale extends even beyond its operational definitions. The engineer calculates the forces on an airframe without measuring them! Are they not there until measured?[2] It would be an extreme view to say they are not there, at least not until the wings fall off. In the same sense, the principles that relate mass and velocity to momentum and energy are felt to apply to the 150-pound football player who is running north at 20 miles an hour and the 300-pound player running south at 15 miles an hour just as they do to balls rolling down slopes. Mass and velocity determine force and energy in the collision between the two players, just as the relevant equations describe, even though the players are not measured. One prediction from the equations, and everyday assumptions about human nature, is that the smaller player is less likely to seek out a repetition of such collisions than the larger, other things being equal. Football players are subject to these scales and the relations there are between them, even when they are not operationalized. Force is there, even when it is not being measured; it existed before it was operationalized, and will exist when operationalism is forgotten. That may be a view that is abhorrent to some philosophies, but it is the ongoing premise that forms the basis of science. If there

---

[2]This view may not be an appropriate representation of variables in quantum mechanics. It would take someone more expert than we are in that field to judge.

were not a widespread belief that scientific scales exist outside their operational definitions, no one would pay scientists to do science! In this view, a scientific scale has an existence beyond its operational definitions.

How, then, is a scientific scale identified? We both measure it through the relations it enters into and, in a seeming paradox, identify its nature, and even verify its existence, through the relations. The paradox is avoided in practice because as scientists we somehow guess that there is a scale and guess at how it can be defined and guess at the relations it will enter into. When we guess right, it all works out, at least roughly. We then become convinced that there is a scale and that we can empirically define it. In the ideal case, we then set about refining the procedures used to define it and the relations it enters into. (This latter process is one that is neglected to a lamentable degree in what otherwise tries and aspires to be behavioral science.) We find alternate manifestations of it, and more relations that it is in. And so on. Sometimes, more often than not, the process fails at some point. If the failures are repeated, we lose interest in the scale, and go on to something else, if for no other reason than that the research support will run out.

Boring's Definition

After this discussion it may be clear that Boring's (1945) reference to what tests measure reflects quite a different view of operational definition than the narrow kind represented by Bergman and Spence (1944), or even Smith (1950). Bergman and Spence's kind of view has its own defects and has had its own insidious effects. It seems to be saying one or both of two things. One is that any score that comes out of any procedure that purports to measure intelligence is a value of the scale, intelligence. If so, this would be Humpty Dumptyism. Even assuming that such issues as finding methods for equating scores from different tests can be solved in a scientifically meaningful way, such a definition is seen to be unsatisfactory to the process of science, much less to engineering-like applications of such scores. Although it does seem to be true that anyone can publish a "test" and say that it measures intelligence, it does not seem to be true that one can willy-nilly call something an intelligence score and expect that it will be accepted in that role by other scientists. Some intelligence tests measure intelligence, and some don't, it seems, and rightfully so.

But there are many different measures of intelligence that are accepted by at least some others. How do we know they are all measuring the same thing? Data relevant to this question occur in hundreds, probably thousands of studies, and the answer, of course, is that it seems they must not be. The criterion that would need to be satisfied, that was identified earlier, is that they should have the same relations to other scales, and demonstrably they do not. Moreover, the diversity cannot be explained by appropriateness criteria such as the ones we use in measuring temperature. They systematically do not agree with each other, much less have the same relations. So, if intelligence is what the tests test, it is too diverse to be called a scientific scale.

There are two fixups to this result that have been adopted. One is to refine kinds of intelligence that are ever more narrow, into Intelligence$_1$, Intelligence$_2$, and so on. Intelligence$_1$ is what a certain subset of tests test; Intelligence$_2$ is what a second set tests, and so on. The narrow versions behave fairly consistently in their relations, so we may accept them as scientific scales, provided we do not insist these relations be very close. Having different Intelligences may be a satisfactory device, but not if one places much store on the generality of scientific scales. Thus we see that "intelligence is what the tests test" is not a satisfactory definition because it seems that this is many different things that have different relations with each other and with other variables, whereas a scientific scale is an entity that has a unitary set of relationships in the sense that scientists find useful.

Commonality

The alternative to diversifying the meaning of Intelligence in the face of multiple partially but imperfectly agreeing empirical definitions of it is to say that "intelligence is what is in common among all these tests." Many of our good friends seem satisfied with this kind of definition, but it is unacceptable to us as the definition of a scientific scale because this Intelligence has no empirical counterpart. It cannot be felt, seen, tasted, heard, counted, or bitten. To argue that scales in, say, physics are defined with a similar degree of abstractness is to confuse a complex observational process in which the ultimate outcome—a computer-enhanced, infrared photograph of a distant galaxy, say—is technologically distant from the source with a process that is not there. To argue, alternatively, that some statistical operation on numbers that stand for observables is a form of operational definition is to mistake a symbolic operation, the one on the numbers, for an empirical one. So "Intelligence is what is common among these intelligence tests" does not define Intelligence as a scientific scale either.

Intelligence is being used here as an exemplar of a number of scales that have been attempted to be defined in this fashion. There are numerous other variables, often with even poorer definition than Intelligence, whose definitions have been accepted by parts of the behavioral science community in a similar fashion. A more fruitful approach to the phenomenon of numerous moderately consistent but not commensurable definitions of a scale might be a program that attempted to find out in a more proactive way what it was that did lead to moderate agreement, and what the empirically meaningful aspects were that led to the divergence. Looking at test names and correlation coefficients, or even reading test items, does not represent a high level of proactivity.

RELEVANCE TO SCALES AND MEASUREMENT METHODS

Part of the reason for this rather long preamble is to provide a background for discussing what measurement is and how it takes place, including why some measurements are felt to be of one kind or level and some of another, and why some are better than others. It should be clear by now that scientific measurement must take place in a scientific context. Scales do not exist in isolation. They are defined in terms of, and on the basis of, the relations they have with each other.

Science is conservative. It prefers cautious noncommittal to free-wheeling error, which is not to say it abhors free-wheeling. This bias says we should not treat our variables as if they have properties they do not have. We can hypothesize such properties, but then we had better go and show that they are present. We do not suggest to engineers and other consumers of science that they treat the variables that way either. This is just as true in the case of tests that inappropriately consign children to institutions as it is of rockets that unexpectedly explode on launch pads.

Measurement is the assignment of numbers to observations in a scientifically valid way. "Scientifically valid" means in a way that is consistent with the description of scientific scales that has been sketched earlier. That is, relations are shown, or could be shown, to other scales. The relations are known to be of a particular kind rather than some other, and the conservatism of science implies that we not read more into the measurements than is there. This is because we may then infer incorrect predictions from the measurements.

Accuracy of measurement is at least as important as the "level" of measurement. The nominal-scale measurement that accurately allocates an individual to the human species is more important than the less accurate ordinal-scale observation that one person is faster at processing a certain kind of information than another person, particularly when only a human can process that information at all.

Scientifically valid scales, then, are defined when empirically definable variables enter into predictable relations with other scales. The more numerous the relations are, and the more different empirical definitions there are that behave in these predictable ways, the more confidence we have in the scale. The scale exists not only when it is being scientifically observed but also in everyday nonscientific contexts; otherwise, what is the relevance of the scale? Also important is the degree to which the empirical relations are close and exact rather than error-filled. Another point is that the scale is presumed to exist not only when it is being scientifically observed but also in everyday nonscientific contexts; otherwise, what is the relevance of the scale? It is also important not to impute characteristics for the scale that have not been scientifically demonstrated; included here is the necessity of not giving unproven quantitative properties to the scale. Measurement, then, is the assignment of numbers to observations in a scientifically valid way.

GENERAL PRINCIPLES OF SCIENTIFIC MEASUREMENT

Why Ordinal Measurement?

A number of arguments can be made supporting the contention that the great majority of behavioral data can only be considered to have ordinal status (Cliff, 1993, 1996). Basically, the arguments center around the idea that a scale should display certain regularities in its effects and relations if interval-level status is to be justified for it, and it is very rare for our scales to display those regularities. Furthermore, a given form of the scale often has no better justification than alternative, monotonically transformed versions of it. A second aspect of the argument is that the observed variables are often surrogates for latent ones, and it seems unlikely that there is a linear relation between the observed variable and the latent one. Although it is true that statistical conclusions can be made from data analyses of these scales according to the principles of statistical description and inference, in spite of the scales' amorphousness, the point is that these conclusions about the variables in their current form may not be invariant under transformation. Furthermore, the inferences and conclusions that investigators make, or want to make, are themselves often ordinal. We have therefore argued (e.g., Cliff, 1993, 1996) for ordinal statistical treatment of data because the conclusions from such treatment will be insensitive to the particular form of the scale that is analyzed.

Defining Scales

The status of a variable as a scale rests on the consistency of its relations with other scales. When a variable is a composite of several observations (Many variables, such as test items, in behavioral science are of that kind.), the relations among those individual observations are of particular importance as groundwork to the definition of the scale. The measurement status of a scale has two aspects. One is defined by the theoretical use of the scale. This refers to the relations that it has with other theoretical scales in models that it is part of. If it has relations that require ratio–scale properties it must be a ratio scale; if they require continuity, it must be continuous; and so on. The second aspect has to do with the empirical counterparts of the theoretical scales. What properties do they display *empirically*? Do the empirical scales display the properties in their empirical relations with other scales that their theoretical counterparts are supposed to have, at least to a reasonable approximation? The difference between emphasizing the latter aspect over the former does much to explain the discrepancy between the pessimistic conclusions of Cliff (1992) and the more optimistic ones of Narens and Luce (1993) with respect to the contributions of abstract measurement theory to behavioral science.

Empirical Definition of Scales

We would like to define the field of behavioral measurement, or psychometrics, as the development and study of methods for fitting models to behavioral data and evaluating the appropriateness of the models for the data. This statement can be said to be a summary of the role this field has always had, but it is worth being explicit about it here. The estimated values of theoretical variables that are thus derived are assumed to be scales. (We feel, by the way, that the recent emphasis in psychometrics has been too heavily toward the fitting process, to the neglect of the evaluation of appropriateness, except on narrow and nearly irrelevant statistical grounds. There is much too little concern with improving the quality of the data.) However, we feel that it is premature to call such a variable derived through a fitting process a scale: The variable needs to exhibit close and regular relations with other, external variables before it can advance to the status of a scale. This is not to denigrate such variables, because, after all, they may summarize a good deal of data, but rather to emphasize that they need to be validated before they can be presumed to have the status of true scientific scales.

Most of this book is concerned with developing these variables that have not yet achieved the status of scales but that have been psychometrically derived to summarize data. To distinguish them from variables that actually have the characteristics we have described as necessary for achieving the lofty status of scales, we refer to them as *assumed* scales.

A behaviorally defined assumed scale, then, is a variable that is derived to summarize a number of observations. It is derived by fitting a model to the data, and the model must fit to a satisfactory degree, otherwise, there is no grounds for even an assumed scale. The fitting can sometimes be done formally and explicitly by a mathematical process that optimizes the fit of a model to the data by finding the numerical values of parameters in the model that fit the data best (in one or more of several quantitative or qualitative senses). The parameter estimates then become the assumed scale or scales. Examples in behavioral science of assumed scales include variables derived via item response theory (IRT) models for responses on objective tests. There, the scale that is of primary interest is a trait scale for the individuals, but the items also are scaled on one or more variables. The trait scores are derived because they are presumed to have some external utility for predicting or explaining behavior in another context such as performance in school. However, by the criteria presented here, these are at best assumed scales.

Another instance comes from multidimensional scaling (MDS) in which measures of psychological similarity between a number of stimuli or concepts are fitted to a model that treats the (dis)similarities as interpoint distances. This results in values for the stimuli on one or more assumed scales. These are used then to explain the degree of similarity. There is in such cases an intimate and direct connection between the models and the variables or scales that are derived from them. There is also, in such cases, an overall measure of how well the model fits the whole collection of data, albeit such measures of fit are often hard to interpret. Sometimes, of course, such measures tell us that the model cannot be the explanation of the data because the departures of the data from the model are too large, even with optimum fits for the parameters. The measurement status of scales derived from models that do not fit is an unresolved, and for the most part ignored, issue.

Sometimes these assumed scales derived via MDS are used to characterize the stimuli for other, external purposes (Cliff, 1972; Cliff & Young, 1968; Green & Carmone, 1972). If the relations that are then shown turn out to be close enough, the variables might be allowed to advance from the status of assumed scales to that of scales. There are hints in the references cited that this might have been possible, but the follow-up research to demonstrate external validity for the assumed scales was not extensive enough, or the relations that were shown were not close enough, to justify that status.

The process of "measurement" is often much more informal in behavioral science than the one described earlier of fitting a model to a rather extensive set of data. A common example is attitude measurement. If an attitude "scale" is composed of several items judged to reflect a certain attitude dimension, the respondent's answers to the items are typically added up to form a score on the attitude, just as if that process were the same as the case where the innkeeper adds up the cost of the drinks served to come to a total score that he is owed. Where is the model here? What is the fitting process? There are a number of models for the process of answering attitude items. In some of them, it does turn out that the sum of item scores is a reasonable estimate of a score on the underlying attitude, provided, of course, that the model fits. In others, it is not. In still others, while the total score is an index of the underlying scale, it is a nonlinear one. How appropriate any of the models might be, how well any of them fits, and how close the measured attitude score is likely to be to the "true" attitude, are all questions that sometimes can be, and even have been, answered in a given application.

Justification for Variables

However, in all likelihood, many of the variables that are statistically analyzed in behavioral science have a psychometric basis that is at best informal, although some of them do have a formal basis, and more could have. By the term *psychometric basis* we mean, at a minimum, an evaluation of the reliability and construct validity, more generally, the *generalizability* (Cronbach, Gleser, Nanda, & Rajaratnam, 1973) of the scores that are used. A further level of psychometric definition would be provided when the score is derived from observations through the fitting of a quantitative model to the data. In that case, the score is an estimate of a scale that is part of the model, but so far it is only an assumed scale. If it is further found that the model *fits* the data adequately, then we are on the way to a scale. In order to be fully validated as such, it should be shown to enter into close and consistent relations with still other variables. It is this process of observation-to-score-to-model-fitting-to-scale, not just the recording of numbers arbitrarily assigned to observations, that represents the modern view of what constitutes psychological measurement (Cliff, 1992; Guttman, 1971; Michell, 1990).

If many or even most behavioral scales provide only ordinal information, it would seem desirable to have methods for deriving scales ordinally, but the amount of specifically ordinal psychometric machinery that exists is rather small, both at the generalizability level or the model-fitting one, compared to what exists for fitting more parametric models to ordinal data. Nevertheless, there is some machinery, and the main purpose of this book is to present what we feel is the soundest portion of it and to expand on that portion as much as possible.

The view presented earlier was that scientific scales are defined through operations in the real world that result in variables that have consistent, and close, relations with each other. Psychometric procedures, however, almost universally operate internally to a particular set of data. This is true whether scales are being defined through a model-fitting process or more informally. The rationale for operating within a set of data has to be that through such a process we hope to identify what we have called assumed scales, variables that behave consistently enough that we can hope that they are scientific scales. Once a variable has achieved assumed-scale status, the further, and equally important, step is to show that this variable enters into relations with other variables that are close enough and frequent enough to justify calling the assumed scale a scale.

A FUNDAMENTAL TYPOLOGY OF DATA

Data Are Binary

At the most basic level, data are binary. We may go on to convert them to numerical scores, but at the most primitive level, they are binary. Several decades ago the late Clyde Coombs proposed a system for the fundamental classification of the types of binary data that can exist (Coombs, 1951, 1964). This system proved to be remarkably satisfactory to those concerned with basic issues in behavioral measurement. It starts with the observation that data represent relations and that they are binary relations. Much behavioral data is binary: Test items are correct or incorrect; questionnaires are answered "yes" or "no" or agree–disagree; commercial product A is preferred or not to product B; stimulus X is similar or not to stimulus Y; artifact P is found or not in grave Q. All these relations are binary.

Even data that seems to be directly quantified can fit the system as a series of dichotomous data. For example, a student's written response to an item on a classroom test may be graded on a 5-point scale, but the grade can be considered as a series of passes versus failures, so that a grade at level four out of five can be thought of dichotomously as passing the first four levels and dichotomously failing the fifth. Other quantified data can be treated similarly to create multiple dichotomies although the process can seem cumbersome for data that presents itself as quasi-continuous numbers such as response times or electrodermal measurements. Nevertheless, at a fundamental level, these variables, like more obvious ones, are binary.

Coombs' System

A major aspect of Coombs' (1951, 1964) system was his suggestion that all types of data could be classified according to three dichotomies. Data represent relations, and the first dichotomy has to do with the nature of the relation represented by a datum. It can represent either a *dominance* relation or a *proximity* relation. Dominance relations are observed when two stimuli are compared with respect to some attribute, and one is judged to be harder, more desirable, or brighter than the other. Similarly, a dominance relation is observed when one team or chess player defeats another. On the other hand, data represent proximity relations when two stimuli or concepts are judged similar or related (1) as opposed to dissimilar or unrelated (0), or two students are seen to be friends (1) versus not friends (0). Thus, one of Coombs' three major distinctions is between data that represent dominance relations versus data that represent proximity relations.

The distinction between dominance and proximity relations is illustrated in the two upper matrices in Table 2.1. The left matrix shows a domi-

TABLE 2.1
Patterns That Define Types of Relations

One-Set Relations

	Dominance							Proximity						
	a	b	c	d	e	f	g	a	b	c	d	e	f	g
a	0	1	1	1	1	1	1	1	1	0	0	0	0	0
b	0	0	1	1	1	1	1	1	1	1	0	0	0	0
c	0	0	0	1	1	1	1	0	1	1	1	0	0	0
d	0	0	0	0	1	1	1	0	0	1	1	1	0	0
e	0	0	0	0	0	1	1	0	0	0	1	1	1	0
f	0	0	0	0	0	0	1	0	0	0	0	1	1	1
g	0	0	0	0	0	0	0	0	0	0	0	0	1	1

Two-Set Relations

	Dominance							Proximity						
	a	b	c	d	e	f	g	a	b	c	d	e	f	g
s	1	1	1	1	1	1	1	1	1	0	0	0	0	0
t	0	1	1	1	1	1	1	1	1	1	0	0	0	0
u	0	0	1	1	1	1	1	0	1	1	1	0	0	0
v	0	0	0	1	1	1	1	0	0	1	1	1	0	0
w	0	0	0	0	1	1	1	0	0	0	1	1	1	0
x	0	0	0	0	0	1	1	0	0	0	0	1	1	1
y	0	0	0	0	0	0	1	0	0	0	0	0	1	1
z	0	0	0	0	0	0	0	0	0	0	0	0	0	1

nance relation among members of a set A = {a, b, . . . g}. The set could be a set of lights of different strengths and the relation might be that the column stimulus is "brighter than" (1) the row stimulus with 0 meaning "not brighter than." Alternatively, the set could be graduate schools to possibly attend with 1 representing "has a better reputation than."

The right matrix represents a proximity relation. Here, 1 means "close to," "similar to," "about the same as," or similar relations, and 0 means the opposite. Both matrices represent ideal, perfectly consistent cases. The key characteristic of a matrix of relations representing dominance is the observation of a triangle of 1s in the upper right of the matrix with a triangle of 0s in the lower left (the elements have to be in the right order).[3] An element dominates all those below it in the order and is dominated by all those above it. In contrast, a unidimensional proximity relation shows a diagonal stripe of 1s with 0s in both the upper left and lower right sections, again when the elements are in the right order. An element here is similar to itself and to those that are next to it in the order.

The examples in the preceding paragraphs represent relations between members of the same set, but Coombs' second distinction was whether the relation was between members of the same set or two different sets. (Coombs' ideas all rest on the assumption that there exist well-defined sets. Defining those sets is often a major part of the scientific enterprise.) So, we can have dominance or proximity relations and the relation can be between members of the same set or two different sets. The most common example of a dominance relation between members of different sets is the dichotomous test item. If a person passes an item (gets it correct), then the person "dominated" the item, whereas if he failed it, the item dominated the person. Much of this book is devoted to analyzing this kind of data to yield assumed scales. On the other hand, questionnaires that are presented in an agree–disagree format are often better interpreted as providing proximity relations because probably the respondent compares the questionnaire item to his self-concept or his internalized opinion, and agrees or disagrees on the basis of the similarity (closeness) of the item to the respondent's self-concept or opinion.

The lower part of Table 2.1 illustrates two-set dominance (left) and proximity (right) relations between members of a set A = {a, b, . . . , g} that defines the columns and a set S = {s, t, . . . , z} that defines the rows. As in the one-set case, a dominance relation is characterized by an upper right triangle of 1s and a lower left block of 0s. The proximity relation shows a diagonal stripe of 1s separating upper right and lower left triangles of 0s. The

---

[3]The positions of the triangles of 1s and 0s could be reversed, depending on how the relation is defined.

dominance relation shows that each row element is dominated by all column elements up to a point, and then it dominates all the rest. For example, a person fails all the hardest items on a test, but then passes all the rest. In the proximity relation, each row element has a band of column elements that are close to it. The fact that the sets are different means that the border between the two kinds of symbols could show as farther up or down or to the right or left, depending on the nature of the data.

It should be emphasized that deciding whether a relation is of the dominance as opposed to the proximity type is not a subjective decision on the part of the investigator. Rather, the distinction should be based on how the data behave. A collection of data relations that represent dominances will show one kind of consistency, whereas they will show quite different consistencies if they represent proximities. A large part of the remainder of this book is devoted to evaluating consistencies in collections of data relations.

So data relations can represent either dominance or proximity, and they can be between members of the same set or different sets. Coombs realized (1951, 1964) that a third distinction was necessary in order to accommodate as broad a spectrum of data as he wanted to do. The third dichotomy splits data where the relation is between a pair of set-elements from data where it is between a *pair of pairs* of elements. All of our examples so far have been instances where there is only one pair, and the pair of pairs circumstance is indeed less frequently encountered. There are, however, examples. In a psychophysical experiment, a subject might be presented with two pairs of musical tones and asked whether the first pair is more different (1) than the second, or not (0). A little consideration will suggest that the data are likely to behave as a dominance relation, but the relation is between pairs of pairs of tones; also, the pairs of pairs are all from the same set.

According to Coombs' scheme, then, there are eight possible types of data depending on whether the binary relation represents a dominance relation or one of proximity, whether the relation is between members of the same set or different sets, and whether the relation is one between pairs or pairs of pairs. We deal with these concepts in more detail later.

MENTAL TESTS AND DATA RELATIONS

A substantial part of this book is devoted to the treatment of mental test data. The basic relation in such data is at the item level, and aside from classroom tests constructed by individual teachers, the great majority of test responses are scored dichotomously: correct or incorrect in the case of ability or achievement tests; gave or did not give the keyed response in the case of a personality inventory. We argue strongly for multilevel responses, but the fact remains that the majority of items are scored dichotomously. These item scores are then summed to provide a total score on the test or personality scale. In the next set of chapters we consider how to evaluate collections of test responses in order to decide whether they may legitimately provide a summed score that may legitimately be called at least an assumed scale.

Chapter 3

Types of Assessment

A CLASSIFICATION OF TEST ITEMS

At the end of chapter 2, it was noted that "Psychometric procedures, however, almost universally operate internally to a particular set of data. The rationale for operating within a set of data has to be that through such a process we hope to identify what we have called assumed scales, variables that behave consistently enough that we can hope that they are scientific scales."

In this chapter a number of different procedures that have been used for making assessments are described. No attempt is made to make this list exhaustive but examples of various types of tests in common use are given and classified. The various types of assessment are classified first in terms of whether the items or tasks require the examinee to provide the answer, called "free response" or "creative answer" tasks, or whether they require a choice between two or more alternatives—the multiple-choice items.

The second basis of classification is whether or not the score on the response to each item is evaluated or scored dichotomously with two ordered categories. Examples of dichotomous tasks would be those evaluated as right–wrong, pass–fail. Other dichotomies include yes–no, agree–disagree, or giving the keyed as opposed to the unkeyed response, or vice versa, to an item of a personality scale such as introversion or manic depression. For scoring purposes, the dichotomous categories are then converted to a 1, 0 scale.

Alternatively, the response or its evaluation may be polytomous with three or more ordered categories. Written responses on a test can be rated as Fail, Poor, Satisfactory, or Excellent, or just rated numerically, such as 0,

1, 2, or 3. Some free-response items on an intelligence test are scored in this way, and for summary purposes the verbal categories are generally converted to numbers as well. On personality tests or attitude scales the respondent could be asked to indicate his or her extent of agreement with a statement by choosing among the ordered categories "Strongly Disagree, Disagree, Neutral, Agree, Strongly Agree." Again the responses on each item would be converted to simple numbers, 0 to 4, or 1 to 5, to provide total scores.

This double classification by response type and number of evaluation categories provides four types of assessment:

1. free answer and dichotomous scoring
2. free answer and polytomous scoring
3. multiple choice and dichotomous scoring
4. multiple choice and polytomous scoring.

A fifth type of assessment is one in which the person is asked to rank stimuli in order of preference as in some ordinal values scales such as the "Rothwell–Miller Interest Inventory Blank" (1988), the Rokeach "Value Survey" (1973), and the Allport, Vernon, and Lindzey (1951) "Study of Values." All five types of scale are discussed in various sections of this chapter and the following chapters.

Of the other ordinal methods, The Rokeach Value Survey involves the simple ranking of two sets of 18 values and the data can not be analyzed for consistency in the way of the Rothwell–Miller. In the Allport et al. *Study of Values* (1951) such ordinal statistics can be applied as shown by Keats (1972) but because the scale is not used to any great extent these days this method is not repeated here.

The four basic types of items are detailed later in this chapter after we describe the concept of "standard scores," which are so widely used in standardized tests.

STANDARD SCORES

Statistical Definition

On formally published or administered tests such as those the reader has encountered at numerous points in her or his academic career, the total of raw scores is converted to one or both of two types of numerical scales. One type is the "standard score." This has several numerical forms, but all are based on the same idea. The mean score of the distribution of raw scores for a group is assigned a convenient numerical value, such as $m = 10.0$, and the standard deviation (SD) of the distribution is also assigned a simple number such as $s = 3.0$. Then a standard score is assigned to each raw score in terms of its position relative to the mean in standard deviation units.

Then, using z to stand for standard score and x for raw score, the following formula (3.1) would be used:

$$z = 10 + 3.0(x - m)/s \qquad\qquad (3.1)$$

A raw score that was one standard deviation above the mean would then receive a standard score of 13.0. Usually, only whole numbers would be used for the standard scores, so the z values would need to be rounded to the nearest integer.

Variations

The standard score scale on other tests may use different scaling factors. Perhaps the one most frequently encountered sets the mean to 500 instead of 10 and the standard deviation to 100 instead of 3.

This is the scale used by the Educational Testing Service for tests such as the "College Boards" and the Graduate Record Examination. Other tests might use a mean of 50 and a SD of 10. In most instances a score reported as an "IQ" is a standard score having a mean of 100 and a SD of 15.0. These other standard scores are computed by substituting the desired mean and SD for the 10 and 3.0, respectively in formula (3.1). Whatever the scale used, the score is meant to reflect position relative to the mean in standard deviation units, so the raw score that was one standard deviation above the mean would be 600 on the 500, 100 scale, 60 on the 50, 10 scale, and 115 on most IQ scales.

A misapprehension that is surprisingly widespread among otherwise sophisticated individuals is that standard scores are normally distributed. They are not. Their distribution is exactly the same as that of the raw scores from which they are derived. Kelley (1947) summarized evidence that he claimed supported the normal distribution conclusion assumption. Wechsler (1939) began developing a series of tests using this assumption, which is questioned below. In practice raw score distributions are at best roughly normal, and often radically nonnormal as shown by Miccieri (1989).

Standardization Groups

In many testing situations, the standard scores that are reported to individuals and institutions are not standardized with respect to the group of examinees who took the test at the same time and/or place as the individual. Instead these reported scores often reflect the examinee's place with respect to a "standardization group." This is a large group of individuals, typically 1,000 or more, on whom the test's scores have been standardized, so the score reported for an individual represents position within this group. In well-designed tests, this group has been selected to be representative of the population for which the test is intended.

FREE-ANSWER WITH DICHOTOMOUS SCORING ASSESSMENTS

This is the type of procedure we have all encountered, beginning in elementary school. It is also widely used in individually administered intelligence measures. In the original Binet test (Binet & Simon, 1916), for example, the child is presented with a task such as copying a square or giving the meaning of a word and the response is scored as 0 or 1. The tester must have a clear basis for making the scoring decision and in a formalized test examples of scoring particular responses that could be given must be available. The most objective type of scoring such items is obtained when the person is asked to respond with a number as in standard types of mental arithmetic items.

One objection to the use of some items of this free-response kind is that the scoring can be somewhat subjective and that this possibility may introduce a further source of error into the score obtained. For this reason, multiple-choice items are sometimes referred to as "objective test items" because the scoring of the response is not subjective and can be done by computers. However, it should be borne in mind that it is only the scoring of the response that is objective and that there is plenty of room for subjectivity in the selection of the particular items and the alternatives between which the person must choose as well as the definition of which is the correct answer. It is really only a question of the stage at which the subjectivity is introduced. In tests that are, or could be, analyzed according to classical test theory (CT), including ordinary classroom tests, a total score on a set of items is computed as simply the sum of the item scores. This is called a "raw score" in the literature on tests. For some purposes that are important, particularly in chapters 4 and 5, the item scores are converted to tied-ranks scores before being summed.

FREE RESPONSE WITH POLYTOMOUS ITEMS

Binet Tests

In the original Binet–Simon test most of the items were creative answer with dichotomous scoring. However, since that time, there has been a tendency for intelligence tests such as those in the Wechsler scales to become polytomous. Thus a vocabulary item "What is an apple?" might get the response "Something you eat" or, alternatively, the response could be "A piece of fruit." Clearly the second response, "A piece of fruit," is more precise than the first so could be given a higher score, say 2, whereas the response "Something you eat" could be given a score of 1 and an incorrect response a score of 0. The item can become trichotomous with three ordered categories. An objection to this type of polytomous scoring is that conservative scorers tend to use the score of 1 more often than more precise scorers.

Binet's items were derived from experts who had had lots of experience with children. They were asked to provide examples of tasks on which success or failure, in their opinion, showed which children were more or less intelligent on the task. The fact that they were able to do this and provide items which formed a scale indicates that the experts understood what was asked of them. However, there was no psychological theory by which the items were chosen. They were in fact chosen on the basis of the extent to which they discriminated between children of different age levels.

Piagetian Tests

In more recent time Piaget (1947), who worked in the Binet–Simon laboratory for some years, developed a theory of operational thinking, and this theory enables the construction of sets of items examining, for example, the operation of conserving judgment of number, weight, and volume when no relevant change was made to the stimuli. For example, if two rows have the same number of beads equally spaced, as below,

```
    0       0       0       0       0
    0       0       0       0       0
```

most children, if not all, will say that there is the same number in each row. However, if the beads in one row were spread farther apart in front of the child, as below,

```
        0       0       0       0       0
  0       0               0               0           0
```

but none added or removed, the preoperational child (usually under age 6) will say there are more beads in the longer row simply because it is longer and ignore the fact that the beads are farther apart.

In administering these Piagetian tasks it is important to ask the child why he or she gave the particular response whether it was correct or not. Some children give an incorrect response with an irrelevant reason. Other children give the correct response without having a satisfactory reason for doing so. Others again give a correct interpretation of the situation following the giving of the correct response. Whatever the subject's response, he or she is then asked why they thought that it was correct, and the item is not positively scored unless this explanation meets the criteria for the level of thinking being tested.

Some psychologists have tried to convert these tasks into free response or multiple-choice items without seeking an explanation for the response given. Tests based on such items have not proved to be satisfactory (see Verweij, 1994). The results of studying Piagetian items requiring the operation of transitivity were given by Verweij (1994). These results show clearly the need to take into account the explanation given by the child for her or his responses to transitivity items. The transitivity concept is illustrated by the principle that if A is taller than B and B is taller than C, then A must be taller than C, and we make considerable use of it in this book, particularly in chapter 7. One Piagetian example uses a simple beam balance for weighing things. The child is shown that when identically sized weights A and B are placed on opposite sides of the balance, A is heavier. When B and C are on opposite sides, B is heavier. The child is asked, "Which is heavier, A or C?" For credit, the child must not only say "A," but must give the correct reason, one showing that she or he understands the implication. This result generalizes to other concrete operational items.

The Porteus Maze Tests

Porteus (1915) provided another early example of dichotomous scoring in intelligence measures. He did pioneering work on the assessment of mental ability. Using a maze test with items similar to the familiar puzzles, he developed a series of mazes spanning a wide range of ages and difficulty. He used these with children who had problems with their school work. If a child made an error on a particular maze he or she was stopped and given a further trial on the same maze. A further error produced a zero score for an easy maze but a further trial or two were allowed on more difficult mazes.

The maze test had advantages over more oral tests when used with deaf children and with those from minority groups who had language problems. He gave very explicit scoring instructions and later showed differences between Australians with an Aboriginal as opposed to an English background, and between pre- and post-lobectomy/lobotomy operations.

However, Porteus did not check the maze test for its applicability for Aboriginal Australians in the way suggested in chapter 10. He also did not emphasize the fact that although there was a difference in the means of IQs in Aboriginal and non-Aboriginal groups, his results showed that there were thousands of Aborigines who were more intelligent than most non-Aborigines. He later worked in Hawaii where he was associated with the Leiter Performance Tests, which were age scales of the Binet type.

CREATIVE RESPONSES

In educational programs, the setting of creative response tasks is very common and has been for centuries. For example, a person may be asked to write an essay on a particular topic or write a report on a project she or he has undertaken. The responses are sometimes scored dichotomously as simply pass/fail but more frequently are given a verbal grade such as Credit/Pass/Fail or a numerical score of án integer, for example, as a mark from 0–10 (i.e. polytomously) or given letter grades A to F. Such tasks may be set in any of the subjects and the person's result recorded as number of subjects passed.

However, with polytomous tasks in an educational setting, the justification for combining the scores in different subjects into an overall result or average is more complex and is open to considerable debate. These matters are discussed in chapter 4.

In clinical psychology, many creative answer tests have been proposed. Some of these are the projective tests, which are beyond the scope of this book. Others such as the Picture Frustration Study (PFS; Rosenzweig, 1960) require a creative response such as a verbal response to a threatening situation, which is then coded (e.g., punitive or impunitive). Such summary scores can be analyzed by item response methods. However, there is much more to be inferred from the verbal responses than the number of punitive responses evaluated against the norms from particular groups, but this topic is beyond the scope of this book.

In the case of organizational and vocational psychology, creative answer items are not often used because of time restraints. Where they are used it is often for selection for a very senior position and dichotomous scoring may not be appropriate. Frederiksen's (1966) In-Basket Test is an example of such a test in which the creative responses to the various items are usually scored polytomously. Vocational preference is assessed using a ranking task such as the Rothwell–Miller *Interest Blank* (1988).

In the industrial setting, people are sometimes assessed by performance on the job. For example, on an assembly line the time a person takes to perform his or her part of the process can be important when this leads to a decrease in the rate of production. These "time and motion" studies as they were called were pioneered in the United States by a psychologist, Elton Mayo. These studies can also provide criteria against which tests may be evaluated.

Creative Items Polytomously Scored

As noted earlier many educational tests involve creative answer tasks such as writing essays or reporting on projects. These are usually scored on a numerical scale ranging, for example, from 0 to 10 or 20 or a letter scale, such as A to F, with or without pluses or minuses.

When large numbers of candidates are attempting the test more than one marker or grader is used. Empirical studies have shown that markers or graders differ surprisingly in the marks they will allocate and some have concluded that a person's final grade may depend as much on the grader as it does on the person's ability in the subject. For this reason multiple-choice items were introduced on a large scale in the 1930s to replace the creative answer or essay-type questions, but these items have their own problems.

Essay or project examinations have been included here because, in recent times, creative answer tasks have again been used to assess students in schools. The SAT (Scholastic Aptitude Test) that is widely used for university admissions includes a written essay and is an example of polytomous grading applied to formalized testing. The terms *alternative* or *performance* and *authentic* assessment have been used to refer to such examinations and the reasons for reintroducing them are pedagogical. It is argued that schooling should be more than the learning of a large number of isolated facts, and using these to answer multiple-choice questions should include the learning of ways to carry out projects and report the results.

Another method of obtaining assessment material is by requiring the student to build up a portfolio of the results of his or her activities in a given area over a certain period of time. This method is sometimes used in schools and is called "authentic testing," because it is based on tasks that have intrinsic meaning to the student. These portfolios can then be assessed by the ordering method described in chapter 5. Despite considerable discussion of performance assessment the problems that led to its abandonment such as reliability, generality, and rater effects are not being examined.

In addition to scoring the degree of correctness of a response, another way to change a creative answer dichotomous cognitive item into a polytomous one with three or more ordered categories is to take into account the speed of response as well as its correctness. Thus, an incorrect response scores 0 and a correct response 1 plus a bonus of 1 or 2 or more if the correct response is given quickly enough. It has been noted in reviews of the WISC III test that there has been an increased tendency to take speed of response into account. This trend has been criticized by those who consider that speed of response is not an important factor in assessing intelligence (Carroll, 1994).

In chapter 5, a method is described for using ordinal test theory to develop ways of dealing with the ordered categories that are often obtained in this type of assessment. Thus, ordinal test theory can be applied to any of the assessment methods being used in educational systems.

Grader Effects

There are a number of ways the differences between graders of creative responses manifest themselves. Rating methods have been studied for many years in the laboratory (see Woodworth, 1938), where it has been shown that raters of the intensity of stimuli differ in the range of responses they use, some preferring a wide range of values others a much narrower range. Furthermore, some raters use predominantly the high end of the scale whereas others prefer to use the low end.

Converting each grader's scores to standard scores with a set mean and standard deviation would overcome these biases to some extent provided that the essays are allocated to graders in an at least approximately random fashion. This method was suggested by experimentalists in 1938 at the time when reliability of grading essays was being questioned but was ignored as a partial remedy for the problems of grading.

The ordinal test theory (OTT) that we describe later is a different and more justifiable approach to this problem of grader variation, again provided there is approximately random allocation of essays. This approach is described in the next three chapters.

The approach of using expert judges to allocate points to creative performance is one that is used in many events at Olympic games and similar sporting situations where diving and skating and other performances are rated. A similar situation exists in musical competitions. However, in these cases each performance is rated by a number of expert judges and so individual bias is reduced. On the other hand, as the object is to rank the performances to discover which is the best, an ordinal approach is likely to be more valid and reliable.

In assessing performance on the job, employers are likely to use ratings by supervisors to decide whether a person should be promoted, given a raise in salary, or even dismissed. Again the problem of individual bias can arise and an unfair result might be obtained. Thus in organizational and vocational settings creative tasks or work performance may be evaluated on polytomous scales. Personal ratings may also be used in assessing the behavior of disturbed people in a clinical environment. In all these contexts problems of differential bias on the part of different raters should be considered and eliminated as much as possible.

Whether or not the creative answer items are scored dichotomously or polytomously using three or more ordered categories there is an arbitrariness in assigning numbers to these categories. Thus, if a response is judged to be correct and speed of response is not to be taken into account, the response is usually given a score of one irrespective of the difficulty of the item. To some it seems anomalous that a correct response to a difficult item is given the same numerical score as a correct response to an easy item, that is, they both receive a score of one. This problem has probably encouraged the increasing use of bonus points based on speed of response.

However, the perceived need to allow for the difficulty of the item really only draws attention to the arbitrariness of the zero–one scoring system. The question that should be asked is whether this arbitrary system extracts the most information that can be obtained from the data. This question is considered quite generally in chapter 4 and elsewhere.

MULTIPLE-CHOICE ITEMS DICHOTOMOUSLY SCORED

Multiple-choice items are the most commonly used items in cognitive tests and are used in educational, vocational, and clinical psychology, and in education generally. One reason for their common use has been mentioned, that is, that they can be objectively scored clerically or by electronic computers. Another reason for using these items is that they can be administered in a relatively short period of time so that a wide range of topics can be covered in a session.

One of the problems with these items is that if only four or five alternatives are presented, there is a reasonable probability that a person can give the correct response to a cognitive test item by a more or less random choice among the alternatives.

A practice aimed at discouraging guessing is to tell the subjects beforehand that they will be penalized for giving wrong answers. One formula for penalizing wrong answers is to use "formula scoring," which assumes that all alternatives are equally likely to be chosen and subtracts the number of wrong answers divided by one less than the number of alternatives. However, if a subject is able to eliminate one or more of the alternatives as is common among able persons, this formula will undercorrect.

The assumption underlying formula scoring was questioned by Brownless and Keats (1958) and Keats and Munro (1992) who carried out studies of guessing using the test–retest procedure where examinees take the same test twice, so scores can be correlated. To avoid the effects of contamination, the scores at one administration were compared with tendency to guess at the other. These workers found that the extent of guessing was negatively correlated with number correct and that the probability of a correct response by guessing was positively correlated with number correct.

These facts are also significant in the evaluation of the "three parameter model" of item response theory discussed in earlier chapters, as well as later ones, as this theory assumes that the probability of a correct response by guessing is not related to the ability of the person, which may well not be true.

Another possible way of reducing the effect of guessing on the number correct score is to have a large number of alternatives that might apply to a small set of items in the way used by Mollenkopf (1950). Alternatively, it has been suggested that respondents should be encouraged to guess on the grounds that if all respondents attempt all items, then formula scoring will be perfectly linearly correlated with number correct score. However, this practice seems to be encouraging the habit of guessing when the correct response is not known. The number correct score is hardly to be considered as the major criterion. Moreover, there will still be variability in the extent to which examinees follow this instruction.

MULTIPLE-CHOICE TESTS WITH POLYTOMOUS SCORING

The most common occurrence of these items is in attitude scales and other self-report scales. The respondent is given a series of ordered categories to select from for each item. One of the most commonly used series is "strongly agree, agree, neither agree nor disagree, disagree, strongly disagree," with the subject having to choose one of these for each of a set of statements. The scores for the categories are usually arbitrary integers such as 2, 1, 0, −1, −2 or their reverse in the case where agreeing with the statement indicates a lower amount of the attitude being measured.

With these items, as with dichotomous scoring of 0 or 1, the question of the justification of the use of one set of arbitrary integers rather than another arises. Likert (1932) attempted to justify the arbitrary integer method in terms of its simplicity and ease of implementation. He also showed that it gave a result that was highly correlated with that obtained by normalizing the distribution on each item and claimed that this validated the method.

Torgerson (1958) referred to this method of quantification using integers as measurement by definition rather than by using a fundamental process. He noted that attempts to become more theoretical lead to item response models, which are more concerned with the characteristics of items than those of subjects tested. This observation is even more true today.

Polytomous items are not treated at great length in standard books on testing. Those that advocate the use of arbitrary integral scoring tend to follow the procedures set out for dichotomous items. Books using item response theory, IRT, have problems with polytomous scoring because the formulations of these theories for polytomous items tend to involve untestable assumptions or require such complex computations as to be impractical.

Our conclusion is that there is no satisfactory method for scoring polytomous items other than the tied-ranks or other ordinal methods of scoring described in chapters 4 to 6.

TYPES OF ITEM PRESENTATION

Types of presentation may be broadly classified as individual or group testing. Individual testing is usually carried out by a single tester presenting items in oral, graphic, or written form to the subject and recording the response or scoring it on a dichotomous or polytomous basis. Examples of individually administered tests are: WAIS, WISC, Binet, Piagetian, British Abilities Scales, and so on, as well as various clinical tests.

The tester may be required to probe the subject's responses by asking, "Can you tell me more about it?" and recording any additional responses or modifying the original scoring. Another type of probe is that used with the items developed by Piaget (1947) where the tester is required to ask the subject to explain why he or she gave the original response. Although there has been some controversy about using this probe on the grounds that it might introduce subjectivity to the testing, we noted earlier that it has recently been shown (Verweij, 1994), that the omission of this step does not produce a consistent ordinal scaling, whereas including it does.

Ordinal Values Scales

The 1988 revision of the Rothwell–Miller "Interest Blank" is composed of nine sets of 12 occupations, one from each of 12 categories of occupations. The respondent is required to rank each of the occupations in a set of 12 in terms of his or her interest in the occupation. In Keats' (1972) *Introduction to Quantitative Psychology*, he referred to this procedure as "quantification by ordering." The method is a precursor to the test theory based on ranks that is a major focus of this book, particularly in chapters 4 and 5.

In the Rothwell–Miller method it is assumed that the subject is ranking the 12 categories of occupations nine times. For this assumption to hold there should be some internal consistency in the rankings of each individual subject. The method used by Kendall (1975, pp. 96–98) to test whether or not a set of rankings has some consistency is noted here and taken up in chapters 4 and 5 on ordinal test theory.

To obtain an overall ranking of the 12 categories by a particular respondent, the rankings of the relevant occupations are summed and the order of the totals for each category determines its ranking from most to least interesting to the subject.

The average of the rankings from 1 to 12 is $6\frac{1}{2} = \frac{1}{2}(1 + 12)$ and as there are 9 rankings, the average of the totals is $9 \times 6\frac{1}{2} = 58\frac{1}{2}$. If the rankings are completely inconsistent, each total occupation's ranking should be close to $58\frac{1}{2}$ and there should be no clear ordering. On the other hand, for perfect consistency, the totals should be multiples of 9. Nine from a particular category ranked 1 gives a total of 9, 9 ranked 2 = 18 and so on, up to 9 ranked 12 = 108. It would be expected that the summed rankings of a particular subject should be somewhere between these two extremes.

To evaluate a particular set of 12 totals of rankings, subtract $58\frac{1}{2}$ from each of the 12 totals and square the difference. Sum the 12 squared differences to form a total sum of squares, S. To determine whether or not these totals of rankings could have arisen by quite arbitrary allocation of rankings one can use χ^2 with $12 - 1 = 11$ degrees of freedom equals $S/117$. For the purpose of interpreting the responses from a particular subject, if the S value is less than 2,303, the responses should be considered worthless because the subject has shown no significant consistency in ranking the categories. In practice this is a very rare occurrence and a subject giving such responses should be examined further.

In testing practice it is common to use coefficient alpha (α) to assess the degree of internal consistency of a test administered to a group of subjects. α is discussed in some detail in later chapters, but for present purposes we merely need to note that it ranges from 0 (completely random) to 1.0 (completely consistent). In the case of the Interest Inventory, it may be shown that (see chap. 4), for an individual subject,

$$\alpha = 9(S - 1287)/8S$$

If this value is $\geq .8$ one can be confident in making further interpretation of the responses.

Methods of Test Administration

In group testing, the tester may have a large group of subjects to test and the tests are presented in printed form. The subject must read the items and record his or her answer on the test itself or on a separate answer sheet. In the latter case the subject must be careful to record the response to an item in the numbered space provided for that item if the items are multiple choice rather than creative answer. However, using separate answer sheets assists with machine marking and saves a great deal of paper and printing.

Although most testing has been group testing, there is a growing tendency these days to administer tests using computers. The subjects must be given thorough instructions and practice so that they know what is expected of them even though they are not very familiar with computers.

One advantage of this method is that the performance can be scored by the computer as the testing is proceeding and the final score available immediately the subject has finished the test. There is an implication that the test is multiple-choice with problems of guessing associated with it.

One advantage computer administration has in common with some other methods of administration is that the test can be adapted to the ability of the subject. The computer can select items that are suitable to the ability of the subject so that the subjects are not given a lot of items that are either too easy or too difficult for the particular subject. This idea was first developed by Binet (Binet & Simon, 1916) but at that time it could only be used in individual testing with the tester scoring the items as the test proceeded. This practice was dependent on the concept of mental age to produce a single scale.

As has been shown by Pfister (1995), it is possible to develop equipment for group testing using one computer recording and scoring responses from up to 60 subjects. The subjects record their responses using a light pen and the alternatives are coded using a bar-code system. This practice saves considerable capital equipment and stationery and again the scores are available within minutes of the completion of the testing.

Although it would be possible to program this equipment to handle adaptive testing, it has not been done so far. However, computerized adaptive testing has been used widely in Educational Testing Service tests.

SUMMARY

In this chapter, four basic types of items or tasks have been described and considered in terms of the way they are scored. The conditions under which these items may be presented have been described. Reference has also been made to a fifth type of test in which subjects are asked to rank the elements in an item such as types of occupations. Various problems have been raised about the usual methods of scoring items. There is clearly a need for general justification of scoring items of all types. It is claimed here that ordinal test theory (OTT) and its use of tied-rank scores provides such a justification. Ordinal test theory is an attempt to establish a theoretical basis, which is more concerned with the characteristics of persons rather than items.

In chapter 4, two general methods of obtaining scores from each item are described in the case of dichotomous items. One, called tied-ranks scoring, is presented and its applications to different types of items described. Its relationship to more conventional ways of scoring items and tests will be derived in the case of dichotomous items.

Item Scores and Their Addition to Obtain Total Test Scores in the Case of Dichotomous Items

ORDINAL MEASUREMENT

Data Are Ordinal

The present authors presume that the objective of psychological measurement is the development of meaningful scientific scales. However, in most instances, behavioral science data are a considerable distance from providing such scales. Much behavioral data are binary, and we will follow the path of noting ways of examining the consistency of such data and deriving scores to summarize it provided that it displays a satisfactory degree of consistency. Such scores are referred to as "assumed scales" or just "scores." These scores are assumed to be ordinal variables, not some higher level such as interval or ratio scales or quasi-continuous variables. If our ideal of the scientific process holds, assumed scales are then to be used in further studies and the relationships they enter into are determined. These may be such as to allow the elevation of the score to interval status and scientific scales. This process is largely beyond the scope of this book.

We realize that this cautious approach runs counter to the prevailing practices both in psychometrics, where mathematical models are fitted to binary data and the resulting numbers are believed to have interval properties, and in other areas of behavioral research, where item scores are simply added up and then considered to be interval-scale variables. We believe that there is no consistent or compelling evidence that variables of either type deserve that status; they fail to demonstrate the regularities necessary for it.

Further, even for the data they summarize, a myriad of alternative, non-linearly related versions would do as well. Furthermore, in the case of psychometric models, they can almost always be shown not to fit the data to which they are applied (exceptions being mostly cases of small sample size), so what is the status of a variable derived using a nonfitting model?

This view may be dismissed as the curmudgeonly reaction of two elderly academicians whom the field has passed by, but we feel that a thoughtful observer will conclude that if the field has passed us by, it has done so going in the wrong direction. So our approach is to develop machinery for ordinal measurement. If that can be accomplished, then perhaps meaningful models can be developed that go beyond ordinality. In the meantime, we provide methods for summarizing data without providing bases for reading more into them than they deserve. We believe that restricting the assumed scales that are derived from simpler behavioral data to ordinal status is required by principles that are basic to science. In particular, one principle is that a variable should not be assumed to have properties that it has not been shown to have or even been shown not to have. One may hypothesize that it has such properties, but the scientist does so only to serve as the basis for research designed to demonstrate them. For the very great majority of variables derived from behavioral data, it has not been shown that the *intervals* have any meaning. Insofar as some of the variables do display a modest level of utility as scientific scales, that is, they relate to other variables, these relations are entirely attributable to their ordinal properties. The intervals do not display any utility or validity except for artificial reasons.

Ranks From Item Scores

Having obtained responses to items of the various kinds described in the previous chapter, one then has the task of identifying scores for these responses. These scores must be such that there is a logical procedure by which they can be added to obtain a meaningful total score on the test or scale. The possible responses are assumed to define an ordinal scale in the sense that a particular response is taken to indicate more (or less) of an ability or attribute relative to those people who respond in a lower (or higher) category. The order on one item must be correlated with an overall order as shown by a rank order correlation of the kind defined by Kendall (1975).

In some types of self-report items this assumption may not be justified. For example, in an anxiety scale with a dichotomous item such as "I am sometimes anxious," the response "no" may be given by a person who never feels anxious as well as a person who feels anxious all of the time. Thus the responses "yes" and "no" do not order the subjects on an anxiety dimension. Such items are referred to as nonmonotic and should be avoided altogether in tests of the kind considered here. If the ordinal scores on items are to be combined in some fashion to form a total score, one aim should be to ensure that the order on this total score is a best estimate, in some sense, of the order of the persons on a variable underlying the responses to the items.

TIED-RANKS SCORES

A method of achieving this aim with dichotomous items is described and discussed in this chapter. This method uses the concept of tied-ranks scores, which is a fundamental concept in one ordinal theory discussed in this chapter and chapter 5 particularly.

The most common method of giving scores to item responses is to allocate successive integers to the ordered responses (i.e., the numbers 0 or 1 for dichotomous items). In the case of trichotomous items or higher order polytomous items the scores 0, 1, 2, etc. or −2, −1, 0, 1, 2, etc. are used. The arbitrariness of this method was noted by Likert (1932) in an article introducing his method of measuring attitudes using polytomous items scored with successive integers. He tried to justify this method of scoring on the grounds of convenience and it must be remembered that computers did not exist at the time he was writing.

Torgerson (1958) referred to this method of arbitrary integral scoring as measurement by fiat. He also noted that people who tried to improve on this method of scoring usually ended up being more interested in the items than in the people being tested. The developments of Item Response Theory since the 1970s confirm this observation.

In the same article, Likert (1932) presented a study reporting a high correlation between total scores obtained by adding these arbitrary integers and those obtained by transforming the integers into standardized normal deviates (via percentiles) and adding these deviates. The method for doing this transformation is described here. However, it should be stressed that there is no logical justification for preferring the normal deviates to the integers on which they are based.

Likert's use of the normal deviates method was based on the misconception that this improved their measurement properties, but the method is described here both for historical reasons and so that it can be compared with a method having theoretical justification. The misconception held by Likert and many others in 1932 is still held by some psychologists today and, indeed, methods in common use such as the Wechsler Tests are based on this misconception. As noted in the previous chapter, this misconception may be attributable to the mutual misunderstanding between mathematical statisticians and empirical scientists concerning the status of the normal distribution noted earlier. Because empirical scientists believed that statisticians had proved mathematically that most variables must be normally distributed, they concluded that those that were not should be transformed so that they were. Thus, there has been a great tendency for psychologists to transform the scores to produce something closer to a normal distribution. This tendency has persisted to the present time, as shown, for example, in the latest editions of the Stanford–Binet test.

The method advocated by Likert (1932) of adding the integral scores allocated to the various response categories is commented on by de Gruijter and van der Kamp (1984) in the following terms: "The simplest way to provide a score or scale value for a person, is by simply adding item scores. This procedure is known as measurement by fiat. There exist only pragmatic reasons for this kind of measurement. For example, the resulting scale could be a useful scale for prediction purposes" (p. 8).

It is shown next that for dichotomously scored items there is a theoretical justification for simply adding item scores of zero and one. However, for more than two alternatives, the best method of scoring is in terms of "tied-ranks" scores (see chap. 5, p. 72).

EVALUATING ITEMS, TESTS AND SCALES

These evaluations are formulated to apply to all forms which order subjects into any number of ordered categories. Essentially they include: internal consistency, reliability, and validity.

Internal Consistency

This property refers to the extent to which items agree with each other in their ordering of the subjects. An item that has a very low average rank order correlation, rho, with the other items should be dropped from the test or scale. Originally the index used to measure this was the Kuder–Richardson formula 20 (KR20; Kuder & Richardson, 1937), which could only be applied to dichotomous items. It estimates the correlation between the total score on a test and the total score on a test having similar statistical properties. It was generalized by Cronbach (1951) to all polytomous items with a coefficient α using item statistics. Guilford (1954) showed that the calculation of α could be simplified by using an analysis of variance of items by persons. Using this method, the variance of persons' scores and the persons by items interaction lead to coefficient α. This concept has been greatly expanded to include more complex contexts into a field called "generalizability," beginning with the work of Cronbach, Gleser, Nanda, and Rajaratnam (1973).

In the testing context, where the variances of the items are usually known, the most useful formula for α is probably

$$\alpha = m(1 - \Sigma s_j^2 / s_x^2) / (m - 1). \tag{4.1}$$

In (4.1) m is the number of items in the test, s_j^2 is the variance of item j, and s_x^2 is the variance of total scores on the test. Examples of its calculation are given in Appendix A, which also includes a computer program for the calculation.

A coefficient mathematically related to α is Kendall's (1975) coefficient of concordance, W, which also measures agreement in the ranking of persons by items. We have:

$$W = [m - (m - 1)\alpha]^{-1} \tag{4.2}$$

with m items. Coefficient W has the advantages that it has a test of significance associated with χ^2 and it is also related to the average of the Spearman ρ rank-order correlation coefficient of each item with every other item. The average ρ coefficient may be more easily understood than either α or W.

Rearranging the formula above relating W to α, one obtains a formula for α:

$$\alpha = [m/(m - 1)][(1 - 1/mW)], \tag{4.3}$$

which indicates that if $MW < 1$, then $\alpha < 0$, that is, that α can be negative. It is difficult to interpret what a negative value for a coefficient of consistency could mean substantively, but in this context it would show that the average covariance between items was negative, a highly undesirable situation if one is looking for internal consistency.

Whereas the agreement between items in ordering people is an important means of evaluating a test, the agreement between people in ordering items is also of considerable significance. This significance was first noted by Guttman (1947); it was also noted by Coombs (1964). They both argued that highly significant agreement implied the existence of a psychological dimension common to the items. As noted by Keats (1995) cultures can only be compared if the psychological dimension defined by items in one culture agrees with that defined in another.

Reliability

Reliability is a measure of the extent to which one measurement agrees with another designed to measure the same thing. Its value may be obtained by repeated testing after a period of time, the examinees not knowing they will be tested twice. The disadvantage of this method is that the subject might have learned how to do some of the items and we get practice effects. Brownless and Keats (1958) and Keats and Munro (1992) showed how this repeat reliability data can be analyzed. An advantage of the retest approach to reliability is that it indicates how large the *validity*, as measured below, of the test can be. Parallel forms of a test, matched on item characteristics, can also be administered with a small time gap to estimate parallel forms reliability by correlation.

Validity

Validity may be defined in terms of the agreement with an ideal measurement. This may be estimated in terms of the correlation of scores on a finite test with those that would be obtained from a universe of items of which the test items are a defined sample. Convergent, discriminative, or construct validity may be estimated using factor analytic approaches not treated here. Predictive validity is the most practical measure and should be examined in practical situations in which tests are used. For example, if SAT scores are intended to indicate or predict how well a student is likely to perform in college, predictive validity would be represented by the correlation between SAT scores and college grade point average. The problem with this method is often in defining an appropriate and reliable criterion measure.

COMBINING ITEM SCORES FOR DICHOTOMOUS ITEMS

Tied-Ranks Scores

This section deals with dichotomous items, those that have two categories, and are usually scored as 0 or 1. Most cognitive tests are in this category as are some attitude scales and personality tests. The section uses the results reported by Keats (1995). Consider an item on which 11 of 100 subjects gave a negative or incorrect response scoring 0 and 89 subjects gave a positive or correct response scoring 1. The 11 subjects showed less of the attribute or ability being tested by the item than the 89 subjects. However, as it is not possible to distinguish between the 11 subjects on this item, they should each be given an average ranking or tied-ranks score of $\frac{1}{2}(1 + 11) = 6$. Those who gave the positive or correct response would be ranked from 12 to 100 but, because it is not possible to discriminate between these subjects on the item, they should be given a tied-ranks score of $\frac{1}{2}(12 + 100) = 56$.

Note that this is 50 more than the score for those giving an incorrect or negative response.

Now consider another item on which 91 subjects gave the incorrect response while only 9 gave the correct response. The tied-rank score for an incorrect response would be $\frac{1}{2}(1 + 91) = 46$ and that for a correct response would be $\frac{1}{2}(1 + 91 + 100) = 96$. Again the difference is 50 or half the number of subjects.

Three points can be made from these results:

1. The tied-ranks score for a correct response on the more difficult item (i.e., 96), is much greater than that for a correct response on the easier item (i.e., 56).

2. The tied-ranks score for an incorrect response on the easier item (i.e., 6), is much lower than that for an incorrect response to the more difficult item (i.e., 46). This is reasonable because people who get the more difficult item wrong will include some more able people than those who get the easier item wrong.

3. In both cases the difference between the tied ranks scores for correct and incorrect responses is $50 = \frac{1}{2}n$ where n is the number of subjects.

Thus the total tied-ranks score across n items for any person will equal $\frac{1}{2}nX + K$ where X is the number of correct responses given by the particular person and K is a constant, which is the same for all persons and equals the total tied-ranks score of a person whose responses were all incorrect. Thus, the total tied-ranks scores are perfectly linearly correlated with the number correct scores or the total integral scores. This relationship holds for all sets of dichotomous items.

The result obtained from relating tied-ranks scores to the number of correct responses is illustrated in Table 4.1 using 100 subjects and dichotomous items.

TABLE 4.1
Relating Tied-Rank Scores to Number Correct Scores for
100 Subjects Attempting Three Dichotomous Items

	Wrong	Right		
Scores	*0*	*1*	*Total*	*Diff.*
Item 1 Frequency	11	89	100	
Tied-Ranks Scores	6	56		50
Item 2 Frequency	49	51	100	
Tied-Ranks Scores	25	75		50
Item 3 Frequency	89	11	100	
Tied-Ranks Scores	45	95		50
Total Tied-Ranks Scores	76	226	300	150

TABLE 4.2
Patterns of Scores on the Three Items of Table 4.1

Total Score	Score Pattern	Total Tied-Ranks Scores
3.	1 + 1 + 1 = 3	Tied-Ranks Total = 226
2.	1 + 1 + 0 = 2	Tied-Ranks Total = 56 + 75 + 45 = 176
	1 + 0 + 1 = 2	Tied-Ranks Total = 56 + 25 + 95 = 176
	0 + 1 + 1 = 2	Tied-Ranks Total = 6 + 75 + 95 = 176
1.	1 + 0 + 0 = 1	Tied-Ranks Total = 56 + 25 + 45 = 126
	0 + 1 + 0 = 1	Tied-Ranks Total = 6 + 75 + 45 = 126
	0 + 0 + 1 = 1	Tied-Ranks Total = 6 + 25 + 95 = 126
0	0 + 0 + 0 = 0	Tied-Ranks Total + 6 + 25 + 45 = 76

With 0 or 1 scoring it is the number correct that determines the score because each one correct adds one to the score. Tied-rank scores give different scores for different items correct. Could this lead to different total tied-ranks scores with the same number correct? This is shown in Table 4.2.

Thus in all cases total tied-ranks scores = $50X + 76$ for all values of X and for all ways this value may be obtained. It is clear that this perfect relationship between total raw score and total tied-ranks score would hold for all items with two ordered categories (i.e., dichotomous items). This is an important justification for the use of 0,1 scoring of dichotomous items. The scoring of polytomous items by the 0,1,2 etc. method can not be justified in this way as is noted in the next chapter.

Measures of Internal Consistency

Because of the perfect linear relationship between the number of correct or positive responses and the total tied-ranks scores, the coefficient of internal consistency most commonly used, α, will be the same whether calculated from the number of correct responses or from the total tied-ranks scores, as noted before. The simplest form of this coefficient was presented by Kuder and Richardson (1937) and the general form by Cronbach (1951). Most current books on tests ignore the relationship between the zero-one scores and the tied-ranks scores and present the tabulations of item data in zero and one form. This also ignores the relationship between α and the concordance coefficient W (Kendall, 1975) and the significance test for both of these.

It also follows that the best estimate of the order of difficulty of the items will be obtained from the order of the number of correct responses to the item. This possibility is explored later in this chapter. A coefficient α or coefficient W for items can also be calculated to indicate the extent to which the persons ordered the difficulty or popularity of the items consistently, as shown later.

An example is now given of calculating both α and W from the same data and showing how they are numerically related (see Table 4.3). The calculations for this Table 4.3 follow Guilford (1954, p. 381) and the formula for α given earlier (4.1). In this example $\alpha = 12/11(1 - 2.03/9.45) = .857$. A point not covered in most texts is the relationship between Kendall's concordance coefficient, W, and α and the use of a chi squared test of significance of reliability and internal consistency (see Keats, 1972, pp. 60–63).

Table 4.4 converts the data from Table 4.3 from dichotomous scores of 0 or 1 to rankings of the 10 subjects in terms of total-tied ranks.

W can be computed most simply here by making use of its analysis-of-variance relationship; it is the ratio of the sum of squares for persons (SS_p) to the sum-of-squares total (SS_t):

$$W = SS_p/SS_t. \tag{4.4}$$

In the tied-ranks context, SS_p is $\Sigma(R_i - R)^2/m$, where R_i is the sum of Person is tied-ranks scores across the m items, and $R.$ is the average of these sums. SS_t is $\Sigma\Sigma(r_{ij} - r. .)^2$, where r_{ij} is Person is tied-ranks score on Item j and $r. . .$ is the average item tied-ranks score. In the example of Table 4.4, SS_p is $[(43.5 - 66)^2 + (53.5 - 66)^2 + \ldots + (93.5 - 66)^2]/12$, or 196.875. Also, reading the elements of the table across rows, SS_t is $[(5.5 - 6.6)^2 + (1 - 6.6)^2 + \ldots + (10 - 6.6)^2]$, or 507.5. Thus,

$$W = 196.875/507.5 = .388.$$

Since Chi^2 = $Wm(n - 1)$ in this situation,

$$\text{Chi}^2 = .388 \times 12 \times 9 = 41.904$$

with 9 degrees of freedom, which is highly significant according to the Table in the Appendix.

The coefficient α may be found from (4.3):

$$\alpha = 12(1 - 1/12W)/(12 - 1) = .857$$

which equals the value obtained by scoring 0 and 1 and applying the standard formula for α.

The advantage of using the ordinal approach is that it not only gives a proper meaning to internal consistency but also a test of significance for the measure of that property.

TABLE 4.3
Data From 12 Dichotomous Items Scored 0 or 1 for 10 Persons

Persons						Items							Total	Square
	1	2	3	4	5	6	7	8	9	10	11	12		
1	1	0	1	0	0	0	0	0	0	0	0	0	2	4
2	1	1	1	0	0	1	0	0	0	0	0	0	4	16
3	1	1	1	1	0	0	0	0	0	0	0	0	4	16
4	1	1	0	1	1	0	0	1	0	0	0	0	5	25
5	1	1	1	1	1	0	0	0	0	0	0	0	5	25
6	1	1	1	0	1	1	1	0	0	0	0	0	6	36
7	1	1	1	1	1	1	1	0	0	0	0	0	7	49
8	1	1	1	1	0	1	1	1	1	1	0	0	9	81
9	1	1	1	1	1	1	1	1	1	1	1	0	11	121
10	1	1	1	1	1	1	1	1	1	1	1	1	12	144
Total	10	9	9	7	6	6	5	4	3	3	2	1	65	517
$p_i q_i$	0	.09	.09	.21	.24	.24	.25	.24	.21	.21	.16	.09	2.03	

66

TABLE 4.4
Tied-Ranks Scores for Persons

Persons						Items							Total
	1	2	3	4	5	6	7	8	9	10	11	12	
1	5½	1	6	2	2½	2½	3½	4	4	3	4½	5	43½
2	5½	6	6	2	2½	7½	3½	4	4	3	4½	5	53½
3	5½	6	6	7	2½	2½	3½	4	4	3	4½	5	53½
4	5½	6	1	7	7½	2½	8½	4	4	3	4½	5	58½
5	5½	6	6	7	7½	2½	3½	4	4	3	4½	5	58½
6	5½	6	6	2	7½	7½	3½	4	4	8	4½	5	63½
7	5½	6	6	7	7½	7½	3½	4	4	8	4½	5	68½
8	5½	6	6	7	2½	7½	8½	9	9	8	4½	5	78½
9	5½	6	6	7	7½	7½	8½	9	9	8	9½	5	88½
10	5½	6	6	7	7½	7½	8½	9	9	8	9½	10	93½
Total Mean	55	55	55	55	55	55	55	55	55	55	55	55	660

Internal Consistency of Persons' Ordering of Items

During the development of test theory, some workers have stressed the need for subjects to order items in the same way. Guttman (1947) made this point very strongly in his definition of the scales that bear his name. Guttman scales require perfect consistency in ordering subjects by items as well as in ordering scale items by subjects. In practice perfect ordering of persons and dichotomous items is not possible and there has been argument from Guttman (1947), Loevinger (1948), and Green (1956) about how to measure degree of scalability. The measure suggested by Guttman (1947) was criticized by Green (1956) who proposed an alternative measure. Cliff (1983) reviewed these and a number of other suggestions, suggesting α as a plausible choice. A high degree of scalability of items from one of these measures was taken to be evidence for the psychological existence of a scale defined in terms of the items.

The probabilistic model of cognitive tests proposed by Rasch (1960) was much more likely to attain the criterion of producing the same order of difficulty of items for the low scorers as for the high scorers. This requirement is the basis for defining a difficulty dimension for items but has been criticized by Lord and Novick (1968) because it implies the rejection of items with too high discriminating power as well as those with too low. The Rasch Model satisfies the ordinal conditions laid down by Luce and Tukey (1964) for conjoint measurement. The conjoint ordering conditions imply consistent ordering of subjects by items and consistent ordering of items by subjects.

However, Item Response Theory (IRT) has attempted to allow for the differential ordering of items by groups of subjects of different ability by introducing a parameter which is defined as a measure of different discriminating power (Lord & Novick, 1968). The extent to which items vary on this parameter will lead to differential ordering of items by subjects of different abilities and so violate one condition of conjoint ordering.

We now present in Table 4.5 an example of the calculations of the extent to which subjects agree on the ordering of the difficulty of the items. The scores for each item in Table 4.5 are the number of the 10 subjects giving the correct response to the item. If p_i equals the proportion of the 12 items answered correctly by Person i, and $q_i = 1 - p_i$, then $\Sigma p_i q_i$ is the sum of the variances for the persons.

By analogy with formula (4.1), the consistency of item ordering by persons, α_I, can be calculated as

$$\alpha_I = n(1 - \Sigma s_i^2 / s_R^2)/(n - 1),$$

where s_i^2 is the person variance, $p_i q_i$, and s_R^2 is the variance of the rights scores for the items, such as those given at the bottom of Table 4.3, reproduced as the first line of Table 4.5. In the present data,

TABLE 4.5
Reanalysis of Data From Table 4.4

Item	1	2	3	4	5	6	7	8	9	10	11	12	Sum
R scores	10	9	9	7	6	6	5	4	3	3	2	1	65
R^2	100	81	81	49	36	36	25	16	9	9	4	1	447

Variance of Item Scores, s_R^2, = $(447 - 65^2/12)/12 = 7.91$.

Persons	1	2	3	4	5	6	7	8	9	10	Sum
p_i	2/12	4/12	4/12	5/12	5/12	6/12	7/12	9/12	11/12	12/12	
$p_i q_i$	.14	.22	.22	.24	.24	.25	.24	.19	.08	.00	1.82

$$\alpha_I = 10(1 - 1.82/7.91)/9 = .855,$$

and the corresponding W is

$$W = .434.$$

From this value Chi squared = $11 \times 10 \times .434 = 47.74$ with 11 degrees of freedom, which is highly statistically significant. Thus the ordering of items by persons is highly consistent to the same extent as the ordering of persons by items. In Chapter 6 we see that the person and item α's are connected through the relative size of s_x^2 and s_R^2.

SUMMARY

This chapter began by emphasizing the need to have an ordinal approach to test theory. According to this theory each item must have a high ordinal correlation, Spearman's ρ, or Kendall's τ both corrected for ties, with the total of the item scores.

Consistent with this requirement, items should show high internal consistency in their ordering of people (i.e., should order the people in approximately the same way as measured by Kendall's W, which is mathematically related to the more commonly used α and which can be tested for statistical significance). These two related requirements give one grounds for believing there may be an underlying dimension defined by the items.

As noted by Guttman (1947), Rasch (1960), and Luce and Tukey (1964), each group of persons with the same item score should order the items the same way as far as difficulty or popularity is concerned. This may be tested by calculating concordance W for person groups ordering the items. This condition is needed for defining an underlying psychological dimension for the items. Item Response Theories with 2 or 3 parameters claim to have obviated this requirement by defining a parameter of item discriminating power. What they have in fact done is to try to improve the goodness of fit of their theory to data that does not meet conditions for interval scaling. This chapter has shown that with dichotomous items, 0 or 1 scores can be used to produce ordinal scores across persons and items. However, in the case of more than two ordered categories of items it becomes clear that scores of 0,1,2. . . do not produce ordinal scores in the same way in most cases.

This fact leads to a situation in which items do not readily convert from integral scores to tied-ranks scores. In the literature many attempts have been made to convert from arbitrary integral scores to interval scores. Indeed, Andrich (1978) has shown that a Rasch assumption will validate the use of arbitrary integral scores as it does with dichotomous items but this assumption does not stand up to appropriate tests. Other writers in this field require strong essential rather than linear independence to obtain generalization to polytomous items and also that the form of the response characteristic curves is known, which can never be true. The next chapter deals with the general application of tied-ranks scoring to polytomous items and its general application in empirical studies.

Chapter 5

Item Scores and Their Addition to Obtain Total Test Scores in the Case of Polytomous Items

SCORING POLYTOMOUS ITEMS

In chapter 4 we presented a method of dealing with dichotomous items which is simplified by the fact that tied-ranks scores with these items are perfectly linearly correlated with the 1 or 0 scores usually used with these items. The use of measures of consistency, W and α, to determine whether items are ordering people consistently was shown to determine the extent to which these items are ordering persons on the same dimension. It was also noted that these same measures could be used to determine whether persons were reacting to a single dimension of items by consistently ordering them. In practice, the consistency of ordering persons may be high but that of ordering items may be low or vice versa. If both are very high the condition known as conjoint ordering is satisfied and this is a necessary but not sufficient condition to form an interval scale. For sufficiency, a condition known as cancellation is required as shown by Luce and Tukey (1964) and mentioned in chapter 2. This condition is almost never tested in applications of Item Response Theory, hence the development of Ordinal Test Theory is necessary.

If there are three or more ordered categories of response the number of possible different score patterns for each total ordered category can be very large indeed. It is most common to use successive integers such as 1, 2, 3, 4, or 5 to stand for the responses to any of five categories, and the total score to be the sum of these item scores. The restriction on the choice of category scores is simply related to order but the size of the interval between item and person as based on their respective tied-ranks scores is quite arbitrary, provided that the order of the categories is preserved. For example, scores of 1, 2, 5, 11, and 15 that have intervals of 1, 3, 6, and 4 could also be used if the responses are only ordinal. Under these circumstances the problem of combining category scores for different item responses by the same person becomes very much greater than was the case with dichotomies as shown in chapter 4.

In the case of dichotomous items, it was shown in chapter 4, Tables 4.4 and 4.5, that the sum of integral 0, 1 scores was perfectly linearly correlated with that of tied-rank scores. However, in the polytomous items in the example in Appendix A this turns out not to be true, since converting integral scores to tied-ranks is a nonlinear transformation. Thus, in this example, the order obtained from the totals of the tied-ranks scores, which give the best estimate of the ordering in the population in a sense related to least squares, is different from that order obtained from the totals of the integral scores.

Example

The method used by Likert (1932), as quoted by Cliff (1996, pp. 48–49) to justify the use of arbitrary integral scores by comparing these with normal deviate scores for each item is best understood by reference to Table 5.1 in order to show the procedure for a particular item. In the Table the ordered categories are indicated by the letters A (*the lowest*) to E (*the highest*), which might correspond to a range from *strongly disagree* to *strongly agree* and be scored −2, −1, 0, +1, +2, respectively on an arbitrary integral scale. For a given sample of 200 subjects the frequencies with which these categories are chosen might be 10, 25, 45, 70, and 50 respectively, as shown in the third row of Table 5.1. In the fourth row the cumulative frequencies are shown, ranging from 10 to 200.

TABLE 5.1
Method of Calculating Normal Deviates

	A	B	C	D	E
Integral scores	−2	−1	0	+1	+2
Frequency	10	25	45	70	50
Cumulative frequency	10	35	80	150	200
Tied-ranks scores	5.5	23	58	115.5	175.5
Tied-percentile ranks scores	2.75	11.5	29	57.75	87.75
Normal deviates	−1.92	−1.2	−.53	.195	1.16
$\lambda = 0, \sigma = 1$					
Wechsler units	4.24	7.4	8.35	10.585	13.48
$\lambda = 10, \sigma = 3$					

The fifth row, labeled tied-ranks scores, refers to the fact that 10 subjects are tied on the item in the lowest category, A, and should be given the average rank for that category, that is, the average of the lowest (1), and highest (10) ranks that are in that category, which here is 5½. Using cumulative frequencies, the 25 subjects in category B would be given a tied rank of 23, the average of 11 and 35, and so on. A general formula for proceeding from cumulative frequencies [CF] to tied-ranks is:

$$\text{tied-ranks} = \tfrac{1}{2}(CF_{(j-1)} + CF_j) + 1 \tag{5.1}$$

where j designates a particular category.

These tied-ranks scores may be converted to tied cumulative percentiles by dividing by $200/100 = 2$ because there are just 200 subjects in this example. The tied percentiles my be converted to normal curve deviates using standard tables (see, e.g., Kendall, 1975, p. 174). These deviates may be converted to scores with a mean of 10 and a standard deviation of 10 as is currently done in the Wechsler scales (Wechsler, 1939, 1997). This Likert–Wechsler procedure, which dates from the 1930s, has no scientific justification but is widely practiced by psychologists and other test users.

Comparing the tied-percentile scores with the arbitrary integral scores shows that the latter have equal differences of 1 between categories whereas the former have differences of 8.75, 17.5, 28.75, and 30, a large range of differences.

Comparison of the integral scores with the Wechsler scores for the same categories shows that whereas the difference between scores for successive categories is unity for the integral scores the values are 3.16, .95, 2.235, and 2.895 using the Wechsler scale scores. Although these differences are by no means trivial they would tend to average out over 20 or more items and so it was possible for Likert to obtain a high correlation between the totals from integral item scores and those obtained through normal deviates.

Advantages of Tied-Ranks

The step made by Likert from the tied-percentile ranks to the normal deviates is quite arbitrary because this step could equally well be made to another theoretical distribution with as much justification. The procedure is also an attempt to go from an ordinal ranking to an interval scale without meeting the conditions of conjoint measurement as discussed in chapter 2. The problem considered here is how to proceed from a ranking on one item to a combination of the rankings from a number of different items.

Such a step could be justified if there were sufficient agreement in the ordering of the subjects by the items to support an assumption that there is a basic ordering of the subjects related to the ordering of the subjects on each of the different items. Kendall (1975) showed that summing the different orderings of persons produced totals, the order of which gave the best estimate of the basic order in two senses related to least squares as noted on page 72 and shown below.

First, Kendall (1975) showed that the average Spearman's ρ (rho) correlation between the order obtained from the totals and the order obtained on each of the items was as great as or greater than the average ρ obtained from any other ordering. However, this demonstration took no account of ties, which would be frequent in the testing and scaling situation and so the conclusion may not hold exactly in all cases. Second, he showed that the estimate of the ordering obtained from the totals of the ranks differs less from a ranking obtained if the items were perfectly correlated than any other estimate of the basic order in a least squares sense. The demonstration holds whether ties are present or not.

McDonald (1985, pp. 90–91) referred to "optimal scaling" of items with more than two categories. This term relates to the procedures proposed for the estimation of weights for integral category scores, which will maximize the average relationship between total score and item scores. In each case the procedure used is aimed at maximizing the ratio of total score variance to the sum of the item score variances. This would have the effect of maximizing the coefficient of internal consistency α defined by Cronbach (1951). As Kendall (1975) has shown, the use of total tied-rank scores does this for ranks. Also, as Cliff (1996, p. 49) noted, this implies that the totals are in the best agreement with what are called the dominances between persons on the individual items. It will be recalled from chapter 3, that the dominances are scores for pairs that are equal to 1, 0, or −1, depending on whether the first score is greater, equal to, or less than the second.

The original work on which these maximizing procedures were based was that of Hotelling (1933) and Kendall's findings were first published in the 1940s. However, until now, nobody has pointed out that using tied-ranks scores achieves the same result as using principal components analysis to estimate optimal category scores.

It is clear that the order obtained from the totals of the tied-ranks scores across items is a better estimate of the basic order than that obtained by adding integer scores, normal deviates, or any other transformation of the tied-ranks scores for each item provided that tied-rank scores for each item are positively correlated with the order from total tied-ranks scores. Thus, one would expect that the α from tied-rank scores would usually be equal to or greater than that obtained from integral scores. This result was obtained in a study reported by Keats (1995) and is presented here in Fig. 5.1.

It may seem odd that, if α is a measure of the internal consistency of the items in ordering the subjects who attempted the scale, that this index can have two different values depending on which method of scoring is used. In the method of calculating α proposed by Cronbach, the subjects ×

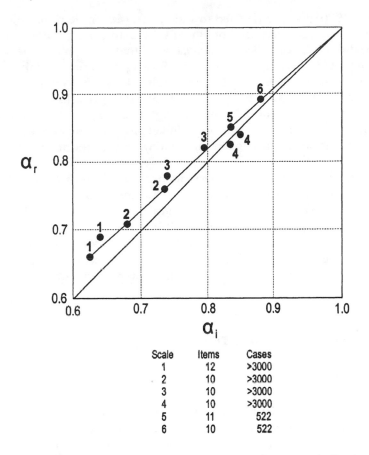

Scale	Items	Cases
1	12	>3000
2	10	>3000
3	10	>3000
4	10	>3000
5	11	522
6	10	522

FIG. 5.1.   Alpha values for item scores (α_i) and tied rank scores (α_r). (See attached Fig. 5.1.)

items analysis of variance is carried out and the between subjects sum of squares (SS_p) and total sum of squares (SS_t), and α is calculated from formula (1.1):

$$\alpha = SS_p / SS_t.$$

These variance values can be calculated using the totals of the integral scores for each subject, as is the usual procedure.

However there is no scientific basis for summing these arbitrary integral values whereas the summing of the tied-ranks scores is justified by the fact that these totals provide the best estimate of the order of the subjects on the variable being considered as shown by Kendall (1975). Thus, the analysis of variance should be carried out on the total tied-ranks scores.

Since 1970, others have tried to scale items with three or more ordered categories using extensions of Rasch's item response theory. Andrich (1978), following Rasch's approach, showed that if one made the assumption that categories were equally discriminating, then the summing of integral scores could be justified. However, this assumption is untestable from item response data. Lee, Poon, and Bentler (1990) developed a very complex model for polytomous items. Although this model led to an increased communality for the items and so was in keeping with the demands of optimal scaling, it cannot be applied without days of computing and is thus not very practical.

With dichotomous items it was found in the previous chapter that the order obtained from total tied-ranks scores was the same as that obtained by summing 0, 1 scores, whereas in general this will not be true for items with more than two ordered categories. If all the categories have the same frequency of response for all items, then tied-ranks scores will produce the same order as that obtained from integral category scores using successive integers. This result is important in considering performance assessment as shown next.

TYPES OF POLYTOMOUS ITEMS

WAIS Items

Although attitude scales and personality tests are the forms of assessment that most commonly use more than two ordered categories, some cognitive tests also use such Items. In the case of the Wechsler Adult Intelligence Scale (1997) and the Wechsler Intelligence Scale for Children (1997) for example, among others, there are hierarchical sets of item scores, subtest scores, and total verbal and performance scores as well as full-scale scores. These tests are worth considering in some detail as the current Wechsler tests are the most commonly used tests of general cognitive ability used today even though they are still based on the unjustified assumptions of Likert and Wechsler in the 1930s.

Most items in these Wechsler tests are scored 0, 1, or 2 or even 0, 1, 2, 3, or 4. In the case of some verbal subtests such as Vocabulary and Comprehension these categories are defined in terms of the correctness and preciseness of the response. For example, if the question is "What is an apple?", the response "Something you eat." is not as precise as "A piece of fruit you can eat." The second of these two responses receives a score of 2 because it is more precise than the first, which scores 1. In the case of some performance items, higher scores are given for faster responses, so again scores of 0, 1, 2, 3, etc. may be awarded.

These item scores are summed to form a subtest score according to the criteria describe earlier, but this score is not as good an estimate of the underlying order of the subjects on the ability tested by the subtest as would be obtained by converting the item scores to tied-rank scores and adding these. The total tied-ranks scores for the subtests yield the best estimate of the order of the subjects on the subtest. The frequency distribution on these totals for the standardization group can be converted to tied-ranks scores for the Comprehension subtest using the formula (5.1) given earlier.

Combining Scores

According to the WAIS norms (Wechsler, 1997) a total scale score of 60 on the verbal subtests corresponds to a Verbal IQ of 101. This total scale score of 60 could be obtained by obtaining a scale score of 10 on each of the six verbal subtests and this would correspond to a total of $300 = 6 \times 50$ on the percentiles using Table 5.3. These percentiles are derived from the normal distribution of the IQs. However a total scale score of 60 could also be obtained by scoring $8 + 8 + 8 + 8 + 9 = 41$ on five of the subtests and 19 on the sixth. The person might have been a number wizard who scored well above average on the arithmetic test but below average on the others. The total percentile score for this person would be 236.9. This score is the same as that of a person who had scale scores of 9 on five subtests and 10 on the sixth with a total of 55 and an IQ of 95 as opposed to 101.

A third way that a total scale score of 60 with IQ = 101 can be obtained, is: $12 + 12 + 12 + 11 + 11 + 2$. The person giving this pattern has scored above average on five subtests but has a very low score on the sixth. the total percentile score for this person is 351.4 which would be close to that obtained by a person with a scoring pattern of $10 + 10 + 11 + 11 + 11 + 11 = 64$ corresponding to an IQ of 105.

TABLE 5.2
Percentiles Corresponding to Various Scale Scores

Scale Score	Percentile	Scale Score	Percentile
19	99.9	9	37.0
18	99.6	8	25.0
17	99.3	7	16.0
16	97.7	6	9.0
15	95.0	5	5.0
14	91.0	4	2.3
13	84.0	3	.7
12	75.0	2	.4
11	63.0	1	.1
10	50.0		

TABLE 5.3
Scale Scores and Percentiles for Five Persons on Each Subtest

Subtest	Scale Scores for Persons					Percentiles for Persons				
	A	B	C	D	E	A	B	C	D	E
1	9	8	10	12	10	37	25	50	75	50
2	9	8	10	12	10	37	25	50	75	50
3	9	8	10	12	11	37	25	50	75	63
4	9	8	10	11	11	37	37	50	63	63
5	9	9	10	11	11	37	37	50	63	63
6	10	19	10	2	11	50	99.9	50	0.4	63
Total	55	60	60	60	64	235	236.9	300	351.4	352
IQ	95	101	101	101	105					

It is to be noted that the IQ values are bunched in the middle at a value of 101 whereas the total percentiles for these persons are spread from 236.9 to 351.4 showing greater discrimination using the percentile method. These values correspond approximately to persons with IQs ranging from 95 to 105 so large differences can be obscured by the standard IQ method.

Although an IQ based on an uneven pattern might be investigated by a psychologist, the Verbal IQ would be that shown and could affect future treatment of the person tested. If Total IQ had been considered the range would have been even greater than that found with only the Verbal IQ.

Scoring Performance Tasks

This type of assessment is also known as "alternative" or "authentic" assessment and is now being increasingly recommended in schools to replace multiple-choice testing. The tasks to be assessed might be essays on a particular topic or a choice of topics, reports on projects carried out by the student, a portfolio prepared by the student on the basis of experience in a particular field during a semester, or other work submitted. However there has been little discussion in the literature of how the reports, essays, and so forth are to be scored. To make the discussion concrete let us consider a school in which there are two classes at the same grade level. Students in both of these classes are given the same assessment tasks from the list given earlier (i.e., reports, essays, etc.).

When these assignments have been handed in, there will be a need to assess them in terms of ordered categories. To remove some of the effects of individual bias, all the essays could be marked by one teacher and the portfolios by the other. The number of score categories is assumed to be seven for both tasks, seven often being a comfortable number of categories for raters to work with. Integers 1 through 7 are assigned according to increasing merit of the responses.

Too few categories would mean that the teachers would simply not distinguish among the levels of passing or among the levels of failing. Using too many categories could require such fine distinctions that the task would seem too difficult for the teacher. What is important is the way the submissions are distributed among the ordered categories. As Woodworth (1938) noted, people who are set rating tasks of this kind differ in the way they use the categories. Some, easy markers, will use the categories 5, 6, and 7 extensively and ignore categories 1 and 2. Hard markers would have a reverse pattern. Other markers will restrict their marks to the central values, 3, 4, and 5 and hardly ever use 1 and 7; others, again, will use the full range of marks fairly evenly.

Because of the various personal biases and their influence on individual marks, it has been suggested that markers should be required to distribute their marks according to a specific distribution. The normal distribution was the most commonly specified one for the reasons given earlier. However, markers found it difficult to "mark on the curve" as it was called. They tended to drift from this curve to one closer to their particular biases.

The main aim of improving the efficiency of scoring is to try to persuade the markers to use all of the categories. The method closest to perfection is for markers to allocate the same number of tasks to each category but raters find this difficult to achieve. A fluctuation of less than the square root of the equal number would be acceptable in practice. In addition, it should be noted that assigning tied-ranks scores, whatever the distribution among the categories, eliminates the major sources of rater effects.

If there are two or more creative tasks contributing to the assessment, it might be informative to consider each pupil's overall performance. Tied-ranks test theory shows that by adding the tied-ranks scores a good estimate of the basic order of ability can be obtained from the order of these sums.

The raters might afterwards wish to determine a qualitative award of, say, Fail, Pass, Credit, Distinction, or High Distinction corresponding to various ordinal positions. This could be done by first defining what an ideal product would contain and then comparing this with the products in category 7 to determine which of these come close enough to this ideal to warrant the award of High Distinction. It is not necessary to award all products in category 7 a High Distinction but if this is not done then none in category 6 should be given the top award. The best estimate of the underlying order should not be disturbed. In the same way, Distinctions should be awarded and so on until the minimum passable product should be defined and only those below this should be failed.

It should be clear that alternative assessment could be and is often used at all educational levels from primary school to university. The method is subject to the same problems of scoring as beset the essay type examinations of the 1930s, which were abandoned in favor of multiple-choice tests. Subjectivity in marking essays can be reduced considerably by using the restrictions on markers that ordinal test theory prescribes, that is, that the number of cases in each scoring category should be about the same. If this ordinal approach is not used, the method can only be partly justified because the scores are subjective. Some justification can still be found for tied ranks because tied-ranks scores equate means and tend to equalize variances.

POLYTOMOUS ITEMS SCORED ACROSS PERSONS

In the case of polytomous items with more than two ordered categories it is possible to calculate total tied-ranks scores for each item in a way analogous to that used for subjects. For a case in which four ordered categories are labeled "strongly disagree, disagree, agree, strongly agree," these scores order the items with regard to the group's overall agreement with them. This interpretation is only justified if there is significant concordance between members of the group in their ordering of items with respect to agreement as measured by Kendall's W or by α. If there is no such concordance, then one wonders whether or not a scale based on these items exists. In the case of perfect concordance in the ordering of items the scale is referred to as a Guttman scale (Guttman, 1947) after the writer who advocated this type of scale, and the method referred to as scalogram analysis.

It is worth noting that the method of dealing with tests and similar assessments is to decide on the scores for persons with a given response pattern and then perhaps consider the ordering of items. In the case of scalogram analysis the order is the opposite: The order of the items in difficulty or popularity is decided first and then the order of the persons. This leads to difficulty in the case of people whose response pattern does not fit perfectly into that order of the items yielding the best scale of items according to the scalogram analysis.

The problem is best understood from the account given by Torgerson (1958, pp. 319–336) and developed by Cliff (1983). In the case of dichotomous items the display of item by subjects has either 1 or 0 in each cell. However, with polytomous items it is preferable to display each item separately in order to see the consistency of response patterns. If perfect scaling is possible, then, when respondents are ordered in terms of total score, the response patterns to a particular item should follow that illustrated in Table 5.4. In the table, an x indicates the category chosen by a subject, and subjects have been ordered in terms of total score. The highest level of response to the item is chosen by those with the highest total scores; those choosing the next category of response are those with the

TABLE 5.4
Scalogram Display for Categories for a Particular Item

		Item			
		a	b	c	d
Subjects in order of total	1.	x			
	2.	x			
	3.		x		
	4.		x		
	5.		x		
	6.			x	
	7.			x	
	8.			x	
	9.			x	
	10.				x
	11.				x
	12.				x

next highest scores, and so on. The pattern represents an idealization, and would not be expected in actuality; instead, there would be some degree of scatter in the table.

SUMMARY

This chapter has dealt with polytomous items with more than two ordered categories for which scores of 1, 2, 3, 4, 5. . . . are customarily but arbitrarily used. However category scores can be arbitrarily spaced provided that the order is preserved. These scores can be transformed to tied-ranks scores and a total tied-ranks score calculated for each person and compared with the total of the arbitrary integral scores. In general, the orders of the persons on the total tied-ranks scores will be different from that obtained from the usual arbitrary integral scores.

The method of calculating tied-ranks scores is demonstrated in Table 5.1, which compares normal deviate scores used in Wechsler's scales and percentile scores with tied-ranks scores. The order of the persons on the total tied-ranks scores will rarely be the same as that obtained by other methods of scoring but has been shown to be the best method of estimating the order on the basic variable as shown by Kendall (1975). Total tied-ranks scores are equivalent to scores obtained from "optimal scaling methods" since they produce maximum internal consistency.

Scores on polytomous items with more than two ordered categories subscale scores in the Wechsler scales could be transformed to provide tied-ranks scores and their totals, but they are not. Because they are not so transformed the final IQ scores may be biased as shown in the data presented in Table 5.4. Allocating scores to essays or project reports is usually done without using ranking methods and this leads to lower reliability because of individual biases in the raters. The method of using ordinal theory in this situation is described in this chapter as is the conversion of total tied-ranks scores to grades.

As was described in chapter 4, for dichotomous items it is possible to calculate total tied-ranks scores for items with more than two ordered categories. If there is perfect agreement among subjects on the order of items and perfect agreement among items on the order of subjects, one would have a perfect scale in the sense defined by Guttman.

In chapter 6, the topic of dominance theory is introduced and developed in the way originated by Cliff (1977, 1979) extended in several ways.

Dominance Analysis of Tests

DOMINANCE RELATIONS

We have seen in the preceding two chapters how assigning tied-ranks scores to test responses can serve as a basis for arriving at meaningful test scores and for evaluating the quality of items and tests. In this chapter we present a different ordinal perspective on test responses and see how it too can be used to form a rationale for test scoring and evaluation.

The methods are based on the idea that a response to a test item provides a *dominance* relation between the person and the item, and through these relations, ordering relations between persons and between items can be inferred. That is, we think of the item as rather like a hurdle. If the person passes the item, he or she dominates the item. If the person fails the item, the item dominates the person; the hurdle was too high.

From these item–person relations we can infer item–item and person–person relations. If a person passes an item that a second person has failed, this may be taken as a dominance relation of the first person over the second. Similarly, if a person fails one item and passes a second, this can be viewed as a dominance relation of the second item over the first. Dominance relations are the basis of the measure of ordinal correlation called Kendall's tau (Cliff, 1996; Kendall, 1975), and tau will later be seen to be an important statistic about a test or a test item.

The dominance reasoning leads to a measure of the amount of information provided by an item. Suppose in a group of n persons n_j have passed Item j, and $n - n_j$ have failed. On this item, the n_j who passed have dominated the $n - n_j$ who failed, so the item has provided n_j times $(n - n_j)$ person-dominance relations. Thus, items passed by just half the persons provide the most information, but we see shortly that there can be reasons for wanting some variability in the proportion of persons passing an item.

There is a parallelism between how items and persons are treated here. Therefore, if Person i has passed x_i out of the m items on a test and failed the rest, that person provides x_i times $(m - x_i)$ *item*-dominance relations.

These ideas provide a simple interpretation of the difference in score of two persons on a test composed of dichotomous items. If Person i has a test score x_i and Person h has a score of x_h, the difference, $x_i - x_h$, is the difference in the number of items passed by i but failed by h, minus the number where the reverse happened, h passed but i failed. We introduce some basic ideas while assuming dichotomous items, but in many cases they extend to polytomous ones.

PSEUDO-ORDERS FROM RANDOMNESS

Having been tested all our educational lives, we may take it for granted that one person having a higher score than another person implies that the first person has more knowledge or ability than the second. Persons using this book are likely to have had a history of scoring higher than others, so this may reinforce the comforting idea of tests ordering persons. There is also the parallel idea that some items are more difficult than others in that fewer people get them correct. But it is desirable to adopt a "show-me" attitude toward these beliefs that test responses order persons on their ability and items on their difficulty.

Suppose there was a computerized test that purported to measure some personality trait by presenting a set of items to which the examinee answered "agree" or "disagree." However, instead of scoring the responses according to some a priori rationale, the computer uses a random number procedure to, in effect, toss a coin to determine whether the response gets a score of 1 or 0 on the item, item scores being summed to give a trait score. The examinees will differ in their total scores, and the "items" will appear to differ in their difficulty or popularity. However, it is easily seen that the whole process is meaningless. It can be made even more persuasive by assigning different "difficulties" to the items simply by assigning different probabilities of getting a positive score to different items, perhaps by assigning a threshold to each item, different thresholds to different items. If the random number corresponding to a response is above the threshold, it receives a score of 1; if below, a score of 0. Now the items really will have different "popularities," but the persons' scores are still meaningless. Many purported personality scales that one finds in magazines have little more meaning than this.

How do we know that a given set of test items provides an order in any meaningful sense? We have seen some methods to evaluate tests in the previous chapters, but in the present one we are first taking a closer look at what lies behind those methods and then will see some ways in which those ideas can be used to evaluate tests.

HOW DICHOTOMOUS ITEMS DEFINE AN ORDER

Basic Response Patterns

To demonstrate that test responses define an order, we first need to consider two dichotomous (right–wrong or yes–no) items and two persons. The following two response patterns where 1 indicates the positive response and 0 the negative, provide the critical information:

Person	Item		Item	
	a	b	c	d
x	1	1	0	1
y	0	1	0	0

In both patterns we see that there is an item that that x gets correct but y gets incorrect, Item a in the first case and d in the second. This is highly suggestive that x can do things that y cannot. Similarly, it appears that a is harder than b and c is harder than d because d is passed by x when c is failed, and b is passed by y when a is failed. Thus, when two items are paired with two persons, these patterns indicate order relations between both items and persons.

However, by themselves the pairs of items and pairs of persons only provide suggestive information, but suppose we have a number of items, and there is never one that y gets correct but x does not. Now our inference that x ranks ahead of y is strengthened. If we consider items across a number of persons, and find that there is no person who passes a but fails b, this is similarly information that a is harder than b.

What sort of data weakens our impression of order? Negative information about the presence of an order comes from looking at combinations of items and persons and finding a different result. Suppose we found a pattern for two items and two persons like the one below:

	e	f
v	1	0
w	0	1

That is, there is an item that *v* gets right and *w* gets wrong, but also an item with the reverse, *w* is correct and *v* is not. There is no consistent ordering information about either the items or the persons here. In fact, the person dominance relations on the two items *contradict* each other; the item-dominance relations provided by the two persons likewise contradict each other.

Now imagine that we have responses from a number of persons on a number of items, and after we order the persons from highest to lowest score and the items from most often wrong to most often right, the pattern in Table 6.1 emerges. This table is similar to the one presented in Table 6.1 as an example of Coombs' (1964) two-set dominance relation. All the 1s are in a rough triangle on the upper right, with all the 0s on the lower left. In any row, as soon as there is a 1, all other entries will be a 1; in any column, as soon as there is a 0, all entries below it will be 0. Thus, for any pair of persons we never get information from one item that is contradictory with information from another, and similarly for items across persons. On the other hand, there are a number of instances that are like one or the other of the two dominance-defining patterns described earlier, so it seems reasonable to conclude that items and persons are ordered. In a sense, the items and persons order each other. It is the pattern in the table that provides a highly logical definition of the way in which responses to items can provide ordering information for persons and items. Insofar as the results on a test look like this, the results can be considered an ordering process.

TABLE 6.1
Perfectly Consistent Test Item Responses: A Guttman Scale

	Items								
Persons	1	2	3	4	5	6	7	8	9
1	1	1	1	1	1	1	1	1	1
2	0	1	1	1	1	1	1	1	1
3	0	1	1	1	1	1	1	1	1
4	0	0	1	1	1	1	1	1	1
5	0	0	1	1	1	1	1	1	1
6	0	0	0	1	1	1	1	1	1
7	0	0	0	1	1	1	1	1	1
8	0	0	0	0	1	1	1	1	1
9	0	0	0	0	0	1	1	1	1
10	0	0	0	0	0	1	1	1	1
11	0	0	0	0	0	0	1	1	1
12	0	0	0	0	0	0	1	1	1
13	0	0	0	0	0	0	0	1	1
14	0	0	0	0	0	0	0	0	1
15	0	0	0	0	0	0	0	0	1
16	0	0	0	0	0	0	0	0	0

However, there are two other important patterns we need to consider:

	g	h	j	k
t	1	1	0	1
u	0	0	0	1

In the one on the left, items g and h are providing the same information about Persons t and u: t can do something that u cannot. Similarly, in the right-hand pattern both persons are providing information that j is harder than k. (We assume that some of the other items and persons are showing the two kinds of ordering patterns illustrated first so as to verify that t comes before u and j is harder than k.) Thus, the pattern involving g and h shows both items *reinforcing* the order of Person t over u, and that involving j and k is reinforcing the order of Item j over k. Note that in a pair of items with a pair of persons (abbreviated below to "pair-pairs"), person-reinforcing patterns and item-reinforcing patterns cannot occur in the same two-by-two section. The responses in Table 6.1 show numerous instances of these reinforcing (or redundant) patterns.

There are two other kinds of patterns, but they provide no information. These are the pair-pairs where both persons get both items correct or both persons get both incorrect. Obviously, no ordering information is provided by such pair-pairs.[1]

Guttman Scales

Because the importance of the pattern in Table 6.1 was first emphasized by Guttman (1947), data that exhibit that pattern are called Guttman scales. A year or two later, and apparently independently, Loevinger (1948) also proposed it as an ideal matrix of test responses.

In the best of psychometric worlds, actual, empirical matrices of test items would look like the table; there would be plenty of the reinforcing and ordering patterns and none of the contradictory ones. In the real world, this is not what happens. There are always some of the contradictory

---

[1] If we consider all the possible response patterns in a pair-pair, there are 16 because each of the four entries could be a 1 or a 0, and $2^4 = 16$. We have only listed six different types, but some of them can occur in more than one way depending on where the 1s and 0s fall. The first two can each occur in four ways because the 0 in the first one could fall in any of the four positions, and the same is true of the 1 in the second. The contradicting pattern can occur in two ways, depending on whether the 1s fall in the upper right and lower left positions or in the upper left and lower right. The two reinforcing patterns can each also occur in two ways; the two 1s could fall in the first or second row in the person-dominance reinforcing pattern; the 1s can likewise fall in the first or second column of the item-dominance reinforcing one. Then there are the all 1s and all 0s patterns. Thus, there are $8 + 2 + 2 + 2 + 1 + 1 = 16$ possible patterns.

ones. However, it often appears that the Guttman scale ideal is an approximation to reality.

In our example where the computer scored items randomly, the pattern would be very different from Table 6.1. Also, it would turn out that if we looked at all the pairs of items in combination with all the pairs of persons, there would be just about as many contradictory pairs of pairs as there are reinforcing ones, whether we counted pairs that reinforce the person order or the item order. (There might be small deviations from equality due to the randomness of the process.) In the second example, where the computer introduced what are in effect real variations in item difficulty, it would turn out that the number of contradictory pair-pairs was about the same as the number of reinforcing *person* pair-pairs. However, there would be more pairs where *item* differences were reinforced than there were contradicting ones. This reflects the fact that there are real, even if arbitrary, differences among the probabilities that the items will receive a positive response.

It is important to realize that there is a symmetry to how items and persons are viewed here. The items are providing information on how persons are ordered, and at the same time the persons are providing information on how items are ordered. Similarly, if the responses in a pair-pair combination display contradictory information about person ordering, they also display it about item ordering. If we were analyzing the responses of persons to a test, no one, including the computer that would examine the pair-pairs, needs to know which direction is items and which persons until the final step of showing some kind of summary.

The one place where the information about items and persons is not symmetric is in the pair-pairs that show reinforcement of relations. There, a pair-pair shows reinforcing information about person relations or about item relations, but never both, as can be seen from the earlier examples.

It seems intuitively obvious that the Guttman pattern provides an order for both items and persons, but this can also be shown to be true in a very strict, abstract mathematical sense, as proven by Ducamp and Falmagne (1968). Interestingly, the ideas can be extended to three-way tables of responses (Collins & Cliff, 1985). For example, suppose one were to measure a group of children on a given set of intelligence items at several specific ages. Ideally, the triangular form would be shown in the person-by-item table at each age. If intelligence represents an ideal developmental process, the triangle of 1s would be small at the earliest age and grow larger (more items passed by each child and each item being passed by more children) at each subsequent age. Another level of idealization is reached if the triangular form is seen for each item, looking at an age-by-person table. Finally, the pattern should also be seen if one looks at an item-by-time table for each child. Thus, the idealized pattern idea generalizes to three-way tables of responses.

"Unique" Relations in Pair-Pairs

We saw earlier that the relations that actually provide information that order persons and items were instances where in a pair-pair there was an item
that one person got correct and the other not, but the reverse did not happen in that pair-pair. That is, one of the two following patterns occurred:

$$
\begin{array}{cc}
1 \quad 1 & \quad 0 \quad 1 \\
\quad\quad \text{or} & \\
0 \quad 1 & \quad 0 \quad 0.
\end{array}
$$

In these patterns, there is a person dominance relation on one item but not
the other, and an item dominance relation on one person but not the
other. There are a number of variations on these patterns: four versions of
the one on the left, depending on where the 0 falls, and four of that on the
right, depending on where the 1 falls.

If we were to consider a particular pair of items, and examined the responses of all the person pairs, we will presumably find a certain number of
person pairs that show one of these two patterns or a variation on them. Indeed, we need to find some because it is these that are the basis of the order. Cliff (1977, 1979) called these relations that occur on one item, or in
one person, but not the other, "unique" relations.

DATA BASIC TO ASSESSING CONSISTENCY

Two-by-Two Tables

Assuming that every person takes every item, it is natural to assign an order
for the persons in terms of the number of items each gets correct and one
for items in terms of how many persons get the item wrong. We would like
to know how close a given matrix of test responses comes to the ideal of a
Guttman scale. If it is fairly close, then we have confidence that score differences are probably real; if not, then they may well be misleading in terms of
measuring some character of the persons.

Examining each pair of items in combination with each pair of persons
would be quite tedious when there are more than a few of each since for m
items and n persons there are $m(m-1)n(n-1)/4$ pair-pairs. A test with 50
items administered to a thousand persons would have well over a half-
billion pair-pairs. Fortunately, the information about how many pair-pairs
there are of each kind can be obtained from summary data that is routinely
available.

TABLE 6.2
Crosstabulation of Responses to Two Items

| | Observed Frequencies | | | | Ideal Frequencies | | |
| | Item 2 | | | | Item 2 | | |
Item 1	Right	Wrong	Total	Item 1	Right	Wrong	Total
Right	90	40	130	Right	100	30	130
Wrong	10	60	70	Wrong	0	70	70
Total	100	100	200	Total	100	100	200

The relevant information can be obtained from the scores of the persons and from 2×2 cross-tabulation tables that many statistical packages provide. Consider Table 6.2 that tabulates the response patterns of 200 persons to Items 1 and 2. The left panel of the table shows that 200 persons took the two items. Of these, 130 got Item 1 correct (so 70 got it wrong); on Item 2, 100 were correct and 100 were incorrect. There were 90 who were correct on both and 60 who were wrong on both; 40 got Item 1 right and Item 2 wrong whereas 10 did the reverse.

Now we consider what this means in terms of the pair-pairs involving these two items and all $200 \times 199/2 = 19,900$ pairs of persons. There must have been a total of $130 \times 70 = 9,100$ instances in which one person was correct on Item 1 and the other incorrect, leading to what we will call person–person dominance relations on the item. In the other 10,800 person–person comparisons, either both persons were right or both wrong, so there is no dominance information.

There were 90 instances of a person being right on both items and 60 persons who were wrong on both items. This means that of the 9,100, there must have been $90 \times 60 = 5,400$ times in which the pair-pairs were of the reinforcing type where one person was correct on both items and the other was incorrect; using r_{jk} to stand here for the number of reinforcing relations on items j and k, $r_{12} = 5,400$. On the other hand, there were also $40 \times 10 = 400$ pairs of the contradictory wrong–right versus right–wrong type. That is, the dominance relations for 400 pairs were opposite on the two items. Letting c_{jk} stand for the number of contradictory person relations, $c_{12} = 400$. The remainder of the ordered pair-pairs on Item 1, $9,100 - 5,400 - 400 = 3,300$, must have been of one of the two ordering types (unique relations) that were described first, those involving three 0s and one 1 or three 1s and one 0.

Similarly, on Item 2, there were $n_2(n - n_2) = 100 \times 100 = 10,000$ person–person dominances. Of the 10,000, there are the same 5,400 that are of the reinforcing type and the same 400 of the contradictory. The only difference from Item 1 is that there were more of the unique type of pair-pairs, $10,000 - 5,400 - 400 = 4,200$ instead of the 3,300 that there were on Item 1.

From the results displayed in Table 6.2 it appears that the two items are closely related because there are many more reinforcing than contradictory relations, 5,400 versus 400. If we want to compare this to the best we could possibly do, we can convert these numbers into some sort of a proportion, comparing the obtained r_{12} and c_{12} to a definition of the best we could possibly do. The most obvious step is to convert the difference to what is known as a tau-a correlation:

$$t_{jk} = (r_{jk} - c_{jk})/n(n-1). \qquad (6.1)$$

This means that $t_{12} = .125$ in the example, and the covariance between the items will be the same.

Comparing to Ideal Patterns

This is a rather low value, and the main reason is that there are many ties when variables are dichotomous. It seems like a good idea to keep the difference as a basic quantity, but to adjust the denominator to make it provide a more realistic expectation. There are a lot of ways to do that, but two are the most obvious. Ideally, all the dominance relations on one item would be reinforced by the other, and there would be no contradictory relations. Therefore, one way to evaluate how we are doing is to compare the difference $r_{12} - c_{12}$ to the total numbers of dominance relations on each of the two items. Since the items differ in difficulty, we get different ratios for the two items: $(5,400 - 400)/130 \times 70 = .55$ for Item 1 and $(5,400 - 400)/100 \times 100 = .50$ for Item 2.

On reflection, we may feel that even this ratio is a bit stringent because not all the relations can be reinforced when the items differ in difficulty or popularity. The best we can expect to do, given the difference in difficulty, is shown in the right-hand panel of Table 6.2. There are no individuals who get Item 2 correct but Item 1 wrong, but there are, and have to be, some who do the reverse because the items differ in difficulty. The best that can be expected, then, given the different item difficulties, is that n_2 get both correct and $n - n_1$ get both incorrect, where n_2 is the *more difficult* item. Thus, if we want to compare our result to the best we could have done, given both of these item difficulties, we divide $r_{12} - c_{12}$ by $n_2(n - n_1)$; in this case that is $(5,400 - 400)/100 \times 70 = .71$. This figure tells us how close we are to the ideal value of 1.00, considering the given item difficulties.

In a given pair of items, the number of relations that are unique to one but not the other can be calculated from the 2×2 cross-tabulation of responses. If the cells of the cross-tabulation table are denoted a, b, c, and d, then the total number of person pairs where there is a relation on Item 1, whose responses define the rows of the table, but who answer the same on

Item 2, is $ac + bd$. This is the number of relations unique to Item 1. Similarly, the number of those unique to Item 2 is $ab + cd$. In Table 6.2, these numbers would be $90 \times 10 + 40 \times 60 = 3{,}300$ for Item 1, and $90 \times 40 + 10 \times 60 = 4{,}200$ for Item 2. In the ideal pattern on the right-hand side of the table, they would be 2,100 for Item 1 and 3,000 for Item 2.

The total number of dominance relations on an item is the sum of the reinforcing, contradictory, and unique relations on it. Therefore, the number that are unique can also be calculated by subtracting the reinforcing and contradictory from the total. Furthermore, we see from the diagrams that in every pair-pair where there is a unique person relation there is also a unique item relation. This fact is used shortly to help us calculate the number of reinforcing item relations on a whole test.

Sums of Types of Relations

As already seen, we can count the number of total, reinforcing, and contradictory person-dominance relations from the cross-tabulations between items and can convert them to ratios that tell us how close the relations between items are. These tabulations can be carried out for each pair of items, and the number of reinforcing and contradictory pairs can be summed across all the tables. We would like there to be a lot more reinforcing pairs than contradictory ones. The number of each can be incorporated into one of several coefficients of overall consistency for the test. We describe some of them next, and it happens that some of these are ones that we have already encountered in the previous two chapters.

Before turning to them, we need to consider a couple of other things that can be calculated from the summary statistics. The first is the total number of person relations that are furnished by the whole set of m items. We saw earlier that each item provides $n_j(n - n_j)$ person relations, so the whole test of m items provides a total of $\Sigma_j n_j(n - n_j)$. Similarly, the n persons provide $\Sigma_i x_i(m - x_i)$ item dominance relations.

It would be desirable to compare the total number of reinforcing item-ordering relations to the number of contradicting ones, as we would do for the person-ordering relations. Looking at 2×2 tables for all $n(n-1)/2$ possible pairs of persons might well be a substantial task if there are a large number of persons, but fortunately this is not necessary. If we look at the examples of pair-pairs that furnish ordering information, or *unique* relations, it is clear that the patterns that furnish unique relations on persons also furnish unique information about items; wherever there is a person relation unique to one item, there is also an item relation unique to one person. We saw earlier that the number of unique person relations can be calculated from the 2×2 tables. These can be summed across all the tables to get a total, just as we can for the reinforcing and contradictory relations.

We let r_p stand for the total number of pair-pairs where there is a reinforcing person relation, c_p stand for the number where there are contradictory person relations, and u_p stand for the total number of unique or ordering pair-pairs. Any person dominance in a pair-pair must be of one of the three types, so

$$\Sigma_j n_j (n - n_j) = r_p + c_p + u_p. \tag{6.2}$$

Similarly, the total number of item dominances can be distributed among reinforcing, contradictory, and person relations:

$$\Sigma_i x_i (m - x_i) = r_i + c_i + u_i. \tag{6.3}$$

The reinforcing and contradictory person relations can be calculated from the 2 × 2 tables, as we noted before. These can be summed across all the tables to give r_p and c_p. The total number of person relations is $\Sigma n_j (n - n_j)$. So, if we want, u_p can be calculated by subtraction.

We also noted that wherever there is a contradictory person relation there is also a contradictory item relation, so $c_p = c_i$. Similarly, wherever there is a unique person relation there is a unique item relation, so $u_p = u_i$. Therefore, if we subtract (6.2) from (6.3), cancel out the equal terms, and rearrange, we can find r_i without doing anything complicated:

$$r_i = \Sigma_i x_i (m - x_i) - \Sigma_j n_j (n - n_j) + r_p. \tag{6.4}$$

This formula allows us to calculate the number of reinforcing item relations simply from the person total scores and the 2 × 2 tables between items. We can use the three equations to calculate indices of person- and item-ordering consistency.

Relations and Statistics

The two main indices of ordinal correlation are Spearman's rho, which we have extensively encountered in the previous two chapters, and Kendall's tau. The latter measure is discussed extensively by Kendall (1975) and by Cliff (1996), and we present the basic concepts concerning it here. It considers each pair of persons, say i and h, on two variables, say x and y, and notes the dominance relation between the two persons on each variable. The number of times the two persons are in the same order on both variables is counted, and the number of times they are in the opposite order is also counted. Then

$$t_{xy} = \frac{\#[(x_i > x_h) \text{ and } (y_i > y_h)] - \#[(x_i > x_h) \text{ and } y_i < y_{ih})]}{\frac{1}{2}n(n-1)}, \quad (6.5)$$

where "#" stands for "the number of pairs in which." That is, tau is the proportion of pairs that are in the same order on both variables minus the proportion in which they are oppositely ordered on the two. In a population, these quantities are expressed as probabilities:

$$\tau_{xy} = Pr[(x_i > x_h) \text{ and } (y_i > y_h)] - Pr[(x_i > x_h) \text{ and } (y_i < y_h)]. \quad (6.6)$$

For many purposes, it is useful to express t in terms of dominance variables, d_{ihx} and d_{ihy}, which are each 1, −1, or 0, depending on whether the scores of i are greater, less, or equal to those of h on the respective variables. In that case,

$$t_{xy} = \frac{\sum_{i>h} d_{ihx} d_{ihy}}{\frac{1}{2}n(n-1)}. \quad (6.7)$$

Various "corrections" to tau can be made to take account of the presence of ties on the variables; however, for our purposes it is simplest to avoid these corrections. The uncorrected form is called "tau-a," but we refer to it here as "tau."

When items are dichotomous, the inter-item covariances as well as the tau and Spearman rho statistics depend on the number of reinforcing and contradictory relations involving the two items. Specifically, the tau between j and k is

$$t_{jk} = 2(r_{jk} - c_{jk})/n(n-1). \quad (6.8)$$

The covariance s_{jk} has the same formula as t_{jk} when the items are scored 1-0:

$$s_{jk} = 2(r_{jk} - c_{jk})/n(n-1). \quad (6.9)$$

The formula for rho-a, r_{Sjk}, is slightly different because of the different constants involved:

$$r_{Sjk} = 3(r_{jk} - c_{jk})/n(n+1). \quad (6.10)$$

It is therefore easy to convert any one of these statistics into the other, and the conversion is the same for any pair of items. Thus, the different statistics are providing the same information. In the example, $t_{12} = 2 \times 5,000/200 \times 199 = .25$, and the covariance s_{12} is the same. The rank-order correlation is $r_{S12} = 3 \times 5,000/200 \times 201 = .37$.

MEASURES OF TEST CONSISTENCY

The quantities discussed earlier, along with some other basic statistical data, allow us to measure the overall consistency of a test. This is typically expressed as a number between 0 and 1.0, the latter representing perfect consistency and the former no consistency at all. Usually a negative value for a consistency index would be interpreted as a chance deviation from zero or possibly some misapplication of the data.

There are several types or levels of consistency we examine. One is the average degree to which items agree with each other. A second is the average degree to which a particular item agrees with other items or, defined somewhat differently, with the order on the whole test. A third level is the extent to which the overall orders derived from two presumably parallel tests agree with each other. The parallel tests may be real or potential. Finally, we can estimate the degree to which information derived from the current test would agree with an ideal order. The "ideal order" will usually be defined here as the order defined by a real or potential universe of test items from which the current test is a sample, an idea that will be discussed further.

Average Interitem Taus

The tau-a between two items depends on the number of reinforcing and contradictory person relations on the two items, as expressed in formula (6.5). It is possible and often useful to examine the whole matrix of interitem taus, and to calculate the average from that matrix; this is the main alternative in the case of polytomous items. However, with dichotomous data, the average tau can be computed more simply by taking advantage of the equality of interitem tau-a and the corresponding covariance that is true in dichotomous items.

Recall that the variance of the ordinary total score on a test, s_x^2, is the sum of the item variances, s_j^2, and covariances, s_{jk}:

$$s_x^2 = \sum_j s_j^2 + \sum_j \sum_{j \neq k} s_{jk}. \tag{6.11}$$

Since, in dichotomous data $s_{jk} = t_{jk}$, this means that

$$\sum_j \sum_{j \neq k} t_{jk} = s_x^2 - \sum_j s_j^2,$$

so

$$\text{Ave}(t_{jk}) = (s_x^2 - \sum_j s_j^2)/m(m-1). \tag{6.12}$$

Formula (6.12) will, of course, also give the average interitem covariance. By comparing the formulas for tau-a and rho-a for dichotomous items (6.8) and (6.10), it can be seen that

$$r_{Sjk} = 3(n - 1)t_{jk}/2(n + 1).$$ (6.13)

The same relation will hold for their averages:

$$\text{Ave}(r_{Sjk}) = 3(n - 1)\text{Ave}(t_{jk})/2(n + 1).$$ (6.14)

Data from five dichotomous items is shown in Table 6.3. First, cross-tabulations of the responses to each pair of items are shown, the "cross-tabulations" of an item with itself showing the number passing and failing the item. The numbers of reinforcing and contradictory person relations on each pair of items are shown next, and these are converted to tau-a's (6.5) in the next section. These may seem rather low, but they are actually somewhat higher than is typical of dichotomous items. Their average is .106. The average r_S is somewhat higher; by (6.11) it is .158.

The item variances and the variance of the total score are also given in the table. These allow us to use (6.9) to calculate the average tau without using the taus themselves:

$$.106 = (3.244 - 1.126)/5 \times 4.$$

Adjustments to the Averages

The average interitem tau is typically fairly low, as was true in the example. In part, this is because the information provided by an individual item is rather weak, so two items cannot agree very strongly. As we saw in Table 6.2, another reason is that there are inherent limitations on the value that tau can take between items. The first limitation is that we are using tau-a here, and between dichotomous items at least half the relations are necessarily tied, so t_{jk} can never be greater than .5 and that value can only be attained when exactly half the examinees pass both items. The maximum attainable value will decrease as the proportion passing an item deviates from .5.

One adjustment to $\text{Ave}(t_{jk})$ that suggests itself then is to compare $r - c$ to the total number of dominance relations that could have been included in it. Recall that there are a total of $n\Sigma n_j - \Sigma n_j^2$ dominance relations provided by the items; however, in arriving at $r - c$ the dominances on an item are considered in relation to each of the $m - 1$ other items, so the total that needs to be considered here is $(m - 1)(n\Sigma n_j - \Sigma n_j^2)$. This provides the basis for a new index:

TABLE 6.3
Crosstabulations of Scores of Five Items

Item		1 P	1 F	2 P	2 F	3 P	3 F	4 P	4 F	5 P	5 F
1	Pass	60	0	35	25	40	20	45	15	50	10
	Fail	0	140	40	105	55	85	75	65	100	40
2	Pass			75	0	50	25	55	20	65	10
	Fail			0	125	45	80	65	60	85	45
3	Pass					95	0	70	25	80	15
	Fail					0	105	50	55	70	35
4	Pass							120	0	100	20
	Fail							0	80	50	30
5										150	0
										0	50

	1	2	3	4	5
Dominances on Item	8,400	9,375	9,975	9,600	7,500
s_j^2	.210	.236	.251	.241	188

Relation Types

Item		Item 2	Item 3	Item 4	Item 5
1	r_{1j}	3,500	3,400	2,925	2,000
	c_{1j}	1,000	1,100	1,125	1,000
2	r_{2j}		4,000	3,300	2,600
	c_{2j}		1,125	1,300	850
3	r_{3j}			3,850	2,800
	c_{3j}			1,250	1,050
4	r_{4j}				3,000
	c_{4j}				1,000

$l_{jk} = s_{jk}$

Item	2	3	4	5
1	.126	.116	.090	.050
2		.144	.101	.088
3			.131	.088
4				.101

$$s_x^2 = 3.244$$

(Continued)

TABLE 6.3
(Continued)

		Number Passing			
			Item		
	1	*2*	*3*	*4*	*5*
n_j	60	75	95	120	150
		$\Sigma n_j = 500$			
Easiness order	5	4	3	2	1

$$k_2 = (r - c)/[(m - 1)(n\Sigma n_j - \Sigma n_j^2)]. \qquad (6.15)$$

k_2 compares $r - c$ to one definition of its maximum. In the data of Table 6.3, summing the r_{jk} gives 62,750 (remembering to use both halves of the data), and c is 20,400, giving

$$.236 = (62,750 - 20,400)/4 \times (200 \times 500 - 55,150).$$

This is more than twice the average tau-a, but still represents a fairly small proportion of the total number of dominances.

However, we saw that even the denominator of (6.12) represents an unrealistic standard when the items differ in difficulty. Even if c were zero, r could not reach this maximum. We saw that the maximum value for r_{12} that could occur in Table 6.2 was $n_2(n - n_1)$ where n_1 was the item with the higher frequency of correct answers.

This kind of limitation occurs for all pairs of items. It could be computed for each pair and added across pairs in order to arrive at the maximum for $r - c$, but this is not necessary when all persons take all items. Some algebra leads to the conclusion that this more realistic maximum for $r - c$ is $2n\Sigma_j(j - 1) n_j - (\Sigma_j n_j)^2 + \Sigma_j n_j^2$. This leads to our final index of average inter-item consistency:

$$k_3 = (r - c)/[2n\Sigma_j(j - 1) n_j - (\Sigma_j n_j)^2 + \Sigma_j n_j^2]. \qquad (6.16)$$

An important consideration in (6.13) is that j refers to the item-easiness order of the items, $j = 1$ meaning the easiest item, and so on. It should also be realized that $r - c$ can be computed from the total score and item variances, as in (6.9)

In the example of Table 6.3, we calculate the denominator terms as follows. Using the last two lines of the table, $2n(\Sigma(j - 1) n_j = 2 \times 200 \times (4 \times 60 + 3 \times 75 + 2 \times 95 + 1 \times 120 + 0 \times 150) = 310,000$; $(\Sigma n_j)^2 = 500^2 = 250,000$; and $\Sigma n_j^2 = 55,150$. Inserting these numbers as the terms in the denominator of

(6.13) gives 115,150, and $r - c$ is 42,350, so $k_3 = .368$. This is higher even than k_2. It may still not seem very impressive, but it actually represents quite a respectable, even high, value for the interitem consistency of dichotomous test items.

Three different indices of average interitem consistency have been presented here, partly to illustrate the reasoning that goes into such an index. In applications, it seems that the first and third are the most useful. Ave (t_{jk}) directly reports the average tau (and/or covariance) between items, whereas k_3 compares this average to a realistic definition of the maximum it could be, given the distribution of item difficulties.

Evaluating Items

The development of an effective test progresses in stages. First, the concept of what the test will try to measure is formulated, whether by individual effort or group discussion, or a combination of both. Next, the items are written; ideally, they are critiqued by knowledgeable reviewers in terms of their apparent relevance to the measurement goal, and suitability for the intended examinee population, and they are revised, if necessary, and some may be discarded. In large-scale testing organizations, this may even be true of the majority of the original pool.

Once sufficient items are available for one or more forms of the test, they are pretested on a group that is considered fairly representative of the target population. This provides statistical information on the behavior of the items that can be used to select them to a further degree. The information takes a number of forms, but we concentrate on a few.

The first data to examine are the proportion passing each item. Items passed or endorsed by only a small percentage or by almost all of the examinees provide little information, so they are usually discarded. The cutoffs to use are somewhat arbitrary, but only a small fraction—5% to 10%—of a test's items should be passed by more than 95% of the examinees. With multiple-choice items, those with percentages passing that are below or near the chance level should usually be discarded, although there can be exceptions.

With multilevel items, the process becomes a bit more complex. Perhaps a useful rule is to discard, or at least examine closely, any items on which 90% of the examinees are tied.

The other property to examine is the consistency of each item. This is reflected by the average tau (or covariance or rank-correlation) of an item with the other items. This average can be heavily influenced by the number of ties on the item, particularly with dichotomous ones. In order to lessen this influence, the averages can be divided by the number of untied pairs on that item. Remember that with dichotomous items this is $n_j(n - n_j)$.

Items with particularly low averages should generally be discarded. To aid in the decision on which items to discard, the complete matrix of interitem taus should also be examined to identify those that have any negative relations with other items or more than a small number of near-zero ones. This information, along with additional statistical indices described shortly, will often lead to a set of items that is more reliable than the full set, contrary to the assertion of Embretson (1999, p. 12).

There is a second index that should reflect the items' consistencies. This reflects the relation between the order on an item and the order on the total score on the rest of the items. With modern computing equipment, these taus can be computed directly. One simply calculates m new total scores that are defined by eliminating each item in turn and computing the total score on the remaining $m - 1$. Then the taus between each item and the total score on its complementary set show the relation of each item with the remainder. This procedure is preferable to computing the taus between items and the original total because the latter includes the item being examined, so the correlation would be inflated. As was suggested with the average-tau procedure just outlined, these item-total taus can be divided by the proportion of pairs not tied on the item in order to get a clearer indication of the degree to which the dominances on the items agree with those from the total scores on the item pool.

Subscores

It is always true that the score that was designed to be unidimensional actually involves several, perhaps many, traits. However, the item selection procedures described earlier are based on the expectation that a substantial majority of items are primarily measuring what was intended. If the original concept was sound, and the items were carefully constructed, then this will usually be true. In that case the interitem coefficients should not vary very much, except as a function of item difficulty. Dichotomous items tend to correlate more highly with other items that are of similar difficulty. A useful procedure is, for each item, to plot its taus with other items as a function of their difficulty. The resulting plot should be curvilinear, having a maximum at difficulties similar to the given item and decreasing from that as an item's difficulty differs from its own in either direction. Examination of such plots may suggest that the relations between items are not homogeneous because some coefficients fall well below the curve. Inspection of the matrix of interitem coefficients may also suggest such a conclusion.

In that case, some procedure can be employed to try to separate items into subsets that are more homogenous with the intention of deriving subscores on each set. Some form of exploratory factor analysis can be used to help in identifying subsets of items that are more homogeneous. Alternatively, a cluster analysis procedure could be employed. The subscores suggested by either procedure may end up being fairly highly correlated, but the idea is that taus within clusters should generally be higher than those between different clusters. Subscores can then be obtained on each cluster. When the subscores are fairly highly correlated, then they can be combined back into a total score. For example, if a test that is designed to measure verbal ability includes some items in a format that requires the examinee to provide or choose a synonym, others use an opposites form, and still others are analogies, the results of the analysis might divide the items into those three subsets. A score can be gotten on each, but a total score on all could still be used. Similarly, in a knowledge test, perhaps there would turn out to be subject matter clusters. Of course, the items may not divide so neatly in terms of format or content; more imagination might be needed to form meaningful subscores.

ORDINAL VALIDITY AND RELIABILITY

A Universe of Items

As has been discussed earlier in this book, the concepts that are the foundation of psychological measurement are those of validity and reliability. Validity has several senses. Sometimes a test is used for a practical purpose of predicting how individuals will perform in some other context. Predicting how students will do at the next level of schooling is the most common example, but there are many other examples—from predicting how candidates for pilot training will perform in that training to selecting police. Such tests should have been shown to have practical validity in the sense of making predictions of performance that are accurate to at least some degree. Such validity has traditionally been called predictive validity.

In research applications the term *validity* more often is taken to mean the extent to which a test measures "what it is supposed to measure." However, the evidence for such validity is often indirect. It rests on the degree to which test items that are intended to measure the same thing agree with each other, called *convergent validation,* while not correlating highly with tests or items intended to measure something different, called *discriminant validation.* When the evidence of this kind is favorable, construct validity has been shown, and the numerical expression of the validity of a specific test is usually its correlation with the construct.

Inasmuch as the construct is an abstraction, correlations with it can never be observed directly. They are estimated from other observed correlations. Both classical test theory (CTT) and item response theories (IRT) are based on equations involving a latent trait that is imperfectly reflected in the observed scores. In one form or another, the latent trait is whatever is shared in common among the items, whatever it is that, taken as a whole, they are the best measure of. CTT, and for the most part IRT, assume that the items are homogeneous in the sense that there is only one latent trait that they share in common.

In CTT, the discrepancy between observed score and latent trait score is called an error of measurement, and the standard deviation of those errors is the "standard error of measurement." In IRT the inaccuracy of measurement is expressed in somewhat different terms, but the idea is similar; a test's validity is the extent to which the observed item responses reflect the examinee's standing on the latent trait.

One of our goals in this book has been to provide a test theory that avoids the idea of a latent trait; there is almost always too much room for various interpretations of what the trait means. However, in most applications, some general meaning has to be attached to the test's scores. What is it that the test score measures or the test order reflects if it is not a latent trait? In interpreting test scores, we use here instead a concept that we think is simpler and more direct, and that avoids the necessity of assuming homogeneity for the test.

This concept is that a test is a sample of items from a real or potential universe of items. So the idea is that the test is a sample in the statistical sense, and the universe is the corresponding population. A verbal ability test is a sample of items from a universe of items that could have been on such a test. Test validity is the degree to which conclusions based on item scores or orders can be generalized to the universe. Different forms of the test are different samples from the universe. The test can be heterogeneous in terms of item form or content, as long as it is assumed that the universe is heterogeneous in a parallel way, although it is generally best if this is only mildly true so that average item intercorrelations remain fairly high.

This interpretation means that the basic ideas of statistical inference can be applied interpreting test scores, orders on tests, and score differences.

Validity of Score Differences

Suppose there are v_{ih} items where individual i ranks ahead of individual h on a test having m items; in the terminology of this chapter, i dominated h v_{ih} times. Similarly, h dominated i v_{hi} times. These frequencies can be transformed to proportions by dividing by m: $p_{ih} = v_{ih}/m$ and $p_{hi} = v_{hi}/m$. The proportions estimate their counterparts in the universe:

$$E(p_{ih}) = p_{ih}'; \tag{6.17}$$

$$E(p_{hi}) = p_{hi}'. \tag{6.18}$$

p_{ih}', then, represents the probability that an item drawn at random from the universe will be one on which i dominates h, and correspondingly for p_{hi}'. A basic validity question is therefore, if $p_{ih} > p_{hi}$, how confident can we be that the same thing is true in the universe, $p_{ih}' > p_{hi}'$?

It turns out that this question can be answered in a straightforward statistical way. Let d_{ih} represent the difference $p_{ih} - p_{hi}$. If samples (tests) of m items are repeatedly taken from the universe, the variance of d_{ih} across the tests will be (Cliff & Keats, 2000)

$$\sigma_{d_{ih}}^2 = [p_{ih}' + p_{hi}' - (p_{ih}' - p_{hi}')^2]/m. \tag{6.19}$$

The sample estimate of $\sigma_{d_{ih}}^2$ (that is, from the test) is similar:

$$s_{d_{ih}}^2 = [p_{ih} + p_{hi} - (p_{ih} - p_{hi})^2]/(m - 1). \tag{6.20}$$

This means that the "significance" of d_{ih}, in the sense of it representing a corresponding direction of difference in the universe of items, can be tested by a t-ratio:

$$t = d_{ih}/s_{d_{ih}} \tag{6.21}$$

with $m - 1$ df. That is, if the t-ratio exceeds the two-tailed significance level in the table, we can reject the hypothesis that $p_{ih}' - p_{hi}' = 0$ at that level. Alternatively, we can use the tabled t-ratio to construct a $1 - \alpha$ confidence interval for the universe difference. The formulation is in terms of dominance relations on items, not just correct versus incorrect, so it applies to polytomous items as well as dichotomous ones, but in the dichotomous case the interpretation of the quantities is somewhat simplified: d_{ih} represents the proportionate difference in total scores: $d_{ih} = (x_i - x_h)/m$. The p_{ih}s are then the proportions of items on which i was correct and h not, and p_{hi} means the proportion of times the reverse happened for that pair.

The formula for the variance of the difference implies a certain degree of complexity for the question concerning which score differences might be significant. Not only does the significance of the difference between individuals vary depending on its size, $p_{ih} - p_{hi}$, but also on $p_{hi} + p_{ih}$. This means that the difference required for significance is smallest when one proportion is zero, the t-ratio then reducing to

$$t = p_{ih}(m - 1)/(1 - p_{ih}). \tag{6.22}$$

This also means that the overall validity of dominance differences on a test is greatest when its score pattern has the Guttman form.

Significant Score Differences

The cutoffs required for significant differences in tests of a given length can be calculated directly by using formula (6.16) in conjunction with the tabled t-values with $(m - 1)$ df and the chosen significance level. Table 6.4 provides illustrations for tests of 10, 20, and 40 items and two-tailed significance levels of .05 and .20. The .05 level may be considered conservative, given that we are making decisions about individual pairs of persons, whereas the .20 is fairly liberal.

The upper section of the table shows, for example, that when there are no items where h dominates i, two items where i dominates h is sufficient to reject $p_{ih}' = p_{hi}$ at the .20 level; however, six where i dominates h are required to reach the same conclusion if there are 2 where h dominates i. The numbers rise to four versus zero and nine versus two when the .05 level is required. To illustrate use of the table, suppose there are five items where Person A is correct and B is not, and one item where B is correct and A not, leading to a difference of four. Because there is one item on which the lower scoring person dominates, the second column of the table applies. We see that the difference of four is significant at the .20 level (upper section), but not the .05 (lower section). Note that in this case the results hold for 10, 20, or 40 items in the test. Dashes are entered in the table to denote instances where the sum of the two numbers exceeds the number of items in the test, so the corresponding dominances are impossible.

Several things can be noted in the table. First, the differences in dominances that imply significance can be rather small, but the required difference increases as the smaller frequency increases. Also, there is virtually no effect of the number of items in the test; the conclusion is almost completely determined by the two frequencies. Although it seems there should be a small test-size effect, implied by the factor $m - 1$ in the formula (6.20), it tends to be counterbalanced by the effect of the degrees of freedom on the critical value of t. It should also be noted that while the frequencies toward the right-hand ends of the rows correspond to numbers that are possible with the assumed number of items, they often correspond to situations that imply a preponderance of contradictory relations as compared to replicated ones. For example, in a test of 10 items, if there are six items where i dominates h and two where the reverse happens, this implies 12 contradictory relations. There are only two items left to go in the other two cells of the 2×2 table for this pair of persons. This implies that there is at most $1 \times 1 = 1$ replicated relation, so the net number of replicated relations is substantially negative, meaning there is a substantial degree of inconsistency. Thus, only the first half or so of the entries in each line will usually represent what will happen with any reasonable test.

TABLE 6.4

Number of Items Where t Dominates h Required for Significance, Given the Number where h Dominates t, for Different Test Lengths and Significance Levels

.20 Level

Number of Items Where h Dominates i

m	0	1	2	3	4	5	6	7	8	9	10	11	12	13	14	15	16
10	2	4	6	—	—	—	—	—	—	—	—	—	—	—	—	—	—
20	2	4	6	8	9	11[a]	12	13	—	—	—	—	—	—	—	—	—
40	2	4	6	8	9	11[a]	12	13	15	16	17	18	20	21	22	23	—

.05 Level

Number of Items Where h Dominates i

m	0	1	2	3	4	5	6	7	8	9	10	11	12	13	14
10	4	7[a]	—	—	—	—	—	—	—	—	—	—	—	—	—
20	4	7[a]	9[a]	10	12	14	—	—	—	—	—	—	—	—	—
40	4	7[a]	9	10	12	14	15	17	18	20	21	23	24	25	—

[a]Next lower number barely misses critical value.

Extension to Ranks and Numerical Scores

We can apply the idea of universe scores to situations where numerical or tied-ranks scores are derived from polytomous items. Let r_{jh} be the score of Person i on Item j; this can be either a tied-ranks score as discussed in chapter 5 or a numerical or category score. Averaging r_{ij} across items gives $r_{i.}$, and the average score of Person h is similarly $r_{h.}$. Define q_{ih} as the difference between the two:

$$q_{ih} = r_i - r_{h.}. \tag{6.23}$$

This is simply the difference in total tied ranks or total item scores divided by the number of items. There is a corresponding difference in the mean scores of i and h in the universe, and we let ψ_{ih} stand for it, and q_{ih} is its unbiased estimate:

$$E(q_{ih}) = \psi_{ih}. \tag{6.24}$$

The sampling variance of q_{ih} across forms of the test that are sampled from the universe, like that of any other mean, depends on the variance of the variable, which here is the score difference on an item, and the sample size, which here is the number of items, m. The relevant variance here is thus

$$s_{ih}^2 = [\textstyle\sum_j (r_{ij} - r_{hj})^2 - mq_{ih}^2]/(m-1). \tag{6.25}$$

Then, as with any other mean, the estimated sampling variance of q_{ih} is s_{ih}^2/m.

Therefore the significance of a mean difference q_{ih} for a given pair of persons can be tested as

$$F = mq_{ih}^2/s_{ih}^2, \tag{6.26}$$

with 1 and $m - 1$ degrees of freedom, and a confidence interval for the difference can correspondingly be constructed as

$$q_{ih} \pm t_{\alpha/2}s_{ih}/m^{1/2}. \tag{6.27}$$

As an example, suppose that a polytomous test has been taken by 200 persons, and Persons A and B have the following tied-ranks scores:

Item	1	2	3	4	5	6	7	8	9	10	$r_{i.}$
Person A	140	125	90	120	85	130	125	100	110	95	112.0
Person B	120	90	100	110	120	85	70	80	120	100	99.5

We see that A's average tied rank is 112.0 while B's is 99.5, giving $q_{AB} = 12.5$. The sum across items of the squared rank-differences, $\Sigma_j(r_{A_j} - r_{B_j})^2$ is 8,625, so according to (6.21), $s_{AB}^2 = (8,625 - 10 \times 12.5^2)/9 = 784.7$. The F-ratio (6.26) is $10 \times 12.5^2/784.7 = 1.99$, which would be significant at the .20 level, but not any more extreme one. The t_{05} for 9 df is 2.26, and the square root of 784.7 is 28.01, so the .95 c.i. for the difference, using (6.27), would be $12.5 \pm 2.26 \times 28.01/3.162$ or about -7.5 to 32.5.

As an example of inference about a score difference based on numerical scores, assume that the 10 test responses used earlier in the tied-ranks example were actually based on a 0 to 4 scale, the free-answer test responses being graded, say, from *unsatisfactory* (0) to *excellent* (4). The responses were as follows:

Item	1	2	3	4	5	6	7	8	9	10	r_i
Person A	4	4	2	4	2	4	4	3	3	2	3.2
Person B	3	2	3	3	4	2	1	2	4	3	2.7

Here, $q_{AB} = 3.2 - 2.7 = .50$, and $s_{AB}^2 = 2.72$, giving $F = .92$, which is not significant at any level. The .95 c.i. is $.50 \pm 1.18$, or $-.68$ to 1.68.

ITEM-UNIVERSE AND SCORE-UNIVERSE RELATIONS

Often one would like to make an evaluation of an item in terms of its estimated ordinal relation with the universe. That is, what is t_{jy}, the tau between Item j and the order on the universe of items? This means we are looking for the relation between dominances on Item j and the direction of dominance in the universe; Person i dominates h in the universe if $p_{ih}' > p_{hi}'$. This simply means that an item drawn at random is more likely to be one where i is correct and h not, than one where h is correct and i not. (In the case of polytomous items, the probabilities refer to one person giving a higher ranking answer than the other.)

Cliff and Donoghue (1992) provided some formulas that allow us to estimate t_{jy}. They noted that Cliff's (1995) ordinal regression theory implies that the tau between item and universe can be estimated from two quantities: the average tau of Item j with other items and the average tau among the other items. The formulas we use are

$$t_j = \sum_{k \neq j} t_{jk}/(m - 1), \tag{6.28}$$

and

$$t_{(j)} = \sum_{k \neq m \neq j}\sum t_{km} /(m-1)(m-2). \tag{6.29}$$

The elements excluded from the sums in the latter formula are the diagonal t_{kk} terms and the taus that are included in t_j. The t_j can be treated as normally distributed quantities that have mean zero and standard deviation equal to $[t_{jj}(t_{(j)} - t_j^2)]^{\frac{1}{2}}$. Then the tau between Item j and the universe can be estimated as

$$t_{jy} = t_{jj}\{2N\{t_j / [t_{jj}(t_{(j)} - t_j^2)]^{\frac{1}{2}}\} - 1\}, \tag{6.30}$$

where t_{jj} is the proportion of pairs not tied on Item j and N is the proportion of the normal curve falling below the ratio in the smaller braces. The estimate seems always to be quite good, and improves as the number of items increases.

This approach can then be used to estimate the tau between the overall order on the test and the universe order. As before, the order on the test is determined so that i ranks ahead of h if $p_{ih} > p_{hi}$. With dichotomous items, this simply means $x_i > x_h$, as we know from the previous section. The tau between test and universe is the measure of agreement between the orders defined by dominances from the p_{ih}, p_{hi} pairs and that defined by the corresponding p_{ih}', p_{hi}'. Then we calculate the average of the t_{jy} estimated by (6.30):

$$a = \sum t_{jy}/m, \tag{6.31}$$

and the average interitem tau:

$$b = \sum_{k \neq j}\sum t_{jk} /(m-1), \tag{6.32}$$

and the square root of the difference:

$$c = (a-b)^{\frac{1}{2}}. \tag{6.33}$$

The tau between test and universe can be estimated from the normal curve function N defined from a and c, that is, the proportion below a/c:

$$t_{xy} = 2N(a/c) - 1. \tag{6.34}$$

Table 6.5 provides an example of using these formulas to obtain an estimate of the validity of dominance relations on a test. The responses on this personality scale are on a 6-point scale reflecting degree of agreement with the item. The diagonal entries, in parentheses, give the proportions not tied on the item. The lower rows of the table give the quantities that lead to estimating the tau between total dominances on the test and the universe

TABLE 6.5
Tau-a Values among Six Items

Item						
Item	1	2	3	4	5	6
1	(.795)	.238	.114	.188	.255	.136
2		(.415)	.155	.198	.249	.165
3			(.329)	.224	.161	.172
4				(.415)	.199	.200
5					(.501)	.189
6						(.292)
t_j	.186	.201	.165	.202	.211	.172
$t_{(j)}$	.191	.184	.202	.183	.179	.210
st. dev.	.404	.244	.202	.243	.260	.230
z	.460	.824	.816	.831	.811	.748
$N(z)$	.677	.795	.793	.797	.791	.773
$2f(z)-1$	.354	.590	.586	.594	.582	.546
t_{jy}	.281	.245	.194	.247	.292	.160

$a = .2365$; $b = .7895$; $c = .2167$; $a/c = 1.091$; $N(a/c) = .862$; $t_{xy} = .724$.

order. Recall that with multilevel items the order on the test is in terms of the number of items where Person i dominated h, compared to the reverse. The first lower row gives the t_j, each item's average tau with the other five items (6.28). The is followed by the $t_{(j)}$, which are the averages of the taus not involving Item j (6.29). The row labeled "st. dev." is the denominator of (6.30), that is, $[t_{jj}(t_{(j)} - t_j^2)]^{1/2}$. This is followed by the z-ratio, which is t_j divided by "st. dev." Then comes the normal-curve proportion N that falls below this z-value, followed by $2N - 1$ and this quantity is multiplied by t_{jy}, which finally gives the estimated taus of each item with the universe.

Then, the quantities a, b, and c of (6.31), (6.32), and (6.33) are shown at the bottom of the table, followed by the normal curve proportion that corresponds to a/c. Since this is .862, application of formula (6.34) shows that the estimated tau with the universe order is .724.

Coefficient α in Dominance Analysis

One of the desirable aspects of a statistical test theory is being able to estimate the parallel form reliability of scores or orders on the basis of internal consistency information from the items. Whereas this is possible for numerical scores and, in a sense, for tied-ranks scores, this cannot be done directly for analyses based on dominances. That is, there is not a way of directly estimating the tau between the order on a current test with the order on a hypothetical parallel test from the taus among the items.

However, the coefficient α for a test, whether based on numerical scores or tied ranks, provides information about the overall order on the test in several ways that can be used to estimate the tau between that order and the order on a parallel test. First, consider the numerator and the denominator of the F-ratio in (6.23). If the squared differences in the numerator are averaged across all pairs of persons yielding a mean for it, which we call Q, and the variances in the denominator are also averaged for the denominator, which we call S, then

$$\alpha = 1 - S/Q. \tag{6.35}$$

Thus, α reflects the averages of these quantities that go into F-ratios for pairs of persons.

Correspondingly, α can be used to estimate the average F-ratio because (6.31) can be rearranged so that

$$Q/S = 1/(1 - \alpha) \tag{6.36}$$

That is, the average F-ratio for differences between scores can be estimated from α. However, this may not be a very accurate estimate of the average F-ratio because a ratio of averages is not the same as the average ratio. The distribution of ratios is likely to be quite skewed, and in that case the ratio of averages is usually rather biased with respect to the average ratio. Nevertheless, (6.32) can be used to get a general idea of the typical significance of interindividual differences on a test.

Arcsine Transformations of α

There is an additional way in which the tau between the observed order and a hypothetical parallel form can be estimated. In the case of a bivariate normal population, there is a well-established relation between Pearson correlation (ρ) and tau. This is (Kendall, 1975, p. 126) that

$$\tau = (2/\pi)\sin^{-1}(\rho). \tag{6.37}$$

In the formula, ρ is a population Pearson correlation expressed in radians. The inverse sine transformation is available on any pocket scientific calculator. Since α is the presumed Pearson correlation between the current test and the hypothetical parallel form, it seems that

$$\tau_{xx'} = (2/\pi) \sin^{-1}(\alpha) \tag{6.38}$$

can be used as an estimate of the tau between the test and a parallel form.

It is true that this relation assumes bivariate normality, and one of our goals in this book is to avoid such assumptions. However, assuming normality may not be as stringent an assumption in this application as it sometimes is if we realize that we are applying this to pairwise difference scores. Differences scores are much more normally distributed than the original scores on which they are based. For one thing, the distribution is necessarily symmetric. For another, the kurtosis of the distribution is substantially reduced, relative to that of the original distribution.

We can investigate the process with the six personality items of Table 6.5. The raw score α for these items is .812, implying a dominance-order tau of .603 by formula (6.34). Although it might be prudent to use caution in applying this formula, it may be fairly realistic. The estimated tau between order on the test and that in the universe was earlier estimated to be .724. According to CTT, the correlation between observed score and universe score is the square root of the reliability, whose estimate here is α. We find .812$^{\frac{1}{2}}$ = .901, and putting this in the inverse sine transformation (6.33) gives .714. This is negligibly different from the .724 we found the other way. Thus, in this instance, the two modes of estimation seem quite consistent.

SUMMARY

A good deal of ground has been covered in this chapter. We began with an argument of how it is that dichotomous items can define an order. It turned out that what was necessary was the consistent display of one of two types of relations between a pair of items and a pair of persons. Such an arrangement provides ordering information about both items and persons. On the other hand, a pair-pair can display a set of relations that is *contradictory*, weakening the idea that there is an order. The idea of order is *reinforced* by the presence of a third arrangement of relations. When responses to items are purely random, then there are an equal number of instances of reinforcing (r) and contradictory (c) relations.

The number of each can be computed from the ordinary two-way tables between all the pairs of items, and the total number of relations can be derived from the item variances. The number of person and item relations that are contradictory are necessarily equal, but the number that are reinforcing are usually different. However, the two are connected through the sum of the item variances and the variance of the persons' total scores. The interitem taus, covariances, and rhos are simple functions of the difference $r_{jk} - c_{jk}$.

There are a variety of indices of the consistency of the set of items that make up a test. Among them are the average interitem tau, covariance, or rho. However, because these are heavily constrained in the case of dichotomous items by the item variances and by differences in item difficulties, adjustments to these averages were suggested. Where interitem relations are variable, it may be true that a test's items should be clustered into subsets that yield subscores.

An important indication of a test's utility is its order's agreement with that on a parallel test. Also useful is an estimate of the degree to which it agrees with the order on whatever it is that the test as a whole is measuring. Here, we consider the test's items to be a sample from a universe of potential items, and it is the overall order on the whole universe that we wish the test to reflect as closely as possible. It turns out to be fairly simple to assess the degree to which the relative position of two individuals on the test is in agreement with their relative position on the universe. This idea can be extended to rank differences or score differences. In addition, it is possible to estimate the overall tau between a test and the universe. Estimating the agreement between the present test and a hypothetical parallel test can only be done more indirectly.

Chapter 7

Approaches to Ordering
Things and Stimuli

ONE-SET DOMINANCE

The reader will recall that in chapter 2 we outlined the system developed by Coombs (1951, 1964) that categorized different kinds of data according to three criteria. One criterion was whether the relation underlying the data represented a *dominance* relation, epitomized by the mathematical relation "greater than" or the relation was one based on *proximity*, or closeness. The second was whether the relation was between members of the same set or different sets. The third, to which we pay little attention in this book, depended on whether the relation as between members of *pairs* of elements, or between *pairs of pairs* of elements. So far, in chapters 4, 5, and 6, we have been concerned with data representing two-set relations, typically persons or examinees, compared to items. In this chapter, we are concerned with cases where the fundamental data represent ordering relations between members of the same set. This has many applications in applied and basic experimental psychology, but also in other social and behavioral sciences.

This chapter also provides the reader with a detailed example of how a scale (a) can be defined according to a set of logical rules or *axioms*, (b) how the validity of these axioms can be examined in data, and (c) how the order that agrees best with the data can be found. Thus, we provide some additional conceptual guidelines to understanding what justifies "measurement."

Sets and Relations

If we are trying to find out whether some physical or psychological things have an order, and, if so, what that order is, we start with the set of things and some empirical operation that compares members of the set. If we have a collection of rocks (the set) and want to order them in weight, a physical property, the operation might be putting one rock on each side of an old-fashioned balance, and seeing which side went down. Note that we are using the balance in a purely qualitative way, comparing one rock to another, rather than comparing each rock against members of a set of standard weights. If we wanted to order them in heaviness—a psychological property—we could give pairs of rocks to a person and ask which member of the pair was heavier. In that case, seeing which was chosen as heavier, along with various procedural details, is the operation.

We can get an order either way. Our society has an intellectual bias that says the order given by the balance is the "real" order, but this is just a bias. The heaviness order can be just as real as the weight order; which order is preferred just depends on what our purpose is. The question that concerns us now is: What is it about the outcome of our operations that will tell us (a) whether we have an order at all, and (b) what the order is.

The prototype for a one-set dominance order is the set of ordinary numbers and the relation >. It is worthwhile in this context to try to shed a lot of semantic baggage associated with the word *numbers* and what we know about the sign > and only pay attention to basic principles. The numbers are just members of a set; > is just a sign we use to designate a relation between the members of the set. We are trying to define what it is that is so special about this set and this sign that enables us to end up with something we call an order for the set.

Characterizing Oneset Dominance

The key properties that produce an order based on a dominance relation can be identified. The first one is that in any pair of numbers a,b, either $a > b$ or $b > a$, unless $b = a$ in the sense that the two are identical. There is more to the relation > than this because with numbers the structure is more complete. It is not as if every time we compare an a to a b the outcome could arbitrarily be *either $a > b$ or $b > a$*; after a few comparisons we will be able to predict the outcome of a comparison most of the time from the outcome of previous comparisons. (Remember, we are not using our knowledge about the identity of the numbers themselves, for example, the number we call 7 > the number we call 6.3 *and all other numbers less than 7*. We are just using the outcomes of comparisons involving >.) The principle that we are able to use is that whenever $a > b$ and $b > c$, then $a > c$, so we quickly can omit making comparisons that are already implied by others. Instead of having to compare every one of a set of n numbers to every other one, which would result in $n(n-1)/2$ comparisons, we only need to make those that are not already implied by others. This results in only needing $\log_2(n!)$ comparisons instead of $n(n-1)/2$, which is 22 instead of 45 for $n = 10$, and 525 instead of 4,950 for $n = 100$ if we were actually making comparisons, but the point here is the generality of the principle. This property of numbers is called *transitivity*. It is fundamental to computer algorithms for rapidly sorting a list into numerical or alphabetic order.

A third, perhaps more obvious principle can also be stated. This is that $a > b$ implies that b is not $> a$. This principle is called *asymmetry*. A fourth principle, that a number is not greater than itself, is called *irreflexivity*. For completeness, we also need to state still another principle, that either $a > b$ or $b > a$. That is, with numbers, we do not allow the equivalent of a "don't know," or "can't say," or "no dice" outcome. These principles, which have been formulated numerous times (Gulliksen, 1946; Krantz et al., 1971; Roberts, 1970) sometimes in slightly different combinations, constitute the requirements for the order properties of numbers that is based on an asymmetric or dominance principle. For convenience of reference, we restate them in a more concise form than has been done so far:

Not $a > a$. (irreflexivity)	(d1)
Either $a > b$ or $b > a$. (connectedness)	(d2)
$a > b$ implies not ($b > a$) (asymmetry)	(d3)
$a > b$ and $b > c$ implies $a > c$ (transitivity)	(d4)

These are the properties that we want both our weight and heaviness scales to have if they are each to be an order. As formal axioms, they can be arranged somewhat differently; for example, the set can be based on $\geq$ instead of $>$, making it reflexive instead of irreflexive, but these four are the essential qualities that a system must have to provide a dominance order.

The four properties can be displayed in a visual form that for me has more intuitive force than the foregoing list. This form is illustrated in Table 7.1. The elements $a, b, c, \ldots h$ of the set which is ordered define the rows and columns of the table, the elements being listed in the order that is appropriate for this set. In the table, 1 stands for the fact that the row element stands in the relation $>$ to the column element. The symbols in the table take on a nice regular form: a triangle of 1s above the main diagonal, and a triangle of zeroes below and including the main diagonal.

This simplicity is a consequence of the properties (d1) to (d4) and of having the objects in the correct order. The four properties correspond to aspects of this triangular simplicity. Irreflexivity means that the main diagonal is all 0s. Connectedness means that, for any pair there has to be a 1 on

TABLE 7.1
A Dominance Order

	a	b	c	d	e	f	g	h
a	0	1	1	1	1	1	1	1
b	0	0	1	1	1	1	1	1
c	0	0	0	1	1	1	1	1
d	0	0	0	0	1	1	1	1
e	0	0	0	0	0	1	1	1
f	0	0	0	0	0	0	1	1
g	0	0	0	0	0	0	0	1
h	0	0	0	0	0	0	0	0

TABLE 7.2
A Scrambled Dominance Order

	c	f	e	a	g	h	d	b
c	0	1	1	0	1	1	1	0
f	0	0	0	0	1	1	0	0
e	0	1	0	0	1	1	0	0
a	1	1	1	0	1	1	1	1
g	0	0	0	0	0	1	0	0
h	0	0	0	0	0	0	0	0
d	0	1	1	0	1	1	0	0
b	1	1	1	0	1	1	1	0

one side of the diagonal or the other. Asymmetry means that it cannot be on both sides. Transitivity means that it is possible to put *all* the 0s below the diagonal, and all the 1s above it. If we scramble the order of the objects, but keep all the properties, then the more chaotic picture seen in Table 7.2 occurs. The latter is still an order; we just have not found it.

FINDING THE ORDER

The process of finding the order is quite simple when the axioms are strictly followed, provided we do not care about efficiency. We can just compare each element to each other one and count the number of "wins" that each gets, and then order the elements in terms of those numbers. There are more efficient processes, such as the "bubble sort" that is incorporated in many computer routines, and a similar method that is described in chapter 8.

Once we have found the correct order, we can assign any set of correspondingly ordered numbers to the objects $a, b, \ldots$, and call those numbers a scale. Now, we no longer need the original table of observations because we can always reproduce them from the well-known properties, which are $(d1)$ to $(d4)$, of the numbers we have assigned. There is an interchangeability between the numbers and the observations, *provided the observations behave like numbers.*

Inconsistent Data

The simple order, characterized by $(d1)$ to $(d4)$ is an ideal, and real data does not often conform to ideals, so we can attempt to modify these requirements to reflect more accurately the way the data behave while still retaining the most essential aspects of the ordering principle. To avoid difficulties that have arisen with this issue in the past, we need to deal with a distinction at the outset. This distinction is between, on one hand, a kind of unavoidable inconsistency between data and any model, reflected by the fact that the data are not perfectly consistent due to random errors of observation or measurement, and, on the other hand, *systematic* departures of the data from a model that are represented by fundamental failures of properties such as $(d1)$ to $(d4)$, on the other. The first kind of inconsistency, which is a kind of unreliability or observational error, would occur if, on replication of the comparisons, for some pairs we find first $a > b$ and, on replication, $b > a$, violating asymmetry. Or we might find some violations of transitivity in a single set of data just because the data-gathering method is not sensitive enough to be completely consistent.

Coombs' (1951, 1964) system did not accommodate such a possibility. He did not make the distinction between *data*, which is never perfectly consistent, even in physics of the most precise kind, and underlying scales that behave in a consistent way except for measurement error that is imposed onto them. In fact, he called his book *Theory of Data* (Coombs, 1964). Data that did not behave consistently did not provide scales, in his view. These biases made it difficult for many empirically oriented researchers to treat his methods as more than abstract curiosities, while leading others, who were more sympathetic to his orientation, to dismiss much of psychometrics as "measurement through error."

The orientation of this book is that systems like $d1$–$d4$ represent ideals rather than requirements for data. When we see that data do not behave exactly like $(d1)$ to $(d4)$, two views may still justify scales. One, an idealistic view (in the colloquial rather than the philosophic sense), is the one that says there really are scales underlying our data that have these properties; it is just that our methods can never be good enough to reveal those scales exactly. A second, pragmatic, justification for deriving scales from imperfect data is that a scale derived from data can still be a useful summary of most of the observed relations, even when it cannot summarize all of them.

In dealing with oneset dominance orders, as in other chapters of this book, we focus on two things. One is how to evaluate the extent to which data are consistent with an underlying order, and the other is how best to estimate what that order is. Before turning to those topics, we describe systems that are similar to simple dominance orders but are attempts at making the requirements that underlie them less demanding.

LESS SIMPLE ORDERS

Semi-Orders

One liberalization of the simple order is the semi-order (Roberts, 1971). It is designed to deal with imperfect sensitivity of a very systematic kind. Suppose subjects are attempting to discriminate stimuli on some psychophysical continuum, such as the pitch of tones, and it is noticed that asymmetry is violated for stimuli that are close to each other on the continuum. For example, perhaps your musical ear is not acute enough to distinguish between semitones in terms of their highness, so that you may say that A and B-sharp are equal in pitch, and on a later trial that B-sharp is equal to A. In fact, you do that for all such pairs of tones that are not separated by a full tone. However, you are still perfectly consistent, and make the correct judgment when there is any full-tone separation. Another example might be one in which a subject is presented with pairs of consumer items and asked which he or she prefers, with the "don't care" or "can't say" or "indifferent" response being allowed.

The observed relations might then look like Table 7.3, which is very like Table 7.1, except that the triangle of 1s is smaller.

It certainly looks as if there is an order here, and it is possible to modify ($d1$) to ($d4$) to accommodate this kind of observation while still giving an order. In fact, this can be stated in a more general way that allows more

TABLE 7.3
A Semi-Order

	a	b	c	d	e	f	g	h
a	0	0	1	1	1	1	1	1
b	0	0	0	1	1	1	1	1
c	0	0	0	0	1	1	1	1
d	0	0	0	0	0	1	1	1
e	0	0	0	0	0	0	1	1
f	0	0	0	0	0	0	0	1
g	0	0	0	0	0	0	0	0
h	0	0	0	0	0	0	0	0

than one failure of discrimination for each stimulus; for example, a subject might not be able to distinguish adjacent full tones, but might always distinguish differences that were more than one full tone, and so on, for greater degrees of insensitivity. An order for all the tones will still result, provided a point is not reached so few discriminations are made that some tones have exactly the same profile of discriminations. A process that works to define an order is to count the number of wins, as before, but also subtract the number of losses. This can be seen to work in Table 7.3; the elements a through f can be ordered in terms of wins, and they are all shown to come before g and h, but g and h have the same number of wins, 0. However, h has six losses whereas g has only five, so g must come before h.

Partial Order

The second important variation is the *partial order*. It is in a sense less satisfactory than the other two in that it ends up with some of the objects tied in the order. This is not because of inconsistency, however. The relations in a partial order look like Table 7.4, which still looks very orderly, but instead of the neat upper triangle of 1s there is now a kind of sawtooth effect. What this means is that the objects can be separated into what are called equivalence classes, subsets whose members are effectively equal to each other. Here, the first class is $\{a,b\}$; the second is $\{c,d,e\}$; the third is $\{f,g,h\}$. Within equivalence classes, relations are symmetric; between, they are asymmetric; also, transitivity is never violated.

Interval Order

A third variation is called an *interval order*. It is similar in idea to the semiorder and partial order in that it allows for some relations to be symmetric, as in "don't know" or "can't say" responses. It differs in that there is less regularity in the pattern of the adjacency matrix. It assumes that each

TABLE 7.4
A Partial Order

	a	b	c	d	e	f	g	h
a	0	0	1	1	1	1	1	1
b	0	0	1	1	1	1	1	1
c	0	0	0	0	0	1	1	1
d	0	0	0	0	0	1	1	1
e	0	0	0	0	0	1	1	1
f	0	0	0	0	0	0	0	0
g	0	0	0	0	0	0	0	0
h	0	0	0	0	0	0	0	0

object that is compared has a sort of range of uncertainty, and this range is a characteristic of the object, one that is not systematically related to the overall position of the object on the scale, and that is not dependent on which other object it is compared to.

An analogy is a "snake race." Suppose in a certain area the snakes like to hold races to see which is faster. Due to technical problems when large groups race, they always race in pairs. However, they do not share the human view that a race is won when any part of a snake's anatomy, that is, the nose, crosses the finish line before another's. In fact, some, usually the shorter snakes, have contended that a race is won when the *tip of the tail* of one snake finishes before the other's tip. This controversy led to considerable acrimony and occasional fatalities until a compromise was reached. In order for there to be a clear win, the tail of one snake must finish before the head of the other. This results in a number of tied or no-contest races, but has been agreed to as a compromise.

When a group of snakes conducts a complete series of races in this pairwise fashion, with winners, losers, and ties determined as described, they would like to know as much as possible of an overall ranking of the contestants. In contrast to the partial and semi-orders, there is uncertainty in a snake race about the length of the snake and length is not necessarily related to speed.

When two snakes race, the only direct information we have is whether the tail of one finished ahead of the head of the other, but further relations are implied. A way to think of the situation is that in pairwise comparisons across n snakes, there are $2n$ things involved, n heads plus n tails. When A is judged to have defeated B, we get two pieces of information: the tail of A finished before the head of B, but also implied is the fact that the head of A also finished before the head of B. When a race between A and B is deemed a tie, there are still two pieces of information: the head of A finished before the tail of B, and the head of B finished before the tail of A. (Otherwise, there would not be a tie.) It is also true that the head of an animal always finishes in front of its own tail, the type of rattlesnake called a sidewinder traditionally not being allowed to compete.

The observed relations can then imply others, sometimes resulting in a nearly complete order. Suppose in a set of races among four snakes, the result is that A defeats each of the three others and B defeats D, but the other two races result in ties. These results are recorded in the upper right section of Table 7.5, recording that the indicated tails finished before the corresponding heads. The lower left section contains the order of heads relative to tails that are directly implied by the upper right observations. That is, there is a 1 corresponding to each zero in the upper right, tails-over-heads section because the implication is that the head finished before the tail. The diagonal sections of Table 7.5, representing head–head and tail–tail re-

TABLE 7.5
Illustration of an Interval Order

| | | Observed Relations | | | | | | | |
| | | Tails | | | | Heads | | | |
		A	B	C	D	A	B	C	D
Tails	A	0				0	1	1	1
	B		0			0	0	0	1
	C			0		0	0	0	0
	D				0	0	0	0	0
Heads	A	1	1	1	1	0			
	B	0	1	1	1		0		
	C	0	1	1	1			0	
	D	0	0	1	1				0

lations are blank because that information is not observed directly. However, in Table 7.6 these upper left and lower right sections show the tail–tail and head–head relations that are implied by these known relations. For example, the head of A must have finished before the head of B because A's tail is known to have done so; A's head finished before its own tail which finished before B's head, so its head finished before B's. It is seen in Table 7.6 that the only relations remaining unknown are between the heads of B and C and the tails of C and D. If there were no unknown relations, the data would constitute a semiorder.

These three variations on simple orders, the semiorder, the partial order, and the interval order, are perhaps less strongly contradicted by observations than the simple order, but they, too, are rarely exactly consistent with a meaningfully large set of data. However, they represent ideals or pat-

TABLE 7.6
Implied Relations in an Interval Order

| | | Tails | | | | Heads | | | |
		A	B	C	D	A	B	C	D
Tails	A	0	1	1	1				
	B		0	1	1				
	C			0					
	D				0				
	A					0	1	1	1
Heads	B						0		1
	C							0	1
	D								0

terns that may be more suitable definitions of order for a given empirical situation than the simple order.

Is There a Scale?

The general strategy, then, is to look at the pairwise relations between elements of a set, be these elements a set of stimuli to be judged, a group of chess competitors, or any other. The relations between the members of the set are examined to see the extent that they display the definitional properties. If that is adequately the case, then we say there is an ordinal scale. If not, there is not.

The alert reader probably wants to know what is meant by "adequately." To take Coombs literally would mean that *adequately* equates with *perfectly*; one inconsistency is enough to destroy the order. On the other hand, we believe one might want to say that orders exist more frequently than that would allow, so we adopt a perhaps wishy-washy attitude and say an order underlies the data when the fulfillment of the axioms is sufficiently close for the purpose to which the scale would be put. This was our approach in preceding chapters in evaluating test-type data. We devote a good deal of attention to evaluating how close a given set of data corresponds to the ideal and to finding the best order from fallible data.

This is not to say that in defining scales one would endorse the stance that accepts the consistency of the relations that define the scale in a given set of data as "good enough for government work" and stops there. One of the activities that seems to characterize scientific progress, as distinct from mere research dithering, is the attention that is paid to refining variables. Rather than simply accepting the degree of inconsistency that occurs, it is preferable to find out where it occurs and then why. Then the observational process, including the set of things that is being scaled, can be revised with an eye toward increasing the quality of the scale. One really good scale is likely to be more scientifically useful than any number of pretty good ones.

There are other important issues in scale construction or definition. One is that the basic observational relations that are used to define the scale should represent genuine observations, not artifacts, and that they should be as independent of each other as possible. Having a set of observations that conform well enough to $(d1)$ to $(d4)$ to justify further processing, then one needs a way of converting the data to a single summary scale. This will be an ordinal scale because there is nothing in $d1$–$d4$ that provides a basis for anything more elevated, such as intervals. To be able to take that step to intervals requires (a) more elaborate data and (b) conformity of it to a more extended set of properties than $d1$–$d4$. We do not go into that here. The interested reader can consult sources such as Cliff (1992), Michel (1990), or Krantz et al. (1971).

EMPIRICALLY DEFINING AND EVALUATING DOMINANCE

Defining a Dominance Relation

Given a set of elements, we hypothesize that there is an underlying order for the elements and wish to discover it. The elements can be anything: lights that vary in brightness, poems to be judged for quality, a group of chess-players, and so on. It often makes sense to look for the order by means of a pairwise dominance relation. If consistency with the axioms described in the previous section is shown, then this can be convincing evidence of an order, provided the dominance relations themselves are convincing. Thus, the first requirement for establishing an order is an empirically valid demonstration of a nontrivial, nonarbitrary dominance relation.

This means that the observed dominance should have several qualities. First, it should reflect the underlying variable that determines the order that we are interested in, and as little as possible of anything else. This is the same validity issue that pervades all of behavioral science; we want the order that results, if there is one, to represent what we think it does, and not something else, so the process of observation should not be confounded by extraneous or artifactual effects. But there is an additional aspect here: We are trying to find out if there is an order, whatever it represents, so we also do not want to be fooled into thinking that there is consistency when in fact the consistency itself is artifactual.

Just assigning numbers to things does not necessarily mean they are ordered in any empirically meaningful way. We must seek other properties of the system of observation that support the idea of order, or quantification of any kind, if an order is to be believed. Also, the process of observation is just as subject to the tenets of control, validity, absence of artifacts, and unambiguous interpretation that define good scientific practice as in any other aspect of research that presumes to be scientific.

A second thing that the dominance process should display is distinctness. In as many cases as possible, we need to have a clearcut decision about which element dominates the other. Ties, or their equivalent, or any ambiguity in the outcome of the comparison, are to be avoided, or at least minimized.

The third thing the observation of dominance should have is independence. This means that there should be no arbitrary, hidden, or artifactual process that makes the outcome of one dominance relation associated with another one, except for the identity of the elements involved. This means that when subjects are judging psychophysical stimuli, there should be little opportunity for subjects to remember how they treated particular stimuli in the past and then try to make the current response consistent with earlier ones. Each dominance relation that is observed should furnish separate information about the elements, uninfluenced by the outcome of any other dominance observation.

TESTING THE DOMINANCE AXIOMS

Once a well-defined process for observing dominances has been established, we need to go on to assessing whether the relation has the properties $(d1)$–$(d4)$. The prototypical case for establishing dominance relations is human comparative judgment as pioneered by the psychophysicists of the 19th century. The most elegant, although not the most efficient, method of ordering stimuli is based on data gathered by the Method of Paired Comparisons (Guilford, 1954).[1] Suppose a set of stimuli are to be ordered in terms of some subjective quality such as brightness, heaviness, desirability as a prize, or suitability for viewing by children. The stimuli are presented in pairs, and the person doing the judging is asked which member of each pair is brighter, heavier, more desirable, or more suitable, and the subject must choose one.

If there is a simple order, even though it may be idiosyncratic to this judge, then the judgments should display the qualities described in $(d1)$–$(d4)$. In the traditional presentation, each stimulus is presented in combination with each other one once, and not with itself. This means that reflexiveness cannot be tested because the stimuli are not compared to themselves. However, connectedness is satisfied if all the pairs are presented, although we will see in the next chapter that connectedness may still hold when not all the pairwise relations are observed directly, provided transitivity holds or is assumed. The relations are asymmetric as a matter of experimental necessity when the pairs are only presented once and a choice is forced each time. So far, there is little in the procedure that gives grounds for convincing us that there is an order here because none of the properties of a dominance order have had the opportunity to be violated.

Evaluating Reflexivity

Evaluation of dominance orders has traditionally focused on transitivity $(d4)$, and we see next how this can be done, but let us assume first that we

---

[1]"Paired Comparisons" is somewhat ungrammatical because, taken literally, it implies that *comparisons* are paired, whereas in actuality it is *pairs* that are compared. Thus, a more accurate phrase would be "pair comparisons" or "pairwise comparisons." These latter terms are encountered occasionally, but the "paired comparisons" terminology is deeply engrained.

are serious about the other axioms. Reflexiveness and asymmetry can be tested if the experimental procedure is altered. When stimuli are not identifiable by the subject, simple tones, for example, we can evaluate reflexivity by presenting each stimulus with itself and eliciting the response. When stimuli are identifiable, it usually does not make sense to compare stimuli to themselves. (An investigator who asks the subject, for example, if she prefers peanuts to peanuts when she goes to the movies is likely to lose a certain amount of credibility.) If the subject—given the opportunity—always reports that a dominates a, the responses are reflexive; if she never reports that a dominates a, it is irreflexive. If there is a mixture, then we have to conclude that the response is neither reflexive nor irreflexive, and so one of the fundamental requirements for an order cannot be established. This deficiency may sometimes be remedied by altering the experimental procedure, perhaps by clarifying the task or altering the response or the basis for judgment.

Unfortunately, the likelihood is that even the best procedure will fail to display perfect consistency of either kind. Then, we may wish to fall back on a quantification of the degree to which there is a consistent tendency one way or the other. A simple way to do this is to calculate a "reflexiveness index" by counting the number of reflexive judgments, subtracting the number of irreflexive, and dividing by the number of stimuli.

If we wish to decide whether there is a significant tendency one way or the other, we can use the number of reflexive responses and the .50 line of a binomial distribution table to test that hypothesis. With multiple subjects, we can pool the data across subjects to evaluate this conclusion, computing the reflexiveness statistic for each subject and averaging these across subjects. A confidence interval for this average can be established by using the variance of the reflexiveness statistics in an ordinary one-sample Student's t procedure.

Asymmetry

When we present each pair only once, we are implicitly assuming asymmetry, that is, we are assuming that when a is found to dominate b in the a,b pair, b does not dominate a. The response process is inherently asymmetrical, so there is no way to test asymmetry. If we wish to test this axiom, it must be given an opportunity to fail, and to provide this we have to present at least some pairs more than once.

In the simplest case, each pair is presented twice, perhaps in opposite orders if the members of the pair are presented sequentially, or on both the left and right positions if they are presented at the same time or in a "home and home" format for an athletic contest. If the relation is truly asymmetric, then the same member of the pair will dominate both times. When complete asymmetry is not present, the degree to which the relation is asymmetric can be expressed in terms of an asymmetry statistic. If responding to each pair is random, the same element will be chosen twice in half the pairs and each will be chosen once in half, so asymmetry can be expressed relative to this baseline. For n things, let f represent the number of pairs where the same member is chosen both times. Then

$$\text{asymmetry} = \frac{f - n(n-1)/4}{n(n-1)/4} \tag{7.1}$$

is a reasonable formula for expressing the degree of asymmetry. A test of significance can be generated from it by squaring the numerator while using the same denominator. The result is a statistic that is approximately distributed as a one-degree of freedom chi-square (Table B.1) under a null model where all choices are random and independent. The formula (7.1) can be generalized to situations where there are k repetitions of each pair by replacing the 4s in it by 2^k. f is then number of pairs having 100% of the k judgments in one direction $(2,0; 3,0; \ldots k,0; \ldots)$. For example, if there are four repetitions of each pair, and ten elements, $2^4 = 16$, and the expected number of pairs where the same element is chosen all four times is $10 \times 9/16 = 5.62$.

Thus, the axioms of reflexivity and asymmetry can be evaluated with the data although data-gathering procedures may need to be extended beyond typical practices in order to do so. Where conformity to these axioms is incomplete, one can quantify the extent to which the data are consistent with them and test models that investigate whether there is at least a significant tendency toward reflexiveness and asymmetry.

ASSESSING TRANSITIVITY

Circular Triads

In assessing the conformity of a set of presumed dominance relations to the axioms, by far the most effort has been devoted to transitivity. Suppose x_1 has been judged brighter than x_2 (whether they are lights, colors, or colleagues), and x_2 has been judged brighter than x_3, and now x_1 and x_3 are compared. Transitivity implies that x_1 should be judged brighter than x_3 and the empirical question is "Is it?" If so, transitivity is supported; if not, it is not. When it is not, the triple x_1, x_2, x_3 is often called a "circular triad" because the "order" implied by the dominance relations seems to go from x_1 to x_2 to x_3 and back to x_1 to x_2. . . . However, following the practice of mathematical graph theory, which has considerable application in this context, we refer to such circularities as "cycles." This term may have a numerical modifier to indicate its length. Thus, a circular triad will be called a "three-cycle" (resisting the temptation to call it a tricycle). Longer cycles are possible: $x_1 >^* x_2 >^* x_3 >^* x_4 >^* x_1 >^* \ldots$ and so on.[2] However, it is always possible to break these longer cycles up into circular triads; the number and nature of the three-cycles that are contained in an n-cycle depends on the direction of the other relations. With four elements, there are $4 \times 3/2 = 6$ relations among the four, of which a four-cycle such as the one above specifies only four relations. A four-cycle always contains two three-cycles. The nature of the other two relations will determine what they are. Longer cycles can always be broken into three-cycles although the number may vary (Kendall, 1975, p. 146). For simplicity, we concern ourselves only with three-cycles.

Empirical cycles usually are assumed to reflect the effect of random error in the comparison process, but the possibility exists that there are true cycles among the elements where a dominance order is expected. Natural examples may occur in ecology where Species 1 may outcompete Species 2, and 2 outcompetes 3, but 3 outcompetes 1. The most familiar example is the rock–paper–scissors game. In it, two competitors, on signal, simultaneously use a hand to display one of: a fist ("rock"), the hand held flat ("paper"), or two fingers extended ("scissors"). The scoring is that rock wins over ("breaks") scissors; scissors wins over ("cuts") paper; but paper wins over ("covers") rock. Thus there is no dominance order among the three because they form a cycle. In an empirical context, the objective of an empirical procedure is to discover an order, but the existence of true cycles would also be of interest, so we must allow for that possibility.

In dealing with dominances, it is a good idea to arrange the dominance relations in an $n \times n$ matrix $\mathbf{A}$ in which an entry of 1 means that the ith row element dominated the jth column element, and an entry of 0 means that it did not. We assume that self-comparisons have not been made, and historically it assumed that the relation is irreflexive, so 0 is entered for the i,i comparison, and we follow that convention here. Tables 7.1 and 7.2 are examples.

Counting Three-Cycles

Searching for three-cycles could be a tedious process, but the number of them that occur in a complete matrix of relations can be found from the number of dominances by each element, the sums of the entries in each row of $\mathbf{A}$:.

---

[2]Note that we are using $>^*$ to denote empirical dominance in order to distinguish it from $>$, which denotes a mathematical relation.

$$a_i = \Sigma_j a_{ij} \tag{7.2}$$

If there are no intransitivities, then one element will win all its comparisons, a second will win all but its comparison with the first, and so on, so their totals will be the integers $n - 1$, $n - 2$, $\ldots$, 1, 0. However, where there are intransitivities, this will not be true. There will be ties among these totals, and more specifically, their variance will be reduced. Kendall (1975) showed that the number of three-cycles, g, is given by

$$g = [n(n - 1)(2n - 1) - 6\Sigma a_i^2]/12. \tag{7.3}$$

This formula is, in effect, comparing the variance of the a_i to its maximum possible value, $(n^2 - 1)/12$. (The same formula would, of course apply to the column totals a_i that give the number of losses by the stimuli.) It is illustrated in Table 7.7, and we find $[6 \times 5 \times 11 - 6(25 + 9 + 9 + 4 + 4 + 0)]/12 = 2$ as the number of three-cycles in those data. Searching the relations reveals that these involve 2,3,5; and 2,4,5. Next, we see a different way of counting intransitivities, one that applies more smoothly to those cases where some comparisons are omitted or tied.

The maximum possible value of g occurs when the a_i are equal. However, this can only occur when n is odd. When it is even, an element is involved in an odd number of comparisons and thus cannot dominate in exactly half of them, so then the most even distribution occurs when half the a_i are equal to $\frac{1}{2}n$ and the other half to $\frac{1}{2}n - 1$. This means that the maximum possible values for g are (Kendall, 1975, p. 146)

$$(n^3 - n)/24, \quad \text{for } n \text{ odd}$$

TABLE 7.7
Illustrative Adjacency Matrix

	Elements						Wins	Net Wins	
Versus	1	2	3	4	5	6	a_i	a_i^2	d_i
1	0	1	1	1	1	1	5	25	5
2	0	0	1	1	0	1	3	9	1
3	0	0	0	1	1	1	3	9	1
4	0	0	0	0	1	1	2	4	−1
5	0	1	0	0	0	1	2	4	−1
6	0	0	0	0	0	0	0	0	−5
a_j	0	2	2	3	3	5			
Σa_i^2								51	

$$(n^3 - 4n)/24, \quad \text{for } n \text{ even.}$$

In our six-element example of Table 3.1, this is $(216 - 24)/24 = 8$.

Circularity Coefficient

Kendall (1975) suggested a coefficient to express the degree of transitivity in the data, one that uses the maximum g that could occur as the baseline. However, it seems preferable to use for this purpose the expected number of intransitive triples under random responding to each pair instead of the maximum number possible. In any triple of elements, a,b,c, there are three pairwise relations, a with b, a with c, and b with c. In any of these three pairs, either member could dominate, so the number of possible outcomes of comparing the members of each pair is $2^3 = 8$. Six of these eight possibilities do not involve a circularity, each resulting in one of the $3! = 6$ possible orders of the three. The other two are the circularities $a \rightarrow b \rightarrow c \rightarrow a \rightarrow \ldots$ and $a \rightarrow c \rightarrow b \rightarrow a \rightarrow \ldots$. Thus, for any triple, the probability of a cycle is $2/8 = .25$. There are n-take-three sets of triples, $n(n-1)(n-2)/6$, so the expected number of three-cycles under the assumption that each comparison is an independent 50–50 event is $\frac{1}{4}[n(n-1)(n-2)/6]$. In the example, where $n = 6$, the expected number under random responding is $6 \times 5 \times 4/24 = 5$. If we call this number e, then a coefficient of consistency c can be defined as $c = 1 - g/e$. In our example, this is $1 - 2/5 = .6$. Expressed in terms of the sum of squared row totals a_i, c is

$$c = \frac{12 \sum a_i^2 - 3n^2(n-1)}{n(n-1)(n-2)}. \tag{7.4}$$

When there are no three-cycles, c is 1.0, and it is zero if the number is the expected number under random responding. In our Table 7.7 example this formula gives $(612 - 540)/24 = .60$.

True circularities, like the one in the rock–paper–scissors game, seem unlikely except under similarly artificial circumstances, so negative values of c presumably occur as random deviations from zero. However, the possibility of true cycles does exist, so consistent negative values for c, or highly significant negative values for it, suggest that the observations should be examined carefully for the possibility of some procedural failure. In the absence of such irregularities, the more interesting conclusion would be that a number of true circularities exist in the relations.

In data where there are what seem to be a large number of circularities, the rather discouraging null hypothesis that the subject is responding at random may be entertained. For reasonable values of n, use can be made of the fact that g can be transformed to approximate a chi-squared distribution (Kendall, 1975) with v degrees of freedom:

$$v = \frac{n(n-1)(n-2)}{(n-4)^2},$$
(7.5)

$$x^2 = \frac{1}{n-4}[4\sum a_1 (a_1 - 1) + 4 - n(n-1)(n-2)] + v.$$
(7.6)

INTERSUBJECT CONSISTENCY

Kendall's Tau and Spearman's Rho

Where there are replications of the dominance relations, such as from several subjects, it is obviously important to see how consistent the orders derived from them are with each other. This consistency is most simply expressed in terms of correlations among the orders derived from the individual replications, and the most appropriate measures of correlation are clearly ordinal ones. As we have seen, the two main indices of ordinal correlation are the Spearman rank correlation, r_S, and Kendall's tau, t. Both have several variations; the differences among them are primarily in the treatment of ties. We repeat their definitions and some of their formulas for ease of reference.

The Spearman coefficient is a Pearson correlation between two sets of ranks, but formulas for it can take advantage of simplicities that occur for means and variances when the data are ranks. Designating q_{ix} and q_{iy} as the ranks on X and Y, respectively, one formula for r_S is therefore

$$r_S = \frac{12\sum q_{ix} q_{iy} - 3n(n+1)^2}{n^3 - n}.$$
(7.7)

An even simpler looking version, perhaps the most commonly encountered of all, simply has $6\Sigma(q_{ix} - q_{iy})^2$, or some equivalent expression, as the numerator.

The formula above has a correlation (cosine of the angle between the vectors of ranks) interpretation only when there are no ties on either variable. However, it is commonly employed, even in the presence of ties, provided that the q_i that are used are the averages of the tied ranks. An alternative is to literally compute the Pearson correlation between the ranks, the latter coefficient being called r_{Sb} (Cliff, 1996; Kendall, 1975). For present purposes we prefer formula (7.7) because it lends itself more easily to multivariate generalizations and because it represents how close two sets of ranks agree, compared to the maximum possible, even in the presence of ties. Applications of the formula for r_S are referred to as correlations even when there are ties.

For two matrices of dominance relations on n things as discussed before, r_S can be used to express the agreement between two sets of wins scores, $a_{i.1}$ and $a_{i.2}$:

$$r_S = \frac{12\sum a_{i1} a_{i2} - 3n(n-1)^2}{n^3 - n} \tag{7.8}$$

With ties among the $a_{i.}$, because of the presence of cycles, the formula can no longer attain the limits of ± 1 although the limitation will not be great unless there are numerous ties relative to the number of pairs.

Kendall's tau is a measure of ordinal correlation that is in some senses more in the spirit of the kind of data discussed here. Like r_S it is typically defined in terms of relations on two variables that are assumed or known to be ordinal, but it can be adapted to the context of individual dominance relations.

Given two ordinal variables X and Y, tau is defined for a population as

$$\tau_{XY} = \Pr[(x_i > x_j) \text{ and } (y_i > y_j)] - \Pr[(x_i > x_j) \text{ and } (y_i < y_j)]. \tag{7.9}$$

That is, it is the probability that a pair of elements is in the same order on both variables minus the reverse probability. Similarly, in a sample of size n, the sample version t is

$$t_{xy} = \frac{\#[(x_i > x_j) \text{ and } (y_i > y_j)] - \#[(x_i > x_j) \text{ and } (y_i < y_j)]}{\frac{1}{2} n(n-1)} \tag{7.10}$$

where $\#$ stands for "the number of pairs." For many purposes, it is useful to express t in terms of dominance variables, d_{ij}, where $d_{yx} = \text{sign}(x_i - x_j)$. That is, d_{yx} is 1, -1, or 0, depending on the direction of the difference between x_i and x_j. Expressing t_{xy} in terms of d_{yx} and d_{yy}, we have

$$t_{xy} = \frac{\sum d_{yx} d_{yy}}{n(n-1)}, \tag{7.11}$$

where the sum runs over all the pairs.

Given two dominance matrices such as may result from a series of pairwise comparisons, t can be used to express the similarity of their elements in a very straightforward way in terms of the sum of products of corresponding elements. For elements where $a_{ij} = 1$, d_{ij} can be defined as $d_{ij} = 1$ and the symmetrically placed element as $d_{ji} = -1$. If there is no decision between i and j, $d_{ij} = 0$. That is, $d_{ij} = a_{ij} - a_{ji}$. Thus, to assess the agreement between two dominance matrices, such as would be used to find the degree of similarity of responses by two respondents, formula (7.11) can be used to calculate the tau. This tau can also be calculated directly from the elements of the adjacency matrices:

$$t_{12} = \frac{2\sum a_{ij1} a_{ij2}}{n(n-1)} - 1. \tag{7.12}$$

Tau, like r_S, is usually employed using variables that are already ordered, so various versions of tau that take account of the presence of ties in different ways are possible (Cliff, 1996). However, here we are applying tau directly to the dominance relations themselves. Thus, in a matrix of dominance relations where direct connectedness holds, the issue of ties does not apply even though, with cycles, there may be ties among the wins scores. The formulas (7.11) or (7.12), can give a correlation between two matrices of dominance relations.

Now that the nature of t and r_S has been reviewed, we show how their average values across a sample of subjects can be calculated from summary information about the dominances.

Average Tau From the Total Dominance Matrix

Since a tau can be computed from two d_{ij} matrices, each derived from their respective a_{ij} matrices, it is always possible to find the average tau between all pairs of replications by computing the taus between all the pairs of replications. However, sometimes the data do not lend themselves to this procedure. For example, pairs may be presented randomly to a subject m times without the constraint of presenting all the possible pairs as repetitions of complete sets, so that two or more trials on the 1,2 pair can occur before any trials of the 1,3 pair. This could also happen, for example, in an athletic context where intraleague games occur according to some external constraints, such as in professional baseball, that prevent the carrying out of the schedule as a set of complete round-robin tournaments. It can also occur that the data are only available in a form that gives only the number of times that i dominated j rather than in the complete sequence of results for each pair.

It turns out that the definition of tau can be adapted to these circumstances to provide an average consistency statistic. All that is necessary is to define the average tau as

$$\bar{\tau} = E d_{ijk} d_{ijl} \tag{7.13}$$

where $k, l = 1, \ldots, m$, the number of replications, and the expectation (E), that is, the average over all possible values of i, j, k, and l, runs across all pairs of elements and pairs of replications. The definition applies whether the d_{ijk}, d_{ijl} are organized into complete matrices, $\mathbf{D}_1, \ldots, \mathbf{D}_k, \ldots, \mathbf{D}_m$, one from each subject, or the pairs can simply be mixed into random or haphazard places in the overall sequence. All we need is the matrix with elements f_{ij}, which indicates the number of replications in which i dominated j, that is, $f_{ij} = \Sigma_k a_{ijk}$. Then $\frac{1}{2} f_{ij}(f_{ij} - 1)$ is the number of pairs of replications in which i dominated j in both, and $\frac{1}{2} f_{ji}(f_{ji} - 1)$ is the number of pairs in which j dominated i on both because $d_{ijk} d_{ijl}$ will be 1 in both of these cases.

On the other hand, $f_{ij} f_{ji}$ is the number of pairs of replications in which i dominated j in one member but j dominated i in the other. The reason is that in these cases $d_{ij1} d_{ij2} = -1$, and there are f_{ij} times in which i and j were ordered one way, and f_{ji} that they were ordered the other way, so the number of times this pair of elements is ordered oppositely is the product of these two numbers. (Note that the reasoning here is similar to some that was used in chapter 6.) The number of replications that are being compared is $\frac{1}{2} m(m - 1)$, and, since $m = f_{ij} + f_{ji}$, this number is equal to $\frac{1}{2} f_{ij}(f_{ij} - 1)$ $+ \frac{1}{2} f_{ji}(f_{ji} - 1) + f_{ij} f_{ji}$. Therefore, the difference between the number of times that a given pair i,j is ordered in the same way and the number of times that it is ordered oppositely is $\frac{1}{2} f_{ij}(f_{ij} - 1) + \frac{1}{2} f_{ji}(f_{ji} - 1) - f_{ij} f_{ji}$, which simplifies to $\frac{1}{2}[(f_{ij} - f_{ji})^2 - m]$. Averaging across all pairs of elements, the average tau is therefore

$$\bar{\tau} = \frac{\sum_{i > j} [(f_{ij} - f_{ji})^2 - m]}{\frac{1}{2} n(n - 1)m(m - 1)}. \tag{7.14}$$

Table 7.8 shows the application of this formula to data where $n = 5$ and $m = 4$.

Kendall (1975, p. 149) presented an algebraically equivalent coefficient that he calls u. He computes it from all the $\frac{1}{2}(f_{ij} f_{ij} - 1)$. However, he does not make the connection between it and the average tau.

Average r_s From Dominance Totals

The average rank-order correlation can also be obtained from summary data as well as by computing the r_ss between all the replications. What is needed are the dominance scores a_{ih} for each stimulus i in each replication h. These are shown for the example in the rightmost column of the data from each subject in Table 7.8. The average r_s among m replications, not taking account of ties, is then given by

TABLE 7.8
Dominances, Choice Frequencies, and Correlations

Dominances

Respondent 1

	c	b	g	p	s	$a_{.1}$
Carrots	0	1	1	1	1	4
Broccoli	-1	0	1	1	1	2
Green beans	-1	-1	0	1	1	0
Peas	-1	-1	-1	0	1	-2
Spinach	-1	-1	-1	-1	0	-4

Respondent 2

	c	b	g	p	s	$a_{.2}$
Carrots	0	0	0	1	-1	0
Broccoli	0	0	0	1	-1	0
Green beans	0	0	0	1	-1	0
Peas	-1	-1	-1	0	-1	-4
Spinach	1	1	1	1	0	4

Respondent 3

	c	b	g	p	s	$a_{.3}$
Carrots	0	0	0	1	1	2
Broccoli	0	0	0	1	1	2
Green beans	0	0	0	1	1	2
Peas	-1	-1	-1	0	-1	-4
Spinach	-1	-1	-1	1	0	-2

Respondent 4

	c	b	g	p	s	$a_{.4}$
Carrots	0	1	1	1	1	4
Broccoli	-1	0	1	1	1	2
Green beans	-1	-1	0	0	0	-2
Peas	-1	-1	0	0	0	-2
Spinach	-1	-1	0	0	0	-2

Choice Frequencies

f_g

	c	b	g	p	s	$\Sigma_h a_{.h}$
Carrots	0	2	2	4	3	10
Broccoli	0	0	0	4	3	6
Green beans	0	0	0	3	2	0
Peas	0	0	0	0	2	-12
Spinach	1	1	1	1	0	-4

TABLE 7.8
(Continued)

	Correlations Between Respondents					
	Tau			r_S		
	2	3	4	2	3	4
1	−.10	.70	.70	−.20	.70	.80
2		−.10	.00		.20	.00
3			.40			.50
		Average = .267			Average = .333	

$$\text{Average } r_S = \frac{3}{(n^3 - n)(m^2 - m)}[\sum_i (\sum_h a_{i\,h})^2 - \sum_i \sum_h a_{i\,h}^2]. \quad (7.15)$$

The formula can be applied to the data in Table 7.8, resulting in an average r_S of .333, agreeing with the average of the six coefficients in the matrix at the lower right corner of the table.

We can also apply the principles used in chapters 5 and 6 with respect to coefficient α in the context of ranked data. In the present case, the interpretation of α is that we are estimating the correlation between the $a_{i\text{.h}}$ obtained from the observed set of m subjects and a corresponding set of values obtained from another, equal-sized group from the same population. The formula for α that applies here is

$$\alpha = \frac{m}{m-1}[1 - \frac{\sum_i \sum_h a_{i\,h}^2}{\sum_i (\sum_h a_{i\,h}^2)}]. \quad (7.16)$$

FINDING THE ORDER IN COMPLETE DATA

Summary Orders for Complete Data

The procedure for finding the underlying order in data that is complete and completely consistent is quite simple and obvious. For each object, count the number of pairs in which it dominates, and order according to this score, the a_i from (7.2). Those who have a more negative view in life may wish to count the number of times each is dominated, and order in reverse of these totals. One can also count both and subtract "losses" from "wins." In fact this version, which we call the "net dominance score," running from $-n + 1$ to $n - 1$ in the completely consistent case, is our preferred one because it applies best to the largest number of situations. The complete-data orders will, of course, be the same in all three cases. These scores are illustrated in Table 7.7.

Although the system of using 1 and 0 to record dominances in a table is quite succinct, and conveys all the information in a simple order, in general it is more informative to use $d_{ij} = a_{ij} - a_{ji}$ as noted earlier or just + and −, as in a dominance diagram (Cliff, 1993, 1996), thus allowing 0 to be used for various purposes such as indicating ties, if allowed. In other circumstances 0 could mean that the pair was not compared, as in systems where, for greater efficiency, not all dominances are observed, or where circumstances have lead to some comparisons being omitted. Where it is necessary to distinguish between tied and not compared, a * or a blank space can be used for the latter.

In the upper part of Table 7.9 the elements of Table 7.7 have been converted to a matrix of dominances, **D**, with elements d_{ij}. The net dominance scores d_i for each object are then defined as

$$d_{i.} = \Sigma_j d_{ij},\qquad(7.17)$$

and

$$d_{i.} = \Sigma_j a_{ij} - \Sigma_i a_{ji},\qquad(7.18)$$

that is, the sum of i's wins minus the sum of i's losses. We call this the "net wins" score.

The numbers derived from such a table as the number of +s in a row, the number of −s in a column, or their differences, the net dominances, can be the scale that summarizes the data, and presumably then used to represent some property of the objects. These numbers are integers so there is a temptation to treat them the same way we treat other integers: the number of eggs in a nest, the number of electrons in an atom, the number of persons in a classroom. In one sense their status as true integers is valid. They directly reflect the number of times an object dominated, or the number of times it was dominated, or the difference in the two, depending on which of the three versions of the scale is used. But that number is partly circumstantial. It depends on how many members there were in the set, as well as on just which other elements were in the set, and it is likely to change when these are changed, perhaps doing so in unexpected ways. So treating it as a true integer is usually inappropriate. What probably does not change with such circumstances is the ordinal properties of that score.

It can be used to attempt to reconstruct the original dominances: For each pair, compare their respective numbers and enter a 1, a 0, or a −1 in a reconstructed dominance table accordingly. Compare this table to the ac-

TABLE 7.9
Dominances Corresponding to Table 7.7
and Reproduced Dominances

Observed Dominances

		Element						d_i
		1	2	3	4	5	6	
Versus	1	0	1	1	1	1	1	5
	2	−1	0	1	1	−1	1	1
	3	−1	−1	0	1	1	1	1
	4	−1	−1	−1	0	1	1	−1
	5	−1	1	−1	−1	0	1	−1
	6	−1	−1	−1	−1	−1	−1	−5

Dominances Reproduced From d_i

		Element					
		1	2	3	4	5	6
Versus	1	0	1	1	1	1	1
	2	−1	0	0*	1	1*	1
	3	−1	0*	0	1	1	1
	4	−1	−1	−1	0	0*	1
	5	−1	−1*	−1	0*	0	1
	6	−1	−1	−1	−1	−1	0

Reproduced With Ties Broken

		Element					
		1	2	3	4	5	6
Versus	1	0	1	1	1	1	1
	2	−1	0	1	1	1*	1
	3	−1	−1	0	1	1	1
	4	−1	−1	−1	0	1	1
	5	−1	−1*	−1	−1	0	1
	6	−1	−1	−1	−1	−1	0

*Disagreement with observed dominance.

tual dominance table. The score communicates the idea that if the number for one element of the scale is higher (more positive) than the number for another that was used in the same set of comparisons, then the first should dominate the second. In a true simple order, "should" becomes "will." However, any monotonic transformation of those integer scores will preserve that property equally well. For those two reasons, the instability of the integer values with respect to changes in circumstances and the fact that the ability to predict ordinal relations is preserved under monotonic transformation, we avoid putting much faith in the integer scores as integers, but we do put faith in them as indicators of order.

Using these scores works just as well when the data are inconsistent in the sense of containing transitivity failures. Two things will then happen, though. First, there will be ties in the number-of-dominances or net dominance scores. In fact, the number of ties is a measure of the degree of inconsistency, as we have seen. Second, the order of the scores will not be completely successful in predicting or accounting for the direction of dominance in a given pair, even when that pair is not tied in total dominances.

It is useful to have a measure of agreement between the observed dominances and the summary scores, and a tau between the observed dominances and those predicted from the summary score is the obvious choice as a coefficient. The predictions are

$$d_{ij}' = \text{sign}(d_{i.} - d_{j}).\tag{7.19}$$

The notation "sign()" means to translate the difference in the parentheses to +1 if it is positive, −1 if negative, and 0 if zero.

A measure of how well the $d_{i.}$ reproduce the d_{ij} is then

$$t_{dd'} = \frac{\sum_{i,j} d_{ij} d'_{ij}}{n(n-1)}.\tag{7.20}$$

Table 7.9 has in the upper section a matrix of d_{ij} among five objects and the resulting net wins scores, in which we see two tied pairs. The middle section has the dominances reproduced from these net wins, and we see that, over the whole matrix, there are 14 pairs where the predicted dominances agree with the observed ones, two where they disagree, and four where the prediction is a 0 because the dominance scores are tied. This gives a tau of $(14 - 2)/20 = .6$, indicating a fairly good level of agreement.

It turns out that a revised prediction process can sometimes increase this tau. The revision is that whenever there is a tie in the $d_{i.}$ we look at the direct comparison of that pair and break the tie in favor of the winner of the direct comparison. (This is a tie-breaking procedure that is often used in athletic leagues.) We indicate this by adding a small increment to the winner's d_i score. This has been shown in the table by adding .1 to the wins score of the tied object that was dominant in the direct comparison of the pair. The set of predicted dominances that results from these revised scores is in the lower section of the table. The elements that are different from the matrix above it have been starred (*) for ease of identification, and we see that the only difference is that four elements have changed from 0 to 1 or −1. These four that were previously zero are all in agreement with the observed relations in the top section, so now there are 18 agreements and two disagreements, yielding a tau of $(18 - 2)/20 = .8$ instead of .6.

This tie-breaking procedure will not always be effective in increasing the tau. For example, if three elements are tied in wins and they are members of a three-cycle, then they will each be a winner in direct comparison with one of the two others, and so each will have its score incremented, thus remaining tied.

What Is the Best Order?

What is the best order, in the sense of providing the highest possible value of (7.20)? So far, we have used the net wins order, and it might seem obvious that the process of using the net dominances and adjusting tied values as indicated would produce the best order in terms of giving the highest possible tau between observed and reproduced dominances, and it often does so, but not in all cases. Table 7.10 is an example. In the left section we have a dominance diagram where eight objects, *a, b, c, d, e, f, g, h*, have been ordered in terms of net wins, with the ties broken as we suggested before. It can be seen that there are six pluses below the diagonal, and the corresponding six minuses above it. This yields a tau between observed dominances and those predicted by the dominance order of $32/56 = .57$. However, if the order is changed somewhat, reversing *c* and *d* and also *e* and *f*, in spite of their net wins differences, there are only four pluses below the diagonal, as can be seen in the right-hand panel where the order is *a, b, d, c, f, e, g, h*. This order will give a tau of $40/56 = .71$.

So, is *a, b, d, c, f, e, g, h* the best order? As in many games, the best ordering can depend on how one keeps score. The system we used above (7.20) was one in which every discrepancy counted equally; it did not matter how much two elements were misordered in the reproduced order. However, it can be argued that degree of discrepancy should be taken into consideration. A second measure of orderliness is $\Sigma d_{ij}(r_i - r_j)$, where r_i is the rank of object i in the order. Here, discrepancies are weighted by how far apart those two objects are in the order. If the order agrees perfectly with the dominances, this sum will be $n(n + 1)(n - 1)/3$. This suggests a different index of agreement between an order and the observed dominances:

$$v = \frac{3\sum d_{ij}(r_i - r_j)}{n(n + 1)(n - 1)}. \tag{7.21}$$

This index is $432/504 = .74$ for the data in the table when the net-wins order is used, but only $336/504 = .67$ for the order that gave the maximum for the tau-criterion. Thus, the net-wins order is better by this criterion.

TABLE 7.10
Ordering to Maximize Two Different Criteria

Net Wins Order

Versus	a	b	c	d	e	f	g	h
a	0	+	−	+	+	+	+	+
b	−	0	+	+	−	+	+	+
c	+	−	0	−	+	+	+	+
d	−	−	+	0	+	+	−	+
e	−	+	−	−	0	−	+	+
f	−	−	−	−	+	0	+	+
g	−	−	−	+	−	−	0	+
h	−	−	−	−	−	+	−	0
Net Wins	5	3	3	1	−1	−3	−3	−5

Maximum Tau Order

Versus	a	b	d	c	f	e	g	h
a	0	+	+	−	+	+	+	+
b	−	0	+	+	+	−	+	+
d	−	−	0	+	+	+	−	+
c	+	−	−	0	+	+	+	+
f	−	−	−	−	0	+	+	−
e	−	+	−	−	−	0	+	+
g	−	−	+	−	−	−	0	+
h	−	−	−	−	+	−	−	0
Net Wins	5	3	1	3	−3	−1	−3	−5

It can be proved that the net wins order always gives the largest value of the weighted criterion (7.21). As a general practice, we feel it is preferable to use net wins rather than trying to maximize tau (7.20) for two additional reasons. One is that it does seem appropriate to exact larger penalties for larger discrepancies, so it can be argued that (7.21) is more appropriate than (7.20). The other is that an order that maximizes (7.20) can only be guaranteed by trying all possible permutations of the objects. This can only be attempted with a dozen sets containing a dozen or fewer objects, even with modern computers.

OVERVIEW

This chapter has reviewed the important properties of a dominance order and suggested how they can be evaluated. A primary principle is that the relations that are presumed to represent dominance should be free of contamination and arbitrariness and that they should lead to clear outcomes. That is, the ordinary canons of good research practice should apply. A second major principle is that the data should correspond closely to the dominance axioms, ($d1$) to ($d4$). However, data will rarely do so perfectly, so quantitative measures of conformity have been presented. We have seen that in many empirical contexts reflexivity ($d1$) cannot be evaluated because an element is not compared to or matched against itself. Furthermore, such comparisons are sometimes nonsensical. Where that is not the case, good empirical practice would suggest that such comparisons take place. Given the likelihood of a lack of complete consistency one way or the other, statistical procedures for evaluating the extent of consistency were suggested.

The connectedness ($d1$) of a relation is usually guaranteed by the empirical procedure. If the relation is observed in all pairs, then we call this *direct connectedness*. As seen in the next chapter, connectedness can be present even when not all relations are observed, provided a certain subset are observed and transitivity can be assumed.

Asymmetry ($d2$) is typically not given an opportunity to fail either. When a pair is presented only once, the relation has to be in one direction or the other, so it is inherently asymmetric. Thus, the relation has to be tested more than once in at least some pairs if asymmetry is to be tested. Statistical methods for evaluating the degree of asymmetry (7.1) and for testing whether there is at least a consistent tendency toward it were suggested.

Most of the interest in evaluating the order axioms has focused on transitivity ($d4$). Central to these evaluations is the circular triad, called here a three-cycle because of its connections to mathematical graph theory. Formulas for counting the number of three-cycles (7.3), expressing the degree of transitivity present (7.4), and testing the data to see if there is a significant tendency toward transitivity were suggested.

Where dominance relations are replicated by using several subjects or in some other way, it is useful to assess the degree of consistency between the subjects. A reasonable way to do this is finding the ordinal correlations between the dominance scores. Either the Spearman rank correlation or Kendall's tau can be used for this purpose, although we have a preference for tau since it seems more in the spirit of what we are trying to assess—the overall consistency of the a_{ij}. Formulas for r_S were presented, (7.5) and (7.6), as were several for tau, (7.7), (7.8), (7.9), and (7.10).

Similarly, the average tau among a set of replications can be found from the elements of the matrix which is the sum of the A_k from the individual subjects or from any total dominance matrix (Equation 7.13). We have also noted that the average r_S among a set of replications can be calculated from the total dominance scores (7.14). Thus, the consistency of presumed dominance relations with the axioms $d1$–$d4$ can be evaluated, as can the consistency of the relations across replications.

The order for the objects is probably best summarized by the "net wins" criterion, with ties broken, where possible, in favor of the winner of the "head-to-head" comparisons. This guarantees that the order will agree better with the data than any other according to the measure (7.21), which takes account of the degree of discrepancy between the observed dominances and the summary order. However, the net-wins order does not necessarily maximize the tau criterion (7.20). Trying all possible permutations is the only way to guarantee a maximum for it.

Chapter 8

Alternatives to Complete Paired Comparisons

DATASETS ARE OFTEN INCOMPLETE

In spite of its elegance, there is a real drawback to using paired comparisons: The number of pairs grows as the square of the number of elements. Ten elements means 45 comparisons, usually a manageable number, but 30 elements means 435 pairs and 100 means 4,950. Thus, there is considerable motivation for trying to reduce the number of comparisons while still retaining as much of the elegance of the pairwise dominance process as possible. Also, in many situations one may wish to employ the dominance concepts to yield an overall order in situations where, for circumstantial reasons, not all pairwise dominance relations are observed, resulting in incomplete dominance matrices. In this chapter we describe methods for arriving at orders from incomplete data, including expanding the methods beyond direct pair comparisons.

One possible cause for incomplete data is inadvertence. There was an intention to have all pairs, but some were accidentally omitted. A second reason is circumstances. A behaviorist observing a species of birds in an area may be recording the dominance relations among individuals, but interactions do not occur between all pairs of birds. Or an economist may observe competition between firms, and have a way of concluding which of a pair is dominant in a series of pairwise competitive markets, but not all pairs of firms are competing directly, perhaps for geographical reasons. Also, a sports buff may want to develop his [sic] own rank order of 115 American college football teams, based on their head-to-head results, but not all teams face each other, at least not to this date.

Then another type of reason for incomplete data is that the investigator planned it that way. This almost always occurs as a means of reducing the number of dominances that are directly observed. Several strategies for reducing the number of comparisons are possible. One is to systematically select a subset of all the possible pairs in advance and then develop as much of the order as is possible from the resulting dominances; sometimes it will even be complete. Another strategy is to present the stimuli in groups and have the respondents partially or completely rank-order them within the groups. The extreme possibility here, of course, is ranking the complete set.

Finally, one can adopt an interactive process that takes advantage of the principle of transitivity. If a relation on a set is assumed to be transitive, then knowing that[1] $a >* b$ and $b >* c$ makes it unnecessary to compare a to c because it is logically implied that $a >* c$.

PLANNED SUBSETS OF PAIRS

Tournaments

If one wants to retain the pair comparisons response format while reducing the number of judgments and selecting at least the initial pairs a priori, then a number of approaches are possible. The commonest example of such a shortcut is the single-elimination tournament in which, at the first round, each contestant is matched with some other one. The loser of this comparison is "eliminated," whereas the winner goes on to another contest. The winners play each other, and the losers are again eliminated. The process goes on, half the remaining contestants being eliminated at each round, until there is a single "winner."

Although seemingly satisfactory to sponsors and audiences of many athletic tournaments, such a process has deficiencies from a measurement point of view. The most important is that there is no way of determining it is other than a purely random process, with the outcome of each contest being merely the equivalent of a coin-flip. Even if the process is highly valid, the procedure is unsatisfactory from another point of view. The contestants' true ranks may not be very well reflected in the overall rankings of the players or teams that results from the tournament. For example, if the two best players or teams meet in the first round, one will be eliminated. This will result in the loser, who has no wins and one loss, being ranked below many weaker players who happen to win in the first round over other weak

---

[1]We use >* here rather than simply > to distinguish an observed dominance relation from the mathematical relation >.

players.[2] This can be particularly upsetting to contestants when there is prize money involved. It also leads only to a partial order rather than a simple one because there is no information on which to differentiate the losers on a given round. This may be unimportant in an athletic context, but will be important in many scientific and applied contexts when one wants to differentiate among the losers as well as the winners.

Systematic Subsets

One attractive system for reducing the number of pairs is a procedure that assures all elements will occur in an equal number of pairs, but only a fraction of the pairs are observed directly. The resulting scale is again the net dominances of each element. Although there can be some concern that the final scale is partially the result of the luck of the draw (i.e., which others a given element is compared against), the investigator may be willing to tolerate that ambiguity in the final results as a reasonable price to pay for reducing the number of pairs. Such a method can easily be extended to the multiple trial or multiple judge contexts discussed later.

Table 8.1 in which an "x" indicates that a pair was used and a "o" that it was not, illustrates the method for 10 elements. In this approach, the pairs that are included always appear as diagonal stripes, here, the xs. For clarity, there is an x in the j,i, position as well as the i,j, but of course only one of these pairs would be used.

In the left matrix of the table there are 25 of these xs, slightly more than half of the complete number, 45, above the main diagonal, which is indicated by dashes. The systematic approach guarantees that each element appears in five pairs, as can be seen by counting xs down any column or across any row. Note that if we assume instead that it is the o that indicates inclusion rather than the x, each element will appear in four pairs for a total of 20 altogether, slightly less than half. We cannot have exactly half the pairs unless n or $n - 1$ is divisible by four, and sometimes not even then.

The right-hand matrix illustrates choosing only a third of the pairs. Again, the selected pairs occur as diagonal stripes, and now there are 15 above the main diagonal. Each element will occur in 15 pairs, and there are actually two other similar ways of choosing different sets of 15 pairs. We can get exactly one third of the pairs because $n - 1$ is nine, which is exactly divisible by three.

---

[2]This kind of perceived injustice is the motivation behind "seeding" in tournaments. In seeding, contestants are ranked on some prior measure of expected performance. Then, pairings for the initial rounds are arranged in such a way that contestants with high prior ranks cannot meet until the later rounds. Another common adjustment is "double elimination," in which it takes two losses to be eliminated. This makes it less likely that a top contestant is eliminated early, but makes the tournament longer.

TABLE 8.1
Balanced Subsets of Pairs

Every Second Pair

	1	2	3	4	5	6	7	8	9	10
1	—	x	o	x	o	x	o	x	o	x
2	x	—	x	o	x	o	x	o	x	o
3	o	x	—	x	o	x	o	x	o	x
4	x	o	x	—	x	o	x	o	x	o
5	o	x	o	x	—	x	o	x	o	x
6	x	o	x	o	x	—	x	o	x	o
7	o	x	o	x	o	x	—	x	o	x
8	x	o	x	o	x	o	x	—	x	o
9	o	x	o	x	o	x	o	x	—	x
10	x	o	x	o	x	o	x	o	x	—

Every Third Pair

	1	2	3	4	5	6	7	8	9	10
1	—	x	o	o	x	o	o	x	o	o
2	x	—	x	o	o	x	o	o	x	o
3	o	x	—	x	o	o	x	o	o	x
4	o	o	x	—	x	o	o	x	o	o
5	x	o	o	x	—	x	o	o	x	o
6	o	x	o	o	x	—	x	o	o	x
7	o	o	x	o	o	x	—	x	o	o
8	x	o	o	x	o	o	x	—	x	o
9	o	x	o	o	x	o	o	x	—	x
10	o	o	x	o	o	x	o	o	x	—

The main aspects of this method are the diagonal stripes and that there are a constant number of elements skipped as we go across a row. In the left matrix we skipped one element, the first pair being 1,3, and in the right, we skipped two. The process of selecting the pairs can be described in symbolic terms. One part of the description is that if the i,j pair is included, then the $(i + 1)$, $(j + 1)$ pair is also. In both examples, the 1,2 pair is used, so the 2,3; 3,4; . . . pairs are also. The second part of the description is that if the i,j pair is used, then the i, $(j + k)$; i, $(j + 2k)$; i, $(j + 3k)$ . . . pairs are also chosen. That is, the chosen pairs are equally spaced across a row (or column) on either side of the main diagonal, and k is the spacing between the chosen pairs in a row. In the left illustration, k is 2; Element 1 is paired with 2, so it is also paired with 4, 6, 8, and 10; in the right one, $k = 3$, so, since 1 is paired with 2, it is also paired with 5 and 8.

The requirement that each element must appear in the same number of pairs means that not all set-sizes can provide a desired fraction, or approximate fraction, of the pairs. The most important of the constraints is that if n is odd, we cannot skip every second pair, as in the left example, and have each element appear in the same number of them. For example, if the last row and column of the matrix on the left of Table 8.1 is eliminated so as to simulate $n = 9$, we see that half the elements appear in five pairs and half in four. There are a number of other restrictions, but often an appropriate set can be found if we can be a little bit flexible.

The constraints on the possibilities depend on the following equation:

$$n = (p - 1)k + 2(j - 1). \qquad (8.1)$$

In it, as before, n is the number of stimuli in the set to be studied; k is the spacing; and j is the first element that is paired with 1. The new symbol is p, the number of pairs in which each element will appear. The equation allows us to choose the spacing, k, and the first element paired with 1, j, for a given number of presentations, p, or to conclude that it is impossible to do what we want to do.

In a typical applied situation, we have a certain number of elements to be ordered, and we have a target of the number of pairs to be used, one that is based on some practical considerations. Let v equal that number. Suppose $n = 36$ and $v = 150$, perhaps because that is about the maximum number of judgments we can expect to get from a group of coerced subjects, or because of the amount of time that is available. With 36 elements, there are 36 × 35/2 = 630 pairs, so 150 is a little less than a quarter of all of them. There needs to be some flexibility about v, because usually we cannot hit it exactly and reach our goal of equal numbers of pairs for each element.

First, we find the ratio $2v/n$, which will be approximately the number of pairs in which each stimulus appears. Here, $2 \times 150/36 = 8.33$, which we round to the nearest whole number, $8 = r$.

Now we choose k. All the numbers in the equation are positive integers. This means that $(r-1)k$ must be less than n; However, this product should be close to n, because j is a fairly small number. So, we divide: $n/(r-1)$, or $36/7 = 5.14$. This suggests we try $k = 5$: $36 = 7 \times 5 + 2(j-1)$ and solve for j. No usable j results because we get $j - 1 = 1/2$, not a whole number, and too small anyway since j must be at least 2. We should have known this was not going to work because 36 is even, so $(r-1)k$ has to be also.

So, we try $k = 4$: $36 = 7 \times 4 + 2(j-1)$. This yields $j = 5$. There is one more restriction: j must be less than $k + 2$, otherwise, we will skip too many pairs before beginning. This does not create a problem here because it means j is allowed to be up to five, which is what we wanted to use. The selection of pairs that results, then, is to start with the 1,5 pair and take every fourth pair to the end of the row; then start with 2,6 and take every fourth; and so on. This means we are using $8 \times 36/2 = 144$ pairs, a few less than the target of 150. The result is shown in Table 8.2.

The process is a bit complex, but usually will result in an appropriate selection of pairs. Sometimes there will be more than one combination of p, k, and j that give about the desired number of pairs. On the hand, however, it may sometimes be impossible to find an appropriate combination. If so, it may be reasonable to discard one or two members of the original set in order to arrive at a satisfactory subset of pairs. The method can also be useful when all pairs are to be included as a way to select a subset of pairs to be included twice in order to assess the reliability of responses.

IMPLIED ORDER RELATIONS

There is a computer-based procedure that gives a complete simple order on the basis of pairwise relations, and does so efficiently. Assuming that there is evidence that at least an approximate order exists for a set, it uses the principle of transitivity. However, here, unlike a simple tournament, losers are matched against losers as well as winners against winners. Moreover, each contestant or stimulus is given credit for winning against all those who have been defeated by (or preferred to), any it has won against, and it is charged with losing to all those who have won against any who have defeated it. The process is also extended to higher orders in terms of defining whom the contestant has won against or has been defeated by. That is, winners over winners over winners and so on, are identified if there are any. This leads to a very efficient ordering procedure when there is underlying simple order. It yields an order in a number of comparisons that is the smallest integer larger than $n\log_2(n)$, which is the theoretical minimum number. This number is 34 for 10 objects, 148 for 30, and 665 for 100, rather than the 45, 435, and 4,950 that were noted earlier as required for

TABLE 8.2
Selected Fraction of the Pairs of 36 Elements

```
-OOOXOOOXOOOXOOOXOOOXOOOXOOOXOOOXOOO
O-OOOXOOOXOOOXOOOXOOOXOOOXOOOXOOOXOO
OO-OOOXOOOXOOOXOOOXOOOXOOOXOOOXOOOXO
OOO-OOOXOOOXOOOXOOOXOOOXOOOXOOOXOOOX
XOOO-OOOXOOOXOOOXOOOXOOOXOOOXOOOXOOO
OXOOO-OOOXOOOXOOOXOOOXOOOXOOOXOOOXOO
OOXOOO-OOOXOOOXOOOXOOOXOOOXOOOXOOOXO
OOOXOOO-OOOXOOOXOOOXOOOXOOOXOOOXOOOX
XOOOXOOO-OOOXOOOXOOOXOOOXOOOXOOOXOOO
OXOOOXOOO-OOOXOOOXOOOXOOOXOOOXOOOXOO
OOXOOOXOOO-OOOXOOOXOOOXOOOXOOOXOOOXO
OOOXOOOXOOO-OOOXOOOXOOOXOOOXOOOXOOOX
XOOOXOOOXOOO-OOOXOOOXOOOXOOOXOOOXOOO
OXOOOXOOOXOOO-OOOXOOOXOOOXOOOXOOOXOO
OOXOOOXOOOXOOO-OOOXOOOXOOOXOOOXOOOXO
OOOXOOOXOOOXOOO-OOOXOOOXOOOXOOOXOOOX
XOOOXOOOXOOOXOOO-OOOXOOOXOOOXOOOXOOO
OXOOOXOOOXOOOXOOO-OOOXOOOXOOOXOOOXOO
OOXOOOXOOOXOOOXOOO-OOOXOOOXOOOXOOOXO
OOOXOOOXOOOXOOOXOOO-OOOXOOOXOOOXOOOX
XOOOXOOOXOOOXOOOXOOO-OOOXOOOXOOOXOOO
OXOOOXOOOXOOOXOOOXOOO-OOOXOOOXOOOXOO
OOXOOOXOOOXOOOXOOOXOOO-OOOXOOOXOOOXO
OOOXOOOXOOOXOOOXOOOXOOO-OOOXOOOXOOOX
XOOOXOOOXOOOXOOOXOOOXOOO-OOOXOOOXOOO
OXOOOXOOOXOOOXOOOXOOOXOOO-OOOXOOOXOO
OOXOOOXOOOXOOOXOOOXOOOXOOO-OOOXOOOXO
OOOXOOOXOOOXOOOXOOOXOOOXOOO-OOOXOOOX
XOOOXOOOXOOOXOOOXOOOXOOOXOOO-OOOXOOO
OXOOOXOOOXOOOXOOOXOOOXOOOXOOO-OOOXOO
OOXOOOXOOOXOOOXOOOXOOOXOOOXOOO-OOOXO
OOOXOOOXOOOXOOOXOOOXOOOXOOOXOOO-OOOX
XOOOXOOOXOOOXOOOXOOOXOOOXOOOXOOO-OOO
OXOOOXOOOXOOOXOOOXOOOXOOOXOOOXOOO-OO
OOXOOOXOOOXOOOXOOOXOOOXOOOXOOOXOOO-O
OOOXOOOXOOOXOOOXOOOXOOOXOOOXOOOXOOO-
```

the complete set of comparisons. A computer algorithm for carrying out the procedure interactively with individual subjects was developed (Cliff, 1975; Kehoe & Cliff, 1975; Reynolds & Cliff, 1975, 1984). Related but more limited methods have been suggested by Cook and Kress (1990), David (1987), and Kendall (1955).

The basis for the method is assuming transitivity. If a relation on a set is assumed to be transitive, then knowing that $a >^* b$ and $b >^* c$ makes it unnecessary to compare a to c because it is logically implied that $a >^* c$. In this way, a subset of observed relations can be used to develop a complete order, and the process will be efficient, provided that the pairs chosen for direct comparison are good choices. In the procedure, a random selection of $n/2$ (if n is even) or $(n-1)/2$ (if n is odd) pairs is matched first. They are presented, one pair at a time, to the subject. Then a "winner" is compared to a randomly selected other winner or a "loser" to another loser. Specifically, a stimulus is selected randomly. If it is a winner, it is matched at random with another winner; if it is a loser, it is matched against a loser. The implication of the result through transitivity is deduced.

After this, and at each subsequent step, the number of observed and implied relations for each stimulus is counted, and the one(s) with the fewest known relations are identified. If two or more are tied in completeness, one of these is chosen at random; then the stimuli that are closest to it in net wins are identified, and one of these is chosen, again at random if two or more are equally close. After a check to make sure that the two have not previously been paired, these two are presented for comparison.

The process is illustrated in Table 8.3 for six stimuli, a, b, c, d, e, and f. There is an $n \times n$ matrix on the left in which the results of the actual comparisons are entered as a 1 in the row of the dominant stimulus and column of the nondominant one, and a 0 in the symmetric position. Unknown relations are blanks. After each entry is made, its implications are deduced: If there is a 1 in Row i and Column j and a 1 in Row j, Column k, this is an implication that i dominates k. That is, i dominated j which dominated k, so therefore i dominates k. The implications are recorded in a second matrix, shown at the right. The implied relations are used in turn to possibly imply still further relations, and so on, until no higher order implications are found. However, there can be no implications until at least two stimuli have more than one observed relation. (With fallible data, there is an issue of when an implication should be believed, and we discuss this in some detail shortly.) For the time being, we will simply assume that all implications are accepted. Running totals are kept of the wins and losses, whether direct or implied, for each stimulus, denoted w_1 and l_1, respectively, the net wins, $w_1 - l_1$, and of the number of relations that are neither observed directly nor predicted for it, $n - 1 - w_1 - l_1$.

For convenience in illustrating, the true order in Table 8.3 is alphabetical, a, b, c, d, e, f. First, each element was randomly matched against another, three matches in all, and it was found that $a >* c$, $b >* d$, and $e >* f$. Then b, a winner, was selected randomly from the six; it was to be paired randomly with another winner, and it happened that e was selected from the other two winners, a and e, the comparison finding $b >* e$. These four observed relations are displayed in the upper left panel of the table with 1s in the row and column of the winners, and 0s in the row and column of the losers, other elements being blank. This matrix will be called **A**.

TABLE 8.3

Illustration of Implied Orders

	Observed Dominances — Elements						Fourth Comparison — Elements						Implications	
	a	b	c	d	e	f	a	b	c	d	e	f	Wins	Losses
a	x		1				x		1				1	0
b		x		1	1	1		x		1	1	1	3	0
c	0		x				0		x				0	1
d		0		x				0		x			0	1
e		0			x			0			x	1	1	1
f		0				x		0			0	x	0	2

b >* e   b >* e >* f

	Fifth Comparison — Elements						Implications	
	a	b	c	d	e	f	Wins	Losses
a	x		1	1			2	0
b		x		1	1	1	3	0
c	0		x	1			1	1
d	0	0	0	x			0	3
e		0			x	1	1	1
f		0			0	x	0	2

c >* d   a >* c >* d

(Continued)

TABLE 8.3
(Continued)

Sixth Comparison

Observed Dominances

Elements

	a	b	c	d	e	f
a	x.		1	1	1	1*
b		x		1	1	1
c	0		x	1	1	1
d			0	x		
e	0	0	0		x	1
f	0*	0	0		0	x

$c >^* e$

Implications

Elements

	a	b	c	d	e	f	Wins	Losses
a	x			1	1	1*	4	0
b		x			1	1	3	0
c			x	1		1	3	1
d			x				0	3
e					x		1	3
f	0*	0	0		x	x	0	4

$a >^* c >^* e >^* f;\ c >^* e >^* f;\ a >^* e >^* f$

Seventh Comparison

Observed Dominances

Elements

	a	b	c	d	e	f
a	x	1	1	1	1	1*
b	0	x		1	1	1
c	0		x	1	1	1
d			0	x		
e	0	0	0		x	1
f	0*	0	0		0	x

$a >^* b$

Implications

Elements

	a	b	c	d	e	f	Wins	Losses
a	x			1	1	1*	5	0
b		x			1	1	3	1
c			x	1		1	3	1
d			x				0	3
e					x		1	3
f	0*	0	0		x	x	0	4

no new implications

152

Eighth Comparison

Elements

	a	b	c	d	e	f
a	x	1	1	1	1	1
b	0	x	x	1	1	1
c	0	x	x	1	1	1
d				x	x	1
e		0	0	x	x	1
f		0	0	0	0	x

$d >* e$

Elements

	a	b	c	d	e	f	Wins	Losses
a	x	1	1	1	1	1*	5	0
b	0	x	x	1	1	1	3	1
c	0	x	x	1	1	1	3	1
d	0	0	0	x	1	1	2	3
e	0	0	0	0	x	1	1	4
f	0*	0	0	0	0	x	0	5

$d >* e >* f$

Ninth Comparison

Elements

	a	b	c	d	e	f
a	x	1	1	1	1	1
b	0	x	x	1	1	1
c	0	x	x	1	1	1
d		0	0	x	x	1
e		0	0	x	x	1
f		0	0	0	0	x

$b >* c$

Elements

	a	b	c	d	e	f	Wins	Losses
a	x	1	1	1	1	1*	5	0
b	0	x	1	1	1	1	4	1
c	0	0	x	1	1	1	3	2
d	0	0	0	x	1	1	2	3
e	0	0	0	0	x	1	1	4
f	0*	0	0	0	0	x	0	5

No implications needed

There is now an implied relation: $b >* f$, because $b >* e$ and $e >* f$ as noted earlier. This relation is entered in the appropriate positions in the right-hand panel, which we refer to as $\mathbf{A}^2$. The w_i and l_i scores, counting both observed and implied relations, are on the far right. There are now three elements that have only one known relation, a, c, and d. Element c was then chosen randomly from these three. It is tied in net wins at -1 only with d, so these two are compared, and $c >* d$. This results in a new implication because previously it was found that $a >* c$, so $a >* c >* d$. These relations and the resulting scores are shown in the second set of panels, labeled Fifth Comparison.

The examination of the resulting scores finds c, e, and f to have the fewest known relations; e is randomly chosen from among the three and matched with c because it is closest to it in net wins. The outcome $c >* e$ results in two direct implications: $a >* c >* e$ and $c >* e >* f$. These provide an indirect or *second-order* implication: $a >* e >* f$. The next set of panels, labeled Sixth Comparison, shows the matrices with the observed (left) and implied (right) relations to this point. The wins and losses are again given at the far right. The next three sets of panels show the completion of the process. Inspecting the next-to-last set of matrices, it is seen that the only relation that is not known is b versus c. The result $b >* c$ is shown in the last set, and all relations are now known, nine directly and six by implication.

At each step, after the first set of matches that compare each element to one other, the process is the same:

1. Select the element with the fewest known or implied relations, choosing randomly among those tied for lowest number.
2. Match that element with the one nearest to it in the order as known so far, choosing randomly among those equally close.
3. Record the outcome of the match.
4. Deduce the implications, direct and indirect, if any, and record those.
5. Count the direct or implied wins and losses and record those.
6. Go back to #1.

The procedure stops, of course, when all relations are known or implied.

The complete order was deduced here from 9 of the 15 comparisons. Thus, even with this small number of objects, 40% of the comparisons were saved. The result can be compared with the theoretical minimum. With six objects, the number of possible orders is $6! = 720$, and $\log_2(720) = 9.49$. This is the average number of comparisons necessary to develop the complete order, and accomplishing it with 9 rather than 10 took a bit of luck. This occurred most obviously in selecting the eighth comparison, d versus e. At that time, d, which had the fewest known relations, 3, with net wins of -3, was equidistant from e, with net wins of -2, and f, with -4. It happened that the random choice came up in favor of e. If the reverse had happened, the $d >*$ f result, which here was deduced when $d >* e$, would have meant that comparing d to e would still have been necessary. Thus, 10 comparisons could have been required except for the result of one of the random selections.

Inconsistency

In the procedure just described there is, however, no opportunity for violations of transitivity to show themselves. In a sense, the outcome is as artificial as the telephonic scale, and the resulting order may be completely arbitrary. In demonstrating an order, here as elsewhere, the ideal is a process where the characteristics of order have ample opportunity to fail, and they do not fail. What is to be avoided is artificial or confounding aspects of the process that will lead to the appearance of order where there is none, or very little. If the strict characteristics of a simple order are false, then we want to quantify the degree to which the relations are consistent in order to know how much confidence to place in the approximate order that results from the data.

There are two motives for any data-gathering process, and they need to be kept separate. One is the desire to answer the question of whether there is an order. To answer that one fully, we need to allow the data ample opportunity to show us that there is not an order. The other motive is to find out the order if there is one. For that purpose, we want a process that is as efficient as possible. But the first question is the one that has precedence. Not until it is established does the second become relevant.

Compensating for Inconsistency

The Achilles heel of the implied orders process is that it assumes perfect validity in the observed relations, which is almost certainly unrealistic. The original research (Kehoe & Cliff, 1975; Reynolds & Cliff, 1975, 1984) employed a variety of ad hoc methods in attempts to make such a system robust to inconsistency and invalidity. These sometimes consisted of requiring that a relation be implied more than once. For example, $a >* b$ and $b >* c$ would not be sufficient in itself to imply $a >* c$, but the presence of additional relations such as $a >* d$ and $d >* c$ would do so because now there are two chains that imply $a >* c$. Such an event is easy to keep track of in the process because it would result in an entry of 2 in A^2 in a cell which is empty in A in matrices like those in Table 8.3.

More commonly, a quasi-statistical decision process was employed. This was particularly necessitated in large sets of stimuli whose relations were fairly unreliable because then it often occurred that there would both be implications that $a >* c$ and that $c >* a$. A simple "majority rules" procedure is unsatisfactory because a completely random process will usually result in one direction or the other being favored. More importantly, the weaker element may be ahead in the short run, resulting in the conclusion that $c >* a$ when the reverse more nearly represents the true state of affairs. This nonoptimum conclusion could turn out to be difficult to overturn with later information once it is established. Furthermore, under some circumstances there may be relations that imply that $a >* c$ as well as implications that $c >* a$. Should these cases be treated as ties or should some majority rules principle be applied?

Cliff and colleagues (Cliff, 1975; Kehoe & Cliff, 1975; Reynolds & Cliff, 1984) attempted to study this issue by simulation. The question studied was How many implied dominances, or what majority of implied dominances, is necessary to conclude that an implied ordinal relation is established in one direction rather than the other? They concluded that when there were as few as two implications of a relation, with no contradicting implications, that was a reliable indication that $a >* c$. When there were implications in both directions, the situation was a bit more complicated, but again a small majority was deemed sufficient.

However, a similar issue arose in chapter 6, and there a formula was developed for the standard error of $p_{ih} - p_{hi}$ (6.15), which facilitated decisions concerning the inference that Person i would be correct on a larger proportion of the items in a universe than Person h. The situation here is very analogous, so those formulas can be applied here as well. Since the frequencies will be small, Table 6.3 can be used, and the modest .20 significance level indicates that two uncontradicted implications are reasonable grounds for inferring an ordinal relation. Where there are implications in both directions, the further entries in the table could be used in making the decision as to whether to assume an implied relation on the basis of a majority decision.

In terms of the interactive process, the requirement that at least three observed relations are needed to imply an unobserved one is rather stringent. It means that the savings in number of judgments required is unlikely to be appreciable unless there are at least 20 things to be ordered. An alternative, perhaps cavalier-seeming, approach is to accept all implications. The reasoning behind this is simply that the odds are in favor of the implication being correct rather than incorrect over a wide variety of circumstances, so one may as well take advantage of any implications that occur.

A second, more empirical, approach is to delay the implication process until a more-than-minimum number of pairs have been presented, perhaps

n pairs chosen at random or in a more systematic way that would guarantee that each element would be involved in the same number of comparisons, as described earlier in this chapter. Again, actual relations would be compared to their implied status in order to evaluate the validity of the implications. The agreement between observed and implied relations is tabulated and an ad hoc rule is derived for deciding when implications are to be accepted. The rule would be applied to those implications derived to that stage, and used for subsequent implications as well.

Evaluating Implied Orders

In chapter 7, we discussed in some detail the evaluation of the consistency of a dominance matrix. This was largely based on counting three-cycles. However, in using the direct implication process, we have avoided the opportunity for three-cycles to occur. If $a >^* b$ and $b >^* c$, we infer that $a >^* c$, so the circularity $\{a >^* b; b >^* c; c >^* a\}$ cannot occur. The dominance matrix will be completely consistent.

Given that dominance relations have been implied, how likely is it that they are correct? For that matter, how likely is it that the observed relations themselves will be consistent? The most natural data on which to evaluate observations and implications is their agreement with relations that have been observed directly. The method is to have a sample of comparisons that are used as a "holdout" or cross-validation sample. These are not entered into the dominance matrix. Some of them will be repeats of observed pairs and some will correspond to implications; these two subsets can be separated. Consider first the holdout relation that are repeats of actual dominances used in the implication process. The directions of the holdout relations are compared to the ones actually observed for those pairs. This can be quantified in formula (7.20) in which the d_y are the observed dominances and the d_y' are the corresponding holdouts and the denominator is the number of pairs summed over.

Then, the same is done for those that holdouts that correspond to implied pairs. Now, the d_y are implied dominances and the d_y' are corresponding holdouts, the denominator again being the number of pairs in the sum. Thus, we have a tau between observed dominances and replicated (holdout) dominances and one between implied dominances and the corresponding holdout values. Finally, we can use (7.17) to evaluate the extent to which the order derived from the dominances and their implications on one hand agree with the holdout dominances on the other. In this application, the d_y are observed holdouts and the d_y' are the values implied by the order that has been derived from the interactive process, the denominator being the number of holdouts.

PARTIAL RANKING METHODS

Because there are so many possible pairwise comparisons, and even the shortcuts described earlier can result in a large number, methods that require fewer responses may be desired. It is often the case that research experience with the stimuli in a domain indicates that they conform reasonably closely to the requirements of the dominance order. In that case, some form of ranking method is appropriate in many applications. However, people find that a full ranking can be a tedious and confusing process when there are more than a dozen or so elements, and this is not surprising. In order to rank a set of things, the observer really has to go through some mental process similar to the pairwise comparisons.

The most effective alternative is usually some variation on ranking or partial ranking of subsets. Gulliksen and Tucker (1961) described methods for systematically composing the subsets in order to balance the presentation of each stimulus and allow it to appear in subsets that contain as many as possible, preferably all, of the other stimuli. They also provide for the assessment of three-cycles.

Complete balancing is only possible with certain combinations of set-sizes and numbers of stimuli, and not for all numbers of stimuli. If dominance information is to be obtained for all pairs, each element must be presented in combination with all others in exactly one set. Using s as the number of sets and k as the number in a set, then for complete balancing it therefore must be that $sk(k - 1) = n(n - 1)$.

A small illustration is provided in Table 8.4 in which 9 stimuli are presented in 12 sets of size three. The stimuli are labeled $a, b, \ldots, i$, the first set containing $a, b, c,$ and the last, $c, f, h.$ When the members of a set are ranked, this provides three dominances; 12 sets then provide 36 dominances, which is the number of pairs in the full set. There is no possible inconsistency within a set, but dominances from different sets can be three-cycles. Gulliksen and Tucker (1961) provided formulas for comparing the number of three-cycles, deduced from the variance of the dominance scores we described earlier, to the maximum possible number.

Their methods assume complete ranking within subsets. However, subjects are often uncomfortable with this, feeling that some discriminations are difficult or arbitrary. Some type of partial ranking is often preferred by them. The simplest approach to indifference or nondiscrimination is to allow "don't know," "can't say," or "equal" responses. An alternative, particu-

TABLE 8.4
Balanced Sets of Three Out of Nine Stimuli

| abc | def | ghi | adg | aeh | afi |
| bdh | bei | bfg | cdi | ceg | cfh |

larly when the set-size is more than three or four, is to choose one liked best and one liked least (or whatever dimension of judgment is appropriate), and then the one liked next best and least, and so. This can be implemented with a computer program that stops asking for choices whenever a "can't say" response is encountered. A variation that is even simpler for the subject is to ask which two or three are liked best and least, or just which are liked and which disliked. The results of the choices in any of these methods are used to imply the obvious dominances.

RATING SCALES

The ubiquitous rating scale is by far the commonest data-gathering approach for getting ordinal judgments from subjects about people, concepts, and things. The term *rating scale* refers to the familiar process in which the respondent is presented with a list of things, say, desserts, and a set of categories, ordered, say, in tastiness, and asked to indicate the category in which each dessert falls. The definition of the categories can take many forms: they can be given verbal labels or not, or just the ends can be labeled; numerals can be used to label the categories. The number of categories can vary from 2 or 3 to 10 or more. Whatever the specifics are, the respondent puts each dessert into one of the categories, and the response is presumed to provide quantitative information.

There is no doubt that rating scales are more efficient than any pair-comparison or direct ranking procedure in terms of the rate at which subjects can provide data. In spite of the fact that there is rarely any reason to believe that they give anything other than ordinal information, the responses are commonly treated numerically: the numbers are averaged, differences are compared, and the like. In this section we briefly consider the rationale for rating scales in the context of the ideas we have presented about the bases of measurement, and we make some suggestions about rating scale methods.

What Information Do Rating Scales Provide?

If one stops to think about it, the fact that rating scales work at all is a remarkable psychological principle. The steps in the process that must occur mentally, must be rather complex, and they rely on the respondent's ability to behave abstractly. There must not only be a concept of the thing to be rated, or often a concept of some aspect of it, but also concepts of the categories that are used in the rating. Moreover, both types of concepts have to behave in a quantitative manner, at least to a reasonable degree. In spite of the apparent complexity, the process works quite well in many situations.

It is rare, however, that there is an empirical basis for calling the resulting numbers more than ordinal. As we have seen in earlier chapters, this would require verification of the conjoint measurement axioms, and this is rarely the case, although there are instances such as Anderson (1962) and Cliff (1972). Indeed, it is not obvious how even the requirements of ordinality can be verified, particularly that of transitivity. The use of ratings therefore seems to be pretty much measurement by fiat, but because their usefulness is beyond doubt, it must have some basis.

There are two general aspects of this basis. One can be that reasonable ordinality has been demonstrated in the past for the ratees. That is, some form of paired comparison procedure has been carried out for these stimuli, or some like them, and found to behave reasonably well. Then, ratings have been obtained of the same stimuli, and their order as determined from ratings has agreed well with that derived from the comparison process. Another area of evidence for ordinality can come from replication of the responses. Surprisingly, it is moderate disagreement among replications, rather than perfect agreement, that provides a logical basis for concluding that rating scales provide ordinal information. This is because the pattern of responses to the items often corresponds quite well to that of an *interval order*, which is discussed in chapter 9. Thus, the ordinal status of rating scales is quite reasonable in a wide variety of contexts.

Constructing Rating Scales

Rating scales are so common, the reader may have occasion to construct, or at least evaluate, an application. Some general advice may therefore be useful. The principles suggested here may seem self-evident or commonsensical, but they are overlooked often enough to justify their presentation.

The most important is that the directions should clearly present the basis for rating. What is the main dimension that is to be considered? If there is a special context or point of view, it should also be stated clearly. An overview of the range of stimuli is also useful because otherwise the respondent may have to change the way he or she is using the scale partway through if unexpectedly extreme stimuli are encountered. These points may be summarized by saying that what the subject is doing should correspond as closely as possible to what the investigator intends.

The number of categories to use should be determined by the fineness of discrimination that is to be expected from respondents, the investigator bearing in mind that random others are unlikely to be as interested in the stimuli as she or he is. Four to nine categories are probably the range that should be considered, although simulations seem to indicate that the quality of results is not affected by the number of categories per se. A related question is whether to use verbal anchors for the scale, and how many. Our preference is to use anchors for the two extremes of the scale since this helps to remind the respondent of the context and perhaps to induce some uniformity in the way the scale is used by different ones. Where scales are bipolar we tend to avoid labeling the middle category as "neutral" or the like in hope of reducing the tendency to be noncommittal. This is facilitated further by using an even number of categories so that there is no middle ground to choose. This tactic must be used judiciously as respondents may object to being forced to choose and retaliate by not answering items at all. Whatever the number and format of the categories, the initial directions should urge respondents to use the whole scale, a suggestion that may be repeated from time to time if there are several pages of stimuli to be rated. The overall objective of getting as much information as possible in as uniform a manner as possible should be the basis for judging the format. Pretesting, and subsequent discussion, with at least a few respondents who are similar to the intended group is often superior to hours of thought or committee discussion of the format and directions.

OVERVIEW

This chapter has dealt with methods for reducing the number of responses that is necessitated by complete paired comparisons. First, some possible reasons for not having dominance information about all pairs were given, including not only deliberate design but inadvertance. Then, after tournaments were mentioned briefly, procedures for selecting systematic subsets of pairs that allowed all the elements to have an equal number of appearances were described. It was noted that, although there are a number of possibilities, some combinations of number of elements and number of presentations per element are not feasible.

Another approach to using pairwise comparisons but not employing all pairs is a computer-based method that systematically selects pairs to be presented so as to maximize the amount of information provided by each pair. Although there are issues that revolve around how best to take advantage of responses that are unreliable, the method has much to recommend it. Then methods that involve the rating or partial ranking of subsets were described. Finally, a brief discussion of ranking methods was provided.

The Unfolding Model

WHY "UNFOLDING"?

In chapters 3 to 6 we have been concerned with a single ordering of persons by items or items by persons. In chapter 7, differences between the orders from different respondents were considered random fluctuations from one underlying order. However, suppose in an intense political campaign, for example, potential voters would give different orderings. It is assumed that these different orderings are substantiated in the way proposed in chapter 7.

In this chapter the orderings will not generally be simple in that the ordering produced by one person may have no relationship with that produced by another. The original linear ordering of items on a single dimension may be perceived as being in one direction by one subject but in the opposite direction by another or even in some quite different direction by a third. This situation can be shown to arise if the items and subjects occupy the same line but the ordering by a subject would reflect the order of the distances of that subject from each item in that dimension.

In a particular case the order of the distances might represent the order of preference for the items by the subject. Figure 9.1 reveals the relationships between the items and the subject (I) and the ordering of the items by the subject in terms of their distances along the folded scale (I). Hence the term "unfolding" to describe the derivation of the items scale from the tabulation of preferences on the individual's I scale.

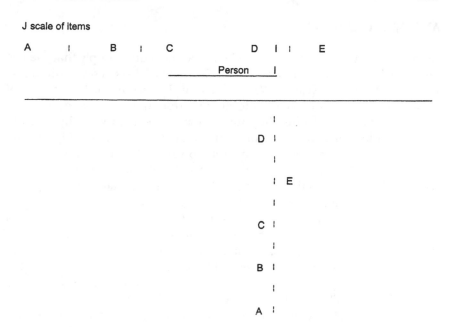

FIG. 9.1.   The vertical scale of Person I corresponds to a preference ordering of D E C B A.

This configuration of points can generate up to 11 different orderings,
depending on the position of the individual I; for example, a subject closest
to Stimulus A will order the others as BCDE and conversely, one closest to
Stimulus E will order the others as DCBA. If the subject closest to A moves
over the midpoint of the interval AB so that it is closest to B, his order will
become BACDE, and so we see that crossing a midpoint will change an order. With five stimuli (S = 5) there are at most 10 distinct midpoints, and so
11 different orderings of the five stimuli will be possible. Of these only
ABCDE and EDCBA will be opposites. With S stimuli in one dimension
there will be a maximum of $\frac{1}{2}S(S-1) + 1$ different orders, but only two of
these will have opposites. These two orders with opposites will correspond
to the order of the stimuli on the straight line. All subjects' orders must end
with one of the two extreme stimuli of the orders with opposites.

The order DECBA applying to Person I can be thought of as consisting
of flags with the letters DCBA on one side of a string folded at Point I,
whereas the letter E is on a flag on the other side of the folded string. If the
string is unfolded, the order of the letters on the straight piece of string will
be EDCBA, which is the order of the points on the line. Hence the aim of
the model is to determine the order of the points from the preference order of the stimuli from each subject. Hence the term *unfolding model* is used.

ANALYZING ORDERS

In writing about the unfolding model researchers often imply that the two sets of variables relate to individuals on the one hand and a set of stimuli on the other. However, Keats (1972) used social class groups ordering types of mass media as the units of an unfolding representation in one dimension. The one-dimensional unfolding model was first put forward by Coombs (1951) but little use was made of it for the next 10 years, possibly because the single dimension was not very common in real empirical data.

Bennett and Hays (1960), as well as McElwain and Keats (1961), published articles that had titles beginning "Multidimensional Unfolding" with the first pair of authors using an algebraic approach and the second a geometrical one. To understand the nature of a two-dimensional display of stimuli and subjects, the simplest case to consider is the one in which there are three stimuli, A, B, and C, and start with one dimension, as in Fig. 9.2.

The order CBA and its opposite ABC cover the right-end open region and the left-end open region, respectively, and reflect the order of the stimuli on the line. The combination AB and its corresponding vertical line mark the point of change from ABC to BAC and similarly for AC and BC and their vertical lines. The two orders ending in B, ACB and CAB are not generated from the figure and confirm the fact that three stimuli in one dimension generate $4 = \frac{1}{2}3(3 - 1) + 1$ orders. If the orders ACB and CAB do occur in the data, then these data do not conform to the model and would require a two-dimensional representation.

In two dimensions, A, B, and C can form a triangle, ABC, which could generate three concurrent perpendicular bisectors of its sides AB, BC, and AC. The six regions defined by these bisectors would correspond to the six orderings of A, B, and C, ABC, ACB, CAB, CBA, BCA and BAC, as seen in Fig. 9.3.

Dimensions and Orders

Some numerical properties of the unfolding model need to be heeded if the model is to be used with real data from empirical studies. These properties are reported in Coombs (1964, pp. 153–180) and in McElwain and Keats (1961).

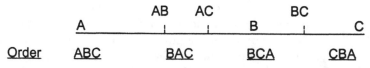

FIG. 9.2.   The possible orderings of three stimuli on a line, and the regions they cover.

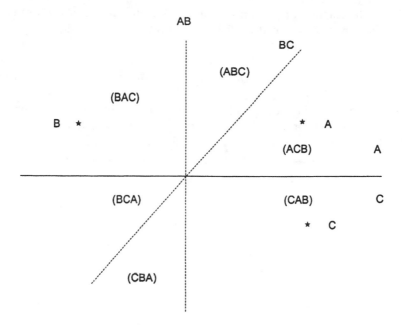

FIG. 9.3. The regions and their orders generated by three points ABC in two dimensions and their perpendicular bisectors.

1. If one dimension is being considered for S stimuli, the largest number of orders to be considered is $_sR_1 = \frac{1}{2}S(S-1) + 1$ with only one order having its opposite also occurring. The order whose opposite also occurs is the order of the stimuli on the straight line defining the dimension.

2. If a second dimension is defined by wrapping the straight line around a circle, the orders defined by the single dimension will all have their opposites also occurring in the circular representation. This will yield a total number of orders of $_sO_2 = S(S-1)$ of orders whose opposites also occur. A distinction is made between R, the total number of orders of S stimuli in a given number of dimensions, D (e.g., $_sR_D$), and O the total number of orders and their opposites that occur with S stimuli in a given number of dimensions, D (e.g., $_sO_D$).

3. Although it is always possible to calculate the value of $_sR_1 = \frac{1}{2}S(S-1) + 1$ for one dimension, it is not obvious how to calculate the maximum number of orders $_sR_2$ for two dimensions. Coombs (1964) gave formulae that lead to the relationship:

$$_sR_2 = {}_{(S-1)}R_2 + (S-1)_{(S-1)}R_1 \qquad (9.1)$$

Thus for four stimuli in two dimensions, the greatest number of orders with or without opposites, $_4R_2$, will equal $6 + 3 \times 4 = 6 + 12 = 18$. Thus, by chaining the calculations it is possible to calculate the greatest number of orders for any number of stimuli in any number of dimensions. The formula for $_sR_2$ generalizes to:

$$_sR_D = {}_{(S-1)}R_D + (S-1)_{(S-1)}R_{(D-1)}.$$ (9.2)

Coombs (1964, p. 154), formula (7.1) quoted an observation by Leisenring which leads to this formula. Parallel formulae to those given for R can be derived for O, the number of orders whose opposites occur.

By combining the formulae relating $_sR_2$, $_{S-1}R_2$, and $_{S-1}R_1$ it may be shown that:

$$_sR_2 = S(S-1)(S-2)(3S-1)/24 + \tfrac{1}{2}S(S-1) + 1$$ (9.3)

or

$$= S(S-1)(S-2)(3S-1)/24 + {}_sR_1$$ (9.4)

and the further extension to:

$$_sR_3 = [S(S-1)]^2(S-2)(S-3)/48 + {}_sR_2,$$ (9.5)

or

$$= S(S-1)(S-2)(S^3 - 4S^2 + 9S - 2) + {}_sR_1$$ (9.6)

so that the values of R, the number of different rankings of S stimuli in two or three dimensions can be calculated more directly.

We note that $_sO_1 = 2$ irrespective of the value of $S > 2$ and $_sO_2 = S(S-1)$. From these values we can use the generalized formula for $_sO_D$ to calculate the greatest number of orders whose opposites occur for any number of stimuli in any number of dimensions. We note that:

$$_sO_D = {}_{(S-1)}O_D + (S-1)_{(S-1)}O_{(D-1)}.$$ (9.7)

and more generally,

$$= S(S-1) \ldots \ldots (S-D+1)$$ (9.8)

Table 9.1 presents $S!$, the greatest number of different orders that can be obtained from S stimuli in $S-1$ or more dimensions and the greatest number of orders that can be represented in D dimensions. This table can be ex-

TABLE 9.1
The Number of Orders With Opposites (O) and Orders With
or Without Opposites (R) With S Stimuli in D Dimensions

		Dimensions D								
		1		2		3		4		5	
S	$S!$	O	R	O	R	O	R	O	R	O	R
2	2	2	2	2	2	2	2	2	2	2	2
3	6	2	4	6	6	6	6	6	6	6	6
4	24	2	7	12	18	24	24	24	24	24	24
5	120	2	11	20	46	72	96	120	120	120	120
6	720	2	16	30	101	172	326	480	600	720	720
7	5040	2	22	42	197	352	932	1512	2556	3600	4320

tended beyond the seven-stimuli case considered in it using formulas presented earlier.

Locating Points

Having used Table 9.1 to determine the minimum number of dimensions required to accommodate a given R orders from S stimuli the question arises as to how the S stimuli are to be arranged to generate the R orders. One can proceed as follows. If there are three stimuli in one dimension, the two orders which are opposites define the position of the stimuli on the line and the stimulus that lies between the other two will not appear last in any of the four orders. This is illustrated in Fig. 9.2 above. With three stimuli in two dimensions, all six possible orders occur, as shown in Fig. 9.3.

With four stimuli, the possible configurations in one or two dimensions have been dealt with exhaustively by McElwain and Keats (1961) and republished in Coombs (1964, pp. 153–180). In Fig. 9.4, the left-hand line generates all seven of the possible orders of four stimuli in one dimension but the right-hand line generates only six because the midpoint of (3), (3) coincides with that of (0), (0) so that one possible order is lost.

With four stimuli in two dimensions, there are only three arrangements that generate all of the 18 possible orders, as shown in Fig. 9.5.

(4)   (0)   (0) (3)   (3)   (0)   (0)   (3)

FIG. 9.4.   Possible arrangements of four points in one dimension.

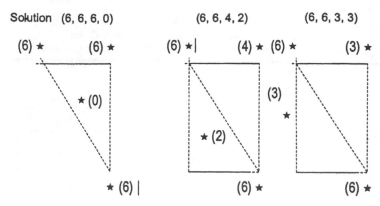

FIG. 9.5.   Three arrangements of four stimuli producing 18 orders.

Reading from left to right in Fig. 9.5, the first configuration, representing the [6,6,6,0] solution, allows for the fact that a stimulus point that is within the triangle defined by [6,6,6,] will never be placed last in any of the possible 18 orders of the four points. The middle figure shows the effect of the point (2) being outside the triangle [6,6,4,] but *inside* the circle and parallelogram defined by the points [6,6,4,]. The point (2) will be ranked last in two of the 18 orders. This solution is referred to as the [6,6,4,2] solution. In the right-hand figure one (3) is a point on the reference circle, triangle, and parallogram while the other (3) is outside the triangle and the parallelogram but inside the circle defined by [6,6,3]. The line [3,3] is closer to the point (6) which begins the two missing orders [6,3,6,3].

The next three orders come from special figures which have lost one or two orders because of their special features. The four orders (2,6,6,2) occur but no others ending in 2, as shown in the middle section of Fig. 9.6. In the lower section configuration the two orders (6,6,0,4) and all orders ending in (0) are missing. In the trapezoid, one order (6,2,6,3) occurs and the stimulus (6), appearing first, is farther from the shorter diagonal than the other stimulus (6).

The preceding figures and descriptions illustrate the ways in which the existence and nonexistence of some of the possible orders among a small set of points implies a particular configuration for them. There are numerous other possible constraints of this type that we do not describe here.

Davidson (1972) built on the work of McElwain and Keats (1961). He proved 10 theorems relevant to the problem of establishing the nondegenerate configurations of S stimuli in D dimensions in the case of the complete set of $_SR_D$ orders appearing in the data. As an example he showed how to use the theory to locate four stimuli in two dimensions given the complete set of 18 orders. His solutions relate to nondegenerate cases.

Following his doctoral research, Davidson studied category theory under Dr. Wallace of the Mathematics Department as a basis for developing

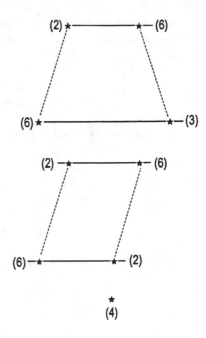

FIG. 9.6.   Degenerate cases with
one or two orders missing.

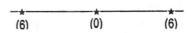

a general method of finding both degenerate and nondegenerate solutions for unfolding data. The results of this research were published in
Davidson (1973). During this period various computer programs were
published for solving the general problem, but these solutions had problems arising from the fact that the spaces studied were nonhomogeneous
as far as unfolding models were concerned. Various sets of data generated
by Davidson's methods were sent for computer solution but no solutions
were forthcoming.

UNFOLDING OF ORDERS VERSUS ANALYSIS
OF INTERSTIMULUS DISTANCES

In 1952, Torgerson published his method of multidimensional scaling of
interstimulus differences as part of his PhD thesis. The distances were
sometimes estimated using the method of paired comparisons or by rating methods. They were treated as interval scales which, of course, the lat-

ter were not. It seemed to be important to compare the two methods of multidimensional scaling, scaling of orders, unfolding, and scaling of distances, using the same set of stimuli. The results of such a comparison were published by Keats (1964) using five Australian political parties at that time as stimuli: the Australian Labor Party (A), the Liberal Party (L), the Country Party (C), the Queensland Labor Party (Q) and the Communist Party (K).

The data were collected by presenting the subject with each of the 10 pairs of political parties and asking which one she preferred and asking her to rate the difference between the two parties on a scale ranging from *little difference* to *a very great difference*. The results of the paired preferences from each of the approximately 500 subjects could be combined to obtain an order of preference providing they were transitive, which they almost always were. In the very rare event of intransitivity the order obtained contained ties.

Almost all of the preference orderings of the five political parties were accounted for in terms of a two-dimensional unfolding model. The point corresponding to the Liberal Party (L) lay inside the quadrilateral formed by K, A, C, and Q and generated the full 46 orderings possible from five stimuli in two dimensions and accounted for more than 95% of the cases. The configuration is shown in Fig. 9.7.

When the 10 differences were analyzed as distances by Torgerson's multidimensional scaling for the full 500 cases they required four dimensions, which were the greatest number that should be needed by five stimuli. However, when the group placing the Australian Labor Party (ALP) first were taken and their 10 differences analyzed that way, they were found to fit neatly into two dimensions, as were the distances for the group placing the Liberal Party (LP) first. However the two representations were found to be very different, as shown in Fig. 9.8.

From this comparison it seems clear that in cases where stimuli have strong feelings associated with them the perception of the relationships between them can be distorted by the preferences. From the point of view of political policies, the Communist party and the Queensland Labor Party were diametrically opposed, so that the Liberal Party's perception of them as being relatively close is a distortion, whereas the Australian Labor Party's view of them as being closer to the Liberal Party and the Country Party in opposing the Communist Party was more realistic.

Another type of analysis was to take the figures from the Torgerson analysis and interpret them as unfolding diagrams and draw in perpendicular bisectors and generate orders. When this is done for the LP group figure, the orders given by that group were obtained, but not those given by the ALP group. A similar result was obtained from the ALP group's figure with their group orders being obtained, but not the LP group's orders. In other

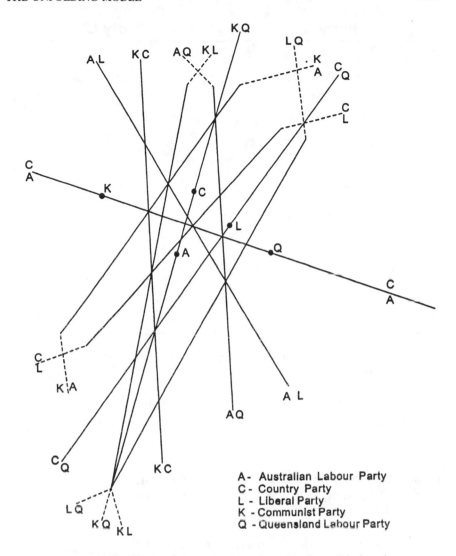

FIG. 9.7.   The unfolding solution for the orders of the five political parties.

words, subjects could perceive the different orders from their own group but not those of the opposing group.

One conclusion that could be drawn from this comparison is that the unfolding approach was suitable for stimuli that produced affective responses but the multidimensional scaling approach was more suitable for the more psychophysical studies where responses are less affected by qualitative responses. Using both methods with the same set of stimuli shows how the

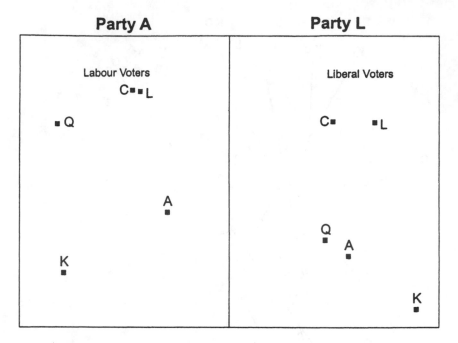

FIG. 9.8.   Comparison of the two representations of differences for the political parties, A and L.

preferences can influence the perception of the stimuli. However, the unfolding approach is impractical in situations in which a large number of stimuli are involved.

COMPARISON BETWEEN MULTIDIMENSIONAL UNFOLDING ANALYSIS AND FACTOR ANALYSIS OF CORRELATED VARIABLES

The data available for this comparison arose from a study of response styles detected in personality tests. The study was reported by Jackson and Messick (1962) on acquiescence and desirability as response determinants on the Minnesota Multiphasic Personality Inventory (MMPI). Each of the 300 items consists of an affirmative statement such as "I do not tire quickly," or "I am worried about sex matters," to which the subject is required to respond with "True," "False," or "Cannot say." The responses provide scores on one or more of several clinical scales such as Depression, Hysteria, or Paranoia.

In the Jackson and Messick study each item was rated by experienced psychologists in terms of how desirable a *true* response could be considered and the 300 items were sorted into five scales ranging from Dy1 for the *highest* desirability through Dy5 for the scale with the *lowest* desirability. Each scale contained 60 items except Dy1 for which only 50 extremely desirable items could be found. The items of the MMPI were administered to subjects who were either students (334), or people in prison (201), or patients from a neuropsychiatric hospital (194). The responses were scored on the 20 scales of the MMPI as well as the five desirability scales and the MMPI validity scales. A variable of acquiescence was defined in terms of the number of items times a subject endorsed. The 29 variables were intercorrelated and factor analyzed to produce nine factors.

The five desirability scales were strictly ordered from Dy1 (*most desirable*) to Dy5 (*least desirable*) and it was possible to order them again in terms of their correlations with each MMPI scale for each sample and tabulate the various orders. From the point of view of the unfolding model, it should be noted that some scales were in two forms; in one a *true* response was scored and in the other a *false* response was scored for the college sample and the hospital sample separately. Thus the order for one form would tend to be the opposite of that for the other. In Table 9.2 the scales Dy1 to Dy5 are represented by the numbers 1, 2, 3, 4, and 5.

Unfolding Dimensions of the MMPI

Two of the 70 orders derived from the samples and 35 personality scales, did not fit the pattern of the other 68. The + occurs because some of the orders contained ties but otherwise agreed with the orders they are added to. The orders fitted into a two-dimensional circular pattern in which two pairs did not appear because of equality of intervals, and all orders had opposites

TABLE 9.2
The Orders of the Correlations With the Desirability
Scales of Each MMPI Scale for Each Sample

Order	Frequency	Midpoint Crossed	Opposite	Frequency
12345	6	——	54321	27 + 3
21345	4	(1,2)	54312	5
23145	2	(1,3)	54132	—
32415	2	(2,3) & (1,4)	51423	1
34251	—	(2,4) & (1,5)	15243	—
34521	2	(2,5)	12543	—
43521	1	(3,4)	12534	8 + 1
45321	2 + 1	(3,5)	12354	3
54321	5	(4,5)	12345	4

```
                      1,4                          Mid-point
          1,2  1,3  2,3  2,5  3,4  3,5  4,5        Mid-points
     x....!....!x...!...x!....!....!x..!..x        Unfolding Dimension
     1         2         3              4    5     Stimulus Points
     1    2   2         3   3    4   4      5 ⎫
     2    1   3         2   4    3   5      4 ⎬  Orders Accounted
     3    3   1         4   5    5   3      3 ⎬  for by the
     4    4   4         1   2    2   2      2 ⎬  Regions
     5    5   5         5   1    1   1      1 ⎭
Freq. 6   4   2         2   2    1  2+1     5
```

FIG. 9.9. Stimulus locations and interval midpoints.

possible, even though one pair did not occur in the data. Figure 9.8 displays the location of the desirability scales and the scales of the MMPI.

The unfolding figure was thus circular and the location of the scales was very similar to that which appears in Jackson and Messick (1962, p. 291) representing the loadings from the factor analysis of the intercorrelations between the variables. The unfolding figures are shown below.

The left-hand column of orders in Table 9.2 form the orders for five stimuli on a straight line with some equal intervals which lead to omissions of possible orders. Figure 9.9 presents this special case with the stimuli 1. . . .5, and midpoints (1,2), (1,3) and so on to (4,5) and the orders from 12345 to 54321.

Notice that the midpoints 2,4 and 1,5, which coincide in Table 9.2, are not included because they have no cases. Also, the 1,4 and 2,3 midpoints coincide, so the former is not labeled. In order to include the orders in the right-hand column of Table 9.2, the first thing to note is that two dimensions are required because more than 11 different orders of five stimuli occur in the data and because more than two orders have their opposites occurring. It should also be noted that most of the orders have their opposites occurring which is true of two dimensional cyclic solutions. Figure 9.10 presents more complete, cyclic unfolding solution.

SOME APPLICATIONS OF THE UNFOLDING MODEL

During the almost 40 years since the formulation of the unfolding model by Coombs (1964), which included the work of McElwain and Keats (1961), there are relatively few published reports using the model. These are typified by having few numbers of stimuli because of the difficulties of analysis when larger numbers, more than 6, are involved. Such sets of stimuli are usually important in the cultures of the subjects and cross-cultural comparisons can be made without needing to check the assumptions needed when the nor-

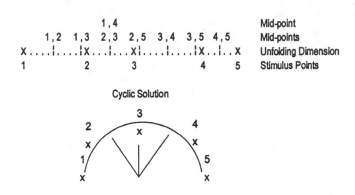

FIG. 9.10. Cyclic solution for the MMPI data.

mal cognitive or attitudinal items are involved as shown in chapter 5. Details of some published examples of the use of unfolding models follow.

Example 9.1

The first example involved four idealized types of persons, Saints, Scholars, Heroes and Artists, and subjects included students from Malay, Chinese and Hindu populations, from Malaysia, and students from Australia of slightly higher age level. The report (see Keats, 1962) was published in the *Journal of Social Psychology* at the request of that journal's editor for cross-cultural reports. The main Malaysia–Australia difference lay in the fact that some Australians tended to rank Saints last whereas almost none of the Malaysians did.

The Malaysian subjects were all asked to rank the four idealized types according to their importance to the community. The Australian subjects were presented with pairs of types and asked to indicate which one was the more important. Very few (13) of these 243 subjects produced intransitive orders and 12 of these were cycles as discussed in the previous chapter. Well over 90% of the subjects in each of the four cultural groups gave orders fitting a 6642 model of the kind shown in Fig. 9.5. Figure 9.11 presents this model with the frequencies for each of the orders for Australian and Malayan subjects separately. The cycles were represented in this figure by centroids of triangles in seven cases.

Example 9.2

A series of examples were presented in Keats (1964) including the political parties already referred to as well as types of crimes and preferences for student accommodation. These examples relate the unfolding diagrams with those of multidimensional scaling of the kind developed by Torgerson (1952).

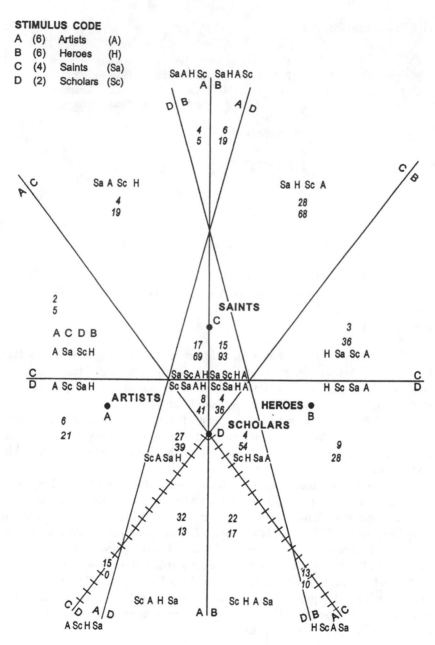

FIG. 9.11. The interrelationship between persons and stimuli in two dimensions with the frequency of Australian (top) and Malayan subjects.

Example 9.3

Another series of studies referred to the importance placed by adolescents on consulting referent others such as parents, siblings, teachers, other adults, and friends on problems related to school performance, personal appearance, popularity, and other aspects of adolescence (Keats et al., 1983). The studies used subjects from Australia, the United States, Malaysia, France, and Norway.

DICHOTOMOUS DATA

Proximity-Based Responses

Our description of unfolding has been based on the assumption that the data consist of rank-orders of n stimuli by m respondents. However, some dichotomous data may be the result of an unfolding type of response process in which the respondent has been required to make a dichotomous response. For example, instead of being told to rank-order the stimuli, the respondent could be asked "Which of these do you like?" or told to "Choose the three you like best" from among a set of possible choices. If the "ideal point" model is descriptive of how the respondent decides which alternatives to choose, he or she will give a positive response to elements that are close to his ideal and negative responses to those that are far from it. When different respondents have different ideals, their selections will differ accordingly. This section describes some methods for inferring ordinal information about stimuli and respondents from the choices.

The reader can recall from chapter 2 the classification system for data developed by Coombs (1964). In it, the contrast between *dominance* and *proximity* was one of three fundamental dichotomies for classifying types of data. Unfolding is a type of proximity response, and, when the basis for choice is unidimensional, the response matrix in situations like that described in the previous paragraph should look like Table 9.3, once the rows and columns are appropriately ordered. That is, dichotomous choice data can be an example of two-set proximity data.

Recovering the Order

With real data, the neat arrangement shown by Table 9.3 can only be approximated, and, when the underlying order for rows and columns is unknown, finding the best orders can be a difficult task. Cliff et al. (1988) suggested a procedure that was quite successful. The data that one starts with is simply a table with dichotomous entries, say, 1s and 0s, and the positive re-

TABLE 9.3
Responses in Ideal Case of Dichotomous Unfolding

						Item					
		1	2	3	4	5	6	7	8	9	10
Person	1	1	1	1	0	0	0	0	0	0	0
	2	1	1	1	1	0	0	0	0	0	0
	3	1	1	1	1	1	0	0	0	0	0
	4	1	1	1	1	1	0	0	0	0	0
	5	0	1	1	1	1	1	0	0	0	0
	6	0	0	1	1	1	1	1	0	0	0
	7	0	0	1	1	1	1	1	0	0	0
	8	0	0	0	1	1	1	1	1	0	0
	9	0	0	0	1	1	1	1	1	0	0
	10	0	0	0	0	1	1	1	1	1	0
	11	0	0	0	0	0	1	1	1	1	1
	12	0	0	0	0	0	1	1	1	1	1
	13	0	0	0	0	0	0	1	1	1	1
	14	0	0	0	0	0	0	1	1	1	1
	15	0	0	0	0	0	0	0	1	1	1

sponses from one person are initially scattered haphazardly across the row. However, if the columns, corresponding to stimuli, were in the best order, the 1s for that person should be bunched tightly together, but reordering columns to bunch one person's responses may result in spreading out another's. Also, there is nothing to tell us whether that one person's responses should be near one or the other end of the continuum or in the middle somewhere.

Note, however, that in the ideal case represented by the table, the positive responses are consecutive in all the rows, so with data we should try to find an ordering that has this effect. Let us number the columns from left to right, 1 to m. A measure of how spread out a person's responses are is the *variance* of the column numbers corresponding to her positive responses. This variance will be as small as it can possibly be if all the positive responses are bunched together in consecutive locations.

This suggests an approach to take with a data matrix whose rows are in an arbitrary order that we believe represents dichotomous unfolding data, or what Coombs (1964) called two-set proximity data: We should reorder the columns so as to minimize the average variance across respondents of the ranks of the endorsed items. Cliff et al. (1988) followed this strategy, implementing it with a computer program. The program examined the effect on the average variance of ranks of interchanging all possible pairs of columns, and interchanged the pair that gave the greatest reduction in average rank-variance. It then looked for another pair to interchange by the same criterion, repeating the process until no further reduction in average rank-variance could be accomplished.

We would like to reorder the rows—corresponding to respondents—in the same way, but here there may be a computing problem due to the possibly large number of pairs of subjects; with 200 subjects there are nearly 20 thousand pairs. It is also likely that the number of steps required to find the best order will be correspondingly large. An alternative is to adopt a simpler approach to ordering rows. After the columns have been optimally ordered, the persons are ordered in terms of the *median* rank of the items that they have endorsed. This should give a reasonable approximation to the optimum order. It can also be used as the starting position for the iterative procedure, thereby greatly reducing the number of required steps. Unfortunately for anyone that might want to apply this kind of procedure, the programs developed by Cliff et al. (1988), are no longer available.

A caveat should be added to the earlier description. The reader may recall that in chapter 7, finding the best order from an inconsistent pair comparison matrix, the "correct" solution depended on the definition of correct. Furthermore, using one of the definitions of optimality, there was no guarantee of obtaining its optimum solution other than trying all possible orders. These issues are present here as well. "Minimum average variance of ranks" is only one possible definition of how bunched together the positive responses are, so a different one might lead to a different order. However, as long as the data are reasonably regular, solutions that are optimum by different criteria should be quite similar. The other caveat is that there is no guarantee that the pairwise interchange of columns until no improvement takes place will itself lead to the order that has minimum variance of ranks. It should work quite well toward achieving that goal, but there is no proof that it does achieve it.

SUMMARY

This chapter assumes that the orders being dealt with are well established but different for different people or groups of people in different cultures. The Unfolding Model represents stimuli and subjects in such a way that the order given by subjects corresponds to the ordering of the distances of each subject's ideal from the stimuli. Examples are given of three, four, or five stimuli in two or three dimensions.

The relationships between the unfolding representations and those given by multidimensional scaling are given for political parties by Keats (1964) and also those given by factor analysis of desirability response scales from a personality test, MMPI, from data from Jackson and Messick (1967, p. 291).

Examples of unfolding analyses of various sets of stimuli are given from the literature. The first was published by Keats (1962) comparing secondary students from Malaysia and Australia and their attitudes to idealized persons. Another example published by Keats et al. (1978) compared the importance placed by adolescents on consulting referent others such as parents, siblings, etc. on matters such as school performance and popularity. Further research could be carried out on stimuli about which subjects may have strong personal feelings, such as religious organizations.

Situations in which the individual's responses are dichotomous but are based on an unfolding-like process are fairly common. Some suggestions concerning how such data can be analyzed were made.

Chapter 10

The Application of Ordinal
Test Theory to Items in Tests
Used in Cross-Cultural Comparisons

INTERCULTURAL COMPARABILITY OF SCORES

In chapters 4 and 5, ordinal test theory was used to introduce the calculation of total tied-rank scores for dichotomous and polytomous items as well as persons. In the case of dichotomous items, chapter 4 stressed the fact that total tied-rank scores for both items and persons are perfectly linearly correlated with the sums of the arbitrary, dichotomous integral scores, 0 and 1. This fact justifies the use of 0 and 1 scoring and implies that the consistency value for items ranking persons, α_p, will be the same for each of the two methods of scoring. In the same way we need to consider, also, the consistency of persons ranking items, α_i, which will also be the same for each of the two methods of scoring.

However, in chapter 5, it was shown that this relationship between total tied-ranks scores and the sums of the arbitrary integral scores of 0, 1, 2, etc. would not be found with polytomous items except in very special cases, for example, the case when the frequencies of choices of the categories are equal or very nearly equal across items. There is no justification in ordinal test theory for the use of arbitrary integral scores for polytomous items. Thus tied-ranks scores are always referred to in this chapter so that the number of alternatives, two or more than two, will not be a problem.

In this chapter we are concerned mainly with the consistency with which persons rank items. In chapter 5 it was shown that this consistency can be measured by using the concordance coefficient formula for W adjusted for ties. This value of W can be tested for significance and also transformed to the value of coefficient of internal consistency, α_1, which is also the most commonly quoted statistic for the consistency of the items in the ranking of persons.

The consistency of persons ranking items is regarded by Guttman (1944) and some later workers as being the criterion for concluding that the items form a scale for the persons tested. The conjoint orderings of persons by items and of items by persons have been regarded as being of great importance as a criterion for scaling by Guttman (1944) as well as by such later scholars as Loevinger (1948), Rasch (1960), Luce and Tukey (1964), and Keats (1967). However, there is no reference in any of these writings to the problem of comparing samples from different cultures on items that are consistently ranked by the two cultures separately. Furthermore, the use of W and α as measures of the consistency of persons ranking items has only recently been suggested by Keats (1997), and in chapter 6 we saw that α's for items and persons are related.

High values of W and α for persons ranking items indicate that the items form a scale for this sample of persons. The conjoint measures for items ranking persons indicate the consistencies of the orders of persons obtained from the scale. The empirical study of conjoint ordering is not only of academic interest but also of interest to cross-cultural psychologists in their attempts to discover whether a test or scale is equally justified in each of two or more cultures. We use the word *cultures* rather broadly to include not only groups that are widely separated geographically but also ethnically defined subgroups that are nominally in the same culture, such as Hispanics, African Americans, or Mennonites living in the United States.

In most accounts of the theory of psychological scaling there is discussion of the use of the parameter α for items ordering people consistently. However, the relationship between α and Kendall's concordance coefficient W is almost never shown. There is also virtually no discussion in the literature of the use of the same parameter α as a measure of the extent to which persons completing a test have ranked items, in terms of difficulty for cognitive items or of popularity in the case of items in an attitude or personality scale. A high value of the internal consistency in ordering items is a strong indication that the items form a scale. Some examples are given in Appendix A of items forming a very consistent scale.

This discussion is essential if comparisons of different national or cultural groups are contemplated, because it must be shown not only that the *items* form a scale in all groups but also that these scales are very highly correlated. However, virtually no journals or books concerned with making linguistic, cultural, or other national comparisons refer to the need to use the values of α for items to determine whether or not the groups involved have the same degree of scaling of items and whether the orders obtained for the items are highly correlated from one group to another. Cultural comparisons are reported without reference to the item characteristics for each of the comparison groups.

In the case of item response theory (IRT), conjoint ordering of items by persons is not insisted upon because an item discrimination parameter is introduced to take care of the possibility that high scorers may have a different ordering of item difficulty or popularity than low scorers. Consistent ordering of items by persons at all performance levels is a necessary but not sufficient condition to produce an interval scale. Harrington (1985) showed that the cancellation axiom must also be satisfied. However, if an item discrimination parameter is introduced, which differs from one item to another as in the IRT with two or more item parameters, the necessary condition of consistent ordering by subjects at each performance level cannot be met and so an interval scale cannot be achieved.

In chapter 1, page 6, the point was made that many developing countries are currently facing problems that led to the development of psychological tests used in developed countries today. Some of the developing countries find it more economical to translate and otherwise adapt tests from developed countries than to construct new tests for their own people. The fact that this practice has led to problems is shown in an article by Zhang Hou-Can of the Beijing Normal University.

Zhang (1992) reported that some Chinese tests in different fields have been developed, but adapted tests still play a large part. The main problems in scoring and interpreting these tests come from cultural differences based on language, knowledge, customs, and values that exist not only between Western and Eastern countries but among Asian countries as well. Even differences between nationalities within China have been found. The results of studies using a variety of tests applied in educational, clinical, and industrial areas are used for demonstration. Ways of solving the problems are also discussed in this article.

The full content of this article shows the extent to which Professor Zhang has undertaken the study of problems of cultural and national differences in testing. Many similar studies have been carried out in the United States and in other countries, but these are not reviewed here.

Muniz, Cuesta, Paz, Navas, and Barbero (1992) reported results of a study of the effects of cultural differences across England, Ireland, Korea, and Spain and seven states of Canada. The data consisted of 63 items from the 281 mathematics questions used in the 1986 National Assessment of Educational Progress. Results showed that for each sample, the 63 items were homogeneous in that they had only one factor. Muniz et al. (1992, p. 186) commented that, "to have a unidimensional test across the countries does not prove that this factor is the same for every country." This possibility was investigated using the three parameter IRT to estimate the difficulty parameter and to compare each sample with the U.S.-sample values. Twenty-three of the 63 items showed bias between at least one sample and the U.S. sample. They conclude homogeneity in each culture does not preclude bias between pairs of cultures.

INTERNATIONAL TEST COMMISSION GUIDELINES

The need for adapting tests to correct for cultural differences led to concern within the International Test Commission (ITC) during the Keats' presidency of that body in the 1990s. After a series of working papers, the Commission published a set of guidelines in the ITC Bulletin (van de Vijvre & Hambleton, 1996), for adapting tests for use in another language and culture. A revision of these guidelines by Tanzer and Sim (1999) is presented here. The guidelines are very general; they do not include the use of a measure of agreement in ordering items by persons in different cultures as the most important criterion for comparability of scores obtained in these cultures.

A statement of the ITC guidelines for test adaptations has been published by Tanzer and Sim (1999, pp. 258–269)[1] with minor modifications by ITC Council in the interest of clarity. The modified guidelines approved by ITC are:

1. The effects of cultural differences which are not relevant [i.e., nuisance factors] or important to the main purposes of the study should be minimized to the extent possible.
2. The amount of overlap in the constructs in the populations of interest should be assessed.
3. Instrument developers/publishers should insure that the translation/adaptation process takes full account of linguistic and cultural differences among the populations for whom the translated/adapted versions of the instrument are intended.
4. Instruments' developers/publishers should provide evidence that the language use in the directions, rubrics and items themselves as well as in the handbook are appropriate for all cultural and language populations for whom the instrument is intended.
5. Instruments' developers/publishers should provide evidence that the choice of testing techniques, item formats, test conventions and procedures are familiar to all intended populations.
6. Instruments' developers/publishers should provide evidence that item content and stimulus material are familiar to all intended populations.

---

[1]We thank the ITC for permission to reproduce these guidelines.

7a. Instruments' developers/publishers should implement systematic judgmental evidence, both linguistic and psychological, to improve the accuracy of the translation/adaptation process of all language versions.

7b. Instruments' developers/publishers should compile evidence on the equivalence of all language versions.

8. Instruments' developers/publishers should ensure that the data collection design permits the use of appropriate statistical techniques [i.e., conjoint ordinal methods] to establish item and/or test equivalence between the different language versions of the instrument.

9a. Instruments' developers/publishers should apply appropriate ordinal statistical techniques to establish the equivalence of the different versions of the instruments.

9b. Instruments' developers/publishers should apply appropriate ordinal statistical techniques to identify problematic components or aspects of the instrument which may be inadequate [i.e., inappropriate] to one or more of the intended populations.

10. Instruments' developers/publishers should provide information on the evaluation of the [construct, predictive etc.] validity in all populations for whom the translated/adapted versions are intended.

11. Instruments' developers/publishers should provide ordinal statistical evidence of the equivalence of tied-ranks scores for all intended populations.

12. Nonequivalent questions between versions intended for different populations should NOT be used in preparing a common scale or in comparing these populations.

13. Instruments' developers and administrators should try to anticipate the types of problems that can be expected and take appropriate actions to remedy these problems through the preparation of appropriate materials and instructions.

14. Instrument administrators should be sensitive to a number of factors related to the stimulus materials, administration procedures and response modes that can moderate the validity of the inferences drawn from the scores.

15. Those aspects of the environment that influence the administration of an instrument should be made as similar as possible across populations for whom the instrument is intended.

16. Instrument administration instructions should be in the source and target languages to minimize the influence of unwanted sources [i.e., nuisance factors] of variation across populations.

17. The instrument manual should specify all aspects of the instrument and its administration that require scrutiny in the application of the instrument in a new cultural context.

18. The administration should be unobtrusive and the administrator–examinee interaction should be minimized. Explicit rules that are described in the manual for the instrument should be followed.

19. When an instrument is translated/adapted for use in another population, documentation of the changes should be provided, along with evidence of the equivalence.

20. Score differences among samples of populations administered the instrument should NOT be taken at face value. The researcher [developer and/or test user] has the responsibility to substantiate the differences with other empirical evidence.

21. Comparisons across populations can only be made at the level of invariance that has been established for the scale on which scores are reported.

22. The instrument developer should provide specific information on the ways in which the sociocultural and ecological contexts of the populations might affect performance on the instrument, and should suggest procedures to account for these effects in the interpretation of results [i.e., test scores and test-taking behavior].

COMPARING POPULATIONS

Although it is important to consider procedures for trying to ensure that tests are applicable in each of two or more cultures, it is also important to consider procedures to ascertain whether or not these procedures have been effective. In Appendix A, the data from the Institute for Child Development in Thailand have such a low value of α for ordering items by subjects that these 10 items cannot be thought of as defining a scale in that culture.

However, in the case of the items used to select potential medical students, the values of α_i from data supplied by Dr. Munro for ordering items was more than .95, as also reported in Appendix A. Such values show that these items can be thought of as forming a potential scale. Unfortunately, in this case no data are available for subjects from a different language culture to which the items have been adapted to determine the extent to which the adaptation has been successful.

Example of Cultural Differences

In the field tests reported as carried out on these ITC guidelines, Hambleton, Yu, and Slater (1999) from the United States and Shanghai, China, used a Chinese translation of a test in English. In French Canada, the arti-clc reported, Jeanrie and Bertrand (1999) used a French translation of the test in English. An example of the problem arithmetic items used in the tests is given in the reference cited:

Aeroplane	Glue	Paint
$4.95	$1.29	$2.19

Chen had $10 to buy a model aeroplane, glue, and paint. At which of the following times could have an estimate been used instead of exact numbers?

A. When Chen tried to decide whether or not he had enough money to buy the plane, glue, and paint.
B. When the clerk entered each amount into the cash register.
C. When the clerk told Chen how much he owed.
D. When Chen counted his change.

Alternative A is obviously the correct answer. It was found that, contrary to the results for most other items, that Chinese students did not do as well as North American students on this item. The difference was 51% correct for Chinese and 74% correct for North American. These numbers may be compared to the overall percentages of 90% correct for the Chinese and 62% correct for the North Americans.

Experience with Chinese students suggests they are most unwilling to make guesses or estimates to arithmetic items and that some of the Chinese students in this study did not answer the question for that reason. It was not because they could not make estimates but rather that they would not.

In all cases there has been little or no reference to the definition of a scale in terms of the consistency of ordering the items by the subjects. Given that there is a well-defined scale in two cultures as judged by the Concordance Coefficient, the ordering of the items in terms of difficulty or popularity in one culture should agree substantially, if not completely, with that in the other. From the graph published by Hambleton et al. (1999), it is clear that the ordering of the 69 items is not the same in the two different languages and cultures of China and French Canada.

Furthermore the spread of difficulty in the Chinese sample was much smaller than that in the English-speaking sample, implying that the Chinese subjects were not ordering the items as consistently as were the North Americans. Where differences in the difficulties of an item in the two cultures were noted, an attempt was made to rationalize the occurrence of these differences. The possible explanation that the items did not form a consistent scale in the Chinese culture was not considered.

Unfortunately, Professor Yu of Nanjing University found that the raw data from this study had been accidentally destroyed during his long absence from China so that further analysis was not possible. In particular, he was not able to report the number of omissions in each sample.

THE ROLE OF ORDINAL TEST THEORY

The role of ordinal test theory in assessing the suitability of a test in two or more languages or cultures was set out by Keats (1997). In the analysis of data from two cultures, five outcomes can occur:

1. The set of items does not form a scale in either culture as tested by the *W* coefficient for ordering items. The cultures cannot then be compared.
2. The set of items forms a scale in one culture but not in the other. The cultures cannot then be compared.
3. The set of items form a scale in both cultures, but the ordering of items in one culture is very different from that in the other as shown by a rank-order correlation. This indicates that the same set of items, translated and/or adapted, has different underlying variables in the two cultures. The cultures cannot then be compared.
4. The set of items forms a scale in both cultures and the order of the items is substantially the same, but a few items show quite different ordinal positions in the two cultures. These biased items should be omitted in cultural comparisons but they may provide information about cultural differences.
5. If none of the foregoing conditions occur, the cultures can be compared by ordinal statistical methods.

The logic of the analysis involved in the methodology was questioned by Bontempo (1993). He wrote "Furthermore, researchers can not simply choose to compare rank orders of item means across languages, with the expectation that even if one sub-population is higher in the dimension of interest than another, well translated items should retain the same relative rank orderings" (p. 151). He notes that if the test theory being used incorporates the parameter of item discriminating power, this expectation will often prove false. The theories considered here do not include the concept of discriminating power for reasons given earlier.

MULTILEVEL RESPONSES

The Kiasuism Scale

Empirical studies of the effects of cultural and language differences have been made using data on the *Kiasuism* scale provided by Ho, Munro, and

Carr (1999) using consistent ordering of total tied-ranks scoring of items within each culture and the ordinal correlations between item total tied-ranks scores for pairs of country samples.

The concept of Kiasuism originated in Singapore and appears to have a number of aspects such as: Greed, Money conscious, Winning, Preventing others from winning, Rushing, and Getting value for money. It has been hailed by Ho as the one national trait that most Singaporeans recognize and acknowledge. The question arises as to the extent to which the 49 Kiasu items define the same scale in different cultures and languages. We report on the results of investigating this question. The data for this study were obtained from the 49-item scale of Kiasuism items scored polytomously using four ordered categories. The example of an item shown in the instructions is:

Circle ONE number only for each answer. There are no right or wrong answers. Here is an example:

Q. Do you enjoy watching television?

NOT AT ALL	A LITTLE	A LOT	DEFINITELY
LIKE ME	LIKE ME	LIKE ME	LIKE ME
1 -------------------- 2 ---------------- 3 --------------- 4			

The items are usually scored using the four arbitrary integers 1, 2, 3, or 4. A preliminary study was carried out in Australia and Singapore for the purpose of selecting items on the basis of discriminating power and the internal consistency of the scale as measured by α. The responses obtained from subjects in the main study were transformed to tied-ranks scores for items by using the computer program in Appendix A. The tied-ranks scores were then used to calculate W and α for each cultural and language sample studied.

Crosscultural Data

Data were available from university students from five different cultural contexts—Singapore (146 cases), Australia (134 cases), India (183 cases), Taiwan (91 cases), and Japan (195 cases). In each case the α value for subjects was statistically significant and approximately 0.9, indicating that the items established an ordering of subjects. For each sample there were also highly significant values of α for items ranked by subjects with values ranging from .95 to .98.

The data were made available by Dr. Don Munro and the computer analysis was carried out by Dr. Mark Chorlton whose assistance is acknowledged with thanks. Spearman's Rho was also calculated for the orders of the total tied-ranks item scores between each of the 10 pairs of cultural and language samples.

Subjects from Singapore, Australia, and India were all tested in English, which is the national language for Singapore and Australia. Taiwanese and Japanese subjects were tested in Chinese and Japanese languages, respectively. The Indian subjects were university students who knew enough English to be tested in that language. The comparisons therefore were for cultural differences among these three English-language cultural groups (i.e., Singapore, India, and Australia). Comparisons involving Taiwan or Japan cultures or both involved both language and culture differences.

Results

It would be expected that the agreement in item ordering might be much lower for comparisons involving the Taiwanese and Japanese because of language and culture differences. This turned out to be true for the Chinese in Taiwan but not for the Japanese. The results of the ordinal comparisons of items are presented in Table 10.1

In Table 10.1, the α values for the total tied-ranks scores for items appear in the diagonals and the ordinal Spearman ρ values between the tied-rank scores for each pair of countries appear in the relevant above-diagonal cells of the table. The largest of the row and column totals is that for the Australian sample, that is 3.888, which includes three of the four highest above-diagonal entries. This result may be due to the fact that the pretest was carried out in Australia. Given the high α_i values it can be assumed that the items form a scale in each country; but the rank-order correlations between items in some pairs of countries are so low as to suggest that the scales are not the same in these pairs.

TABLE 10.1
Coefficient α for Tied-Ranks Items Scores in Each Culture
and Spearman's ρ Between Orders for Each Pair of Cultures

Cultures	Japan	Singapore	Australia	India	Taiwan
Japanese	.984	.659	.813	.519	.475
Singaporean		.983	.711	.510	.495
Australian			.979	.717	.660
Indian				.973	.664
Taiwanese					.950
Total	3.450	3.338	3.888	3.391	3.244

Thus the Kiassu questionnaire might possibly be suitable for comparing Japanese and Australian university students because the popularity of the items correlates .813 between the two samples. However, the Japanese subjects should not be compared with those from Singapore, India, or Taiwan cultural contexts. With correlations of .717 and .711 respectively, the instrument would be less suitable for comparing subjects from India and Singapore with Australians, but they should not be compared with each other on this dimension using this instrument because the key correlation is as low as .510.

Conclusions

In view of the low correlation between the popularities for Taiwan and any other culture, there is no basis for comparing people from Taiwan with those from any of the other countries considered in this study. This result could perhaps be attributed to the language and culture differences observable in Taiwan when compared with the other cultures.

The only differences in raw score, which can justifiably be tested using this scale, are Australia with India, Japan, and Singapore. From Table 10.2 the only significant difference is that of 14.7 on the Kiasu scale between Australia and Singapore.

To interpret this difference one must consider that Kiasuism is a syndrome that amalgamates:

1. Greed
2. Grabbing
3. Selfishness
4. Fear of losing out
5. Striving for one's best
6. Competitiveness
7. Exhausting all means of doing things that may or not be dependent on the intentions, attitudes, needs of the person, and that may or may not be at the expense of another person.

Motivations associated with this syndrome are:

1. Wanting to be first
2. Not wanting to be last
3. Keeping up with the crowd

TABLE 10.2
Average Kiasu Raw Scores for Five Countries

Country	Cases	Mean	SD
Singapore	146	85.49	13.60
Taiwan	91	95.92	19.46
Japan	195	98.51	17.94
Australia	134	100.20	17.65
India	183	100.31	19.00

From the results of Ho (1998, p. 123) in terms of total of raw item scores for the five countries, it can be seen that the preceding table can be constructed.

From these results of the country comparisons it is clear that the Australian university students were much higher on the Kiasu scale than the Singapore students, which means that the Australians were much more self-centered in terms of the Kiasu scale than were the Singaporeans. From the data on rank order correlations between total tied-rank scores for items, these two countries are comparable on the Kiasu scale and there is a statistically significant difference between them. The other pairs of countries that are comparable are Australia and Japan and Australia and India. In neither case are the differences between the means for the two countries statistically significant.

SUMMARY

From the analyses of crosscultural data it can be seen that ordinal test theory leads to the use of the rankings of items by subjects to demonstrate the possibility of a latent scale. In the data from the Kiasu Scale it was clear that the items formed a latent scale in all countries. The rank order correlations between the orders in the pairs of countries suggested that the latent scale was not the same in each of pair of cultures.

Comparisons of ethnic groups' performances on tests have resulted in controversial conclusions for many years. We have pointed out here that it is obvious a test is not measuring the same thing in two groups unless the order of difficulty or popularity of the items is very similar. The fact that such comparisons of relative difficulty have hardly ever been made makes virtually all such comparisons moot. Until it has been demonstrated that a test is measuring the same thing in different groups, comparisons of the groups' average performances is irrelevant. Group differences may simply mean that the groups are doing different things with different relative success.

This chapter has emphasized the need to test the hypothesis that a set of items defines a scale by calculating the extent to which the items are ordered the same way by subjects with widely different total tied-ranks scores on the test.

Given a statistically significant large W and thus α of sufficient size for ordering items, the consistency of the items in ordering the subjects should also be examined by W and α. Given satisfactory results from this form of analysis for two different cultural or national groups, the orderings of the items by the two groups must be correlated to determine whether or not the scales in the two groups are sufficiently close to make comparisons on the common dimension plausible. In practice, as shown by the example using the Kiasuism Scale, it is very difficult to construct scales sufficiently close to each other in pairs of cultures. Of the 10 comparisons only 3 had comparable scales and, of these, one pair performed significantly differently on their common scale. It would be interesting to speculate on what may have caused the large difference between the Singapore and Australian samples on the Kiasuism Scale and carry out further empirical studies.

Appendix A

**FLOW CHART FOR A PROGRAM TO CARRY OUT
A COMPLETE ITEM ANALYSIS OF ITEMS IN A TEST
OR SCALE USING A SMALL PERSONAL COMPUTER**

In most books on testing, the methods of item analysis described apply only to dichotomous items scored 1 or 0. However, methods for polytomous items with any number of ordered response categories should also be made available. In case of either dichotomous or polytomous items the scores used mostly in practice take arbitrary integral values such as 0 or 1 for dichotomous items and 1, 2, 3, 4 or 5 for polytomous items. As we have seen, there is no scientific justification for such scoring. The statistical tests applied almost always relate only to the extent to which the items, b, consistently order the persons, p. However, for a complete examination of a test or scale it is also necessary to study the extent to which the persons consistently order the items and so justify the assumption of a latent dimension underlying the subjects' performances. Table A.1 illustrates the method of analysis that could be used for dichotomous items as well as other polytomous items.

The data in the table were part of those collected by the Behavioral Science Research Institute in Bangkok using some items from an intrinsic motivation scale. They consist of the responses X_{ij} given by $n = 10$ persons, p_i to $M =$ ten 5-category items, b_j, with categories numbered $1 \ldots 5$. The totals for each person and for each item are also given.

From these item-person data it is possible to calculate the consistency, α_p, with which the items order the persons and also the consistency α, with

TABLE A.1
Raw Data for 10 Persons and 10 Items

Persons	Items										Total
	1	2	3	4	5	6	7	8	9	10	
1	5	4	3	4	3	3	3	4	3	4	36
2	2	5	3	4	3	3	2	5	5	5	37
3	2	4	4	5	3	4	3	5	5	4	39
4	5	3	4	4	1	3	2	4	5	5	36
5	2	5	5	3	4	5	4	3	5	5	41
6	3	5	5	4	3	4	2	4	5	3	38
7	2	4	5	5	2	5	5	4	5	4	41
8	2	5	3	4	3	4	3	3	5	4	36
9	2	5	5	5	3	4	3	5	5	5	42
10	1	4	4	5	2	3	3	3	3	4	32
Total	26	44	41	43	27	38	30	40	46	43	378

which the persons order the items.[1] The first step in computing the αs is to square the entries, as shown in Table A.2.

TABLE A.2
The Squares of the Cell Entries in Table A.1

Persons	Items									
	1	2	3	4	5	6	7	8	9	10
1	25	16	9	16	9	9	9	16	9	16
2	4	25	9	16	9	9	4	25	25	25
3	4	16	16	25	9	16	9	25	25	16
4	25	9	16	16	1	9	4	16	25	25
5	4	25	25	9	16	25	16	9	25	25
6	9	25	25	16	9	16	4	16	25	9
7	4	16	25	25	4	25	25	16	25	16
8	4	25	9	16	9	16	9	9	25	16
9	4	25	25	25	9	16	9	25	25	25
10	1	16	16	25	4	9	9	9	9	16
	84	198	205	189	79	150	98	166	218	189

The grand total of the squares = 1576. This grand total of 1576, less the correction term, $(\Sigma X_{ij})^2/mn = 378^2/(100) = 1428.84$, produces a total sum of

---

[1]Gratitude is expressed to Dr. Intasuwan, Director of the Institute, for making these data available.

squares (SS_T) of deviations from the mean = 147.16 since 378 is the grand total from Table A.1. The sum of squares for persons (SS_P) and for items (SS_I) may be found from the row and column totals squared, respectively.

	Row Totals Squared	Columns Totals Squared
	1296	676
	1369	1936
	1521	1681
	1296	1849
	1681	729
	1444	1444
	1681	900
	1296	1600
	1764	2116
	1024	1849
Total	14372	14780

Persons and Items SS may be obtained by subtracting the correction term 1428.84 from each of these two totals, divided by 10, which gives 8.36 and 49.16. The two-way ANOVA table may be presented as:

TABLE A.3
Analysis Of Variance

	Sum of Squares	D.F.	Variance	
Persons	8.36	9	.93	N.S.
Items	49.16	9	5.46	$p < .01$
Interaction	89.64	81	1.106	N.S.
Total	147.16	99		

The coefficient α_p for persons = $(.93 - 1.1)/.93 = -.18$. Thus the lack of consistent differentiation between persons by the items leads to a negative α_p. However, α_i for items = $(5.46 - 1.1)/5.46 = .80$, which indicates a considerable degree of consistency in the persons' differentiation between items. A relationship can be shown between α_p and α_i by equating the interaction term with a value of 1.1 in this case; see chapter 4. Thus:

$$(1 - \alpha_p)\text{Var}_p = \text{Interaction Variance} = (1 - \alpha_i)\text{Var}_i.$$

and by equating the first and third terms and re-arranging:

$$\alpha_i = 1 - (1 - \alpha_p)\text{Var}_p/\text{Var}_i.$$

Although this analysis corresponds to the standard ANOVA recommended in books on test construction, it can be objected to on the grounds that it assumes that the arbitrary integers 1,2,3,4, and 5 correspond to equally spaced units on a scale of measurement. Critiques of this assumption refer to it as measuring by fiat. It is much more justifiable to assume that the item scores simply order the subjects, and these orders should be combined in some justifiable way to produce a proper ordering of the persons. The method of doing this uses tied-ranks scores (see Keats, 1995 and chapter 5), and the modification of the flowchart to use this more efficient method is presented next. In practice, researchers may wish to use both methods. It has been found that the tied-ranks scores yield greater internal consistency than the arbitrary integral scores (see Keats, 1995). It should be recalled that in the case of dichotomous items, the 0,1 scoring produces the same order as the tied-ranks scoring and so the previous formulae are appropriate.

For this form of analysis it is important to consider the ordering of items by persons. See Table A.4 for a consideration of Person 1 and the scores given to the 10 items.

TABLE A.4
Tied-Ranks Scores for Items

Score values as arbitrary integers	1	2	3	4	5
Person 1			b_3	b_2	b_1
			b_5	b_4	
			b_6	b_8	
			b_7	b_{10}	
			b_9		
Frequencies	0	0	5	4	1
Cumulative frequencies	0	0	5	9	10
Tied-ranks scores	0	0	3	$7\frac{1}{2}$	10

Thus the scores for Person 1 for items are transformed from:

b1	b2	b3	b4	b5	b6	b7	b8	b9	b10	Total
5	4	3	4	3	3	3	4	3	4	36

to tied-ranks scores of:

10	7½	3	7½	3	3	3	7½	3	7½	55

Corresponding tied-ranks scores for Persons 2,3....10 can be similarly shown in Table A.5.

TABLE A.5
Tied Ranks Scores for Other Persons 2-10

| Persons | Items | | | | | | | | | | Total |
	1	2	3	4	5	6	7	8	9	10	
2	1½	8½	4	6	4	4	1½	8½	8½	8½	55
3	1	5½	5½	9	2½	5½	2½	9	9	5½	55
4	9	3½	6	6	1	3½	2	6	9	9	55
5	1	8	8	2½	4½	8	4½	2½	8	8	55
6	3	9	9	6	3	6	1	6	9	3	55
7	1½	4	8	8	1½	8	8	4	8	4	55
8	1	9½	3½	7	3½	7	3½	3½	9½	7	55
9	1	7½	7½	7½	2½	4	2½	7½	7½	7½	55
10	1	8	8	10	2	4½	4½	4½	4½	8	55

Note that the row totals corresponding to individuals all equal 55 so that the individual differences have been eliminated by transforming to tied-ranks scores for the items. Proceeding to analysis of variance, the sum of squares for persons is zero. The total sum of squares is 640.5 and the sum of squares for items is 301.6. See Table A.6, from which it may be calculated that $\alpha_{i,} = (33.51 - 4.18)/33.51 = .875$ which is higher than the value of .80 obtained with the untransformed data, and this is in keeping with the findings of Keats (1995).

TABLE A.6
Analysis of Variance

	Sum of Squares	D.F.	Variance	
Items	301.6	9	33.51	$p < .01$
Persons	Nil	9	Nil	
Interaction	338.9	81	4.18	
Total	640.5	99		

TIED-RANKS SCORES FOR ITEMS

Just as it was shown to be possible to transform the arbitrary integral item scores for each person into tied-ranks scores, it is possible to transform the integral scores for each item into tied-ranks scores for each person on that item.

If we consider Item 1 with scores for each of the 10 persons:

Score values	1	2	3	4	5
Frequency	1	6	1	0	2
Cumulative frequency	1	7	8	8	10
Tied-Ranks Score	1	4½	8	8½	9½

Thus the integral scores 1. . . .5 on Item 1 for each person are transformed to tied-ranks scores:

b1	Interaction	1	Tied-Ranks
p1	5	to	9½
p2	2	to	4½
p3	2	to	4½
p4	5	to	9½
p5	2	to	4½
p6	3	to	8
p7	2	to	4½
p8	2	to	4½
p9	2	to	4½
p10	1	to	1
Total	26	to	55

Thus the corresponding scores for Items 2 to 10 for each person are seen in Table A.7.

TABLE A.7
Tied-Ranks Scores for Items 2–10

Persons	Items									Total for 10 items
	2	3	4	5	6	7	8	9	10	
1	3½	2	4	6½	2½	6	5½	1½	4	45
2	8	2	4	6½	2½	2	9	6½	8½	53½
3	3½	5	8½	6½	6½	6	9	6½	4	60
4	1	5	4	1	2½	2	5½	6½	8½	45½
5	8	8½	1	10	9½	9	2	6½	8½	67½
6	8	8½	4	6½	6½	2	5½	6½	1	56½
7	3½	8½	8½	2½	9½	10	5½	6½	4	63
8	8	2	4	6½	6½	6	2	6½	4	50
9	8	8½	8½	6½	6½	6	9	6½	8½	72½
10	3½	5	8½	2½	2½	6	2	1½	4	36½
Total	55	55	55	55	55	55	55	55	55	

Table A.8 shows the ANOVA of these tied-ranks scores. The SS_T from the mean of the 100 numbers is 658.5 and the SS_p is 111.35.

TABLE A.8
Analysis of Variance

	S of S	D.F.	Variance	
Persons	111.35	9	12.37	N.S.
Items	nil	9	nil	
Interaction	547.15	81	6.755	
Total	658.5	99		

Then Internal Consistency of items ordering persons:

$$\alpha_p = (12.37 - 6.755)/12.37 = .45$$

which is still not statistically significant from the analysis of variance but is higher than the negative value obtained from the integral scores, suggesting some degree of consistency in the way individuals are ranked by the items.

RELATIONSHIPS TO KENDALL'S CONCORDANCE COEFFICIENT W

The objection has been noted that neither the arbitrary integral scores nor the tied-ranks scores lie on an interval scale. However, Kendall's W has been shown to be subject to a χ^2 test and also, when tied ranks are used to be related to α by the equation:

$$W = (m - [m - 1]\alpha)^{-1}$$

where m is the number of rankings.

Thus the α values $-.18, .45, .80$, and $.875$ correspond to W values of $.085$, $.17, .35$, and $.47$. It should be noted that W can never be negative whereas α can be. This makes W more satisfactory as it is difficult to interpret what negative internal consistency could mean. Because of the algebraic relationship between α and W we have a third definition of α in addition to the Kuder–Richardson correlational definition and the Cronbach analysis of variance definition. The third definition is in terms of ordinal consistency and is appropriate for tied ranks scores. The formula for χ^2 is $m(n - 1)W$ with $n - 1$ degrees of freedom, where n is the number of things (i.e., objects or persons) ranked (see Kendall, 1975 p. 98). In the present example, m and n are both equal to 10. and χ^2 values for each W are 7.65, 15.3, 31.5, and 42.3, with 9 degrees of freedom and only the last two values being statistically significant.

The totals of tied-ranks scores provide the best estimate of the underlying rank order of the persons or items as shown by Kendall (1975, pp. 101–102) in a least squares sense. This result explains the usually higher internal consistencies of tied-rank scores. Cliff (1996, pp. 49 and 170) draws attention to W and its relationship to the average Spearman's ρ, which he expresses a preference for.

CONJOINT ORDERING

The tied-ranks procedure yields the best estimate of the order of the persons on the one hand and the best estimate of the order of the items on the other. However, there is no single table that produces both of these orderings in one operation. The table that produces the best order for persons produces no ordering for items.

PRINTOUT FROM THE PROGRAM

In the printout from this program, all the values of W, α and χ^2 as well as the total tied-ranks scores for items and persons and their orders should be listed.

As an example of the results obtained from the computer program calculating α, W, and chi^2 for a given set of data the results are given in Table A.9. The test of 25 items of five ordered response categories related to the satisfaction 194 students reported with aspects of their degree course. Their responses ranged from (0) *no satisfaction* to (4) *completely satisfied*. Data were made available by Dr. Don Munro and analyzed using a program written by Mr. Scott Brown with Dr. Mark Chorlton.

It is to be noted that the α values for the raw data for subjects are slightly higher than those for tied-ranks data. A similar relationship holds for items. The results for subjects for the three tests analyzed here are contrary to those reported by Keats (1995) for six other tests but it must be realized that the size of the α values reported here is much greater than that reported in Keats (1995). Further results are needed on this topic but there may be no consistent gain in internal consistency from shifting from raw scores to tied-rank scores for either subjects or items unless the α values are somewhat low in the first place.

TABLE A.9
Data From the Satisfaction Scale

			Raw Results			
Source	df	MS	α	W	χ^2	p-value
Subjects	193	7.493	0.957	0.493	2295.070	0.00000
Items	24	87.372	0.996	0.585	2822.628	0.00000
Interactions	4632	0.321				
Total	4849	1.037				

			Subject-Ranked Results			
Source	df	MS	α	W	χ^2	p-value
Subjects	193	0.000	0.000	0.000	0.000	0.50000
Items	24	1094.234	0.964	0.127	614.465	0.00000
Interactions	4632	38.850				
Total	4849	42.527				

			Item-Ranked Results			
Source	df	MS	α	W	χ^2	p-value
Subjects	193	22887.014	0.913	0.323	1504.408	0.00000
Items	24	0.0000	0.000	0.000	0.000	0.50000
Interactions	4632	1997.755				
Total	4849	2819.3015				

Another topic needing exploration is the correlation between raw scores and tied-rank scores separately for subjects and items. This topic is examined for all data available and reported next.

CORRELATIONS BETWEEN RAW SCORES AND TIED-RANKS SCORES

In the case of the Satisfaction Test reported earlier, the correlation between the item raw scores and the item tied-ranks scores was .812, whereas for persons raw scores and persons tied-ranks scores the correlation was much higher at .932. In the data from the Importance Rating Scale the corresponding correlations were .849 and .877, which were much closer together.

Appendix B

STATISTICAL TABLES

The following tables will be provided from standard sources:

TABLE B.1
Critical Values of the Chi-squared Distribution

	α						
df	.500	.250	.100	.050	.025	.010	.005
1	0.455	1.32	2.71	3.84	5.02	6.63	7.88
2	1.39	2.77	4.61	5.99	7.38	9.21	10.6
3	2.37	4.11	6.25	7.81	9.35	11.3	12.8
4	3.36	5.39	7.78	9.49	11.1	13.3	14.9
5	4.35	6.63	9.24	11.1	12.8	15.1	16.7
6	5.35	7.84	10.6	12.6	14.4	16.8	18.5
7	6.35	9.04	12.0	14.1	16.0	18.5	20.3
8	7.34	10.2	13.4	15.5	17.5	20.1	22.0
9	8.34	11.4	14.7	16.9	19.0	21.7	23.6
10	9.34	12.5	16.0	18.3	20.5	23.2	25.2
11	10.3	13.7	17.3	19.7	21.9	24.7	26.8
12	11.3	14.8	18.5	21.0	23.3	26.2	28.3
13	12.3	16.0	19.8	22.4	24.7	27.7	29.8
14	13.3	17.1	21.1	23.7	26.1	29.1	31.3
15	14.3	18.2	22.3	25.0	27.5	30.6	32.8
16	15.3	19.4	23.5	26.3	28.8	32.0	34.3
17	16.3	20.5	24.8	27.6	30.2	33.4	35.7
18	17.3	21.6	26.0	28.9	31.5	34.8	37.2
19	18.3	22.7	27.2	30.1	32.9	36.2	38.6
20	19.3	23.8	28.4	31.4	34.2	37.6	40.0
21	20.3	24.9	29.6	32.7	35.5	38.9	41.4
22	21.3	26.0	30.8	33.9	36.8	40.3	42.8
23	22.3	27.1	32.0	35.2	38.1	41.6	44.2
24	23.3	28.2	33.2	36.4	39.4	43.0	45.6
25	24.3	29.3	34.4	37.7	40.6	44.3	46.9
26	25.3	30.4	35.6	38.9	41.9	45.6	48.3
27	26.3	31.5	36.7	40.1	43.2	47.0	49.6
28	27.3	32.6	37.9	41.3	44.5	48.3	51.0
29	28.3	33.7	39.1	42.6	45.7	49.6	52.3
30	29.3	34.8	40.3	43.8	47.0	50.9	53.7

TABLE B.2
Two-tailed α-levels of the t Distribution

	.500	.200	.100	.050	.020	.010	.001
1	1.000	3.078	6.314	12.706	31.821	63.657	636.619
2	0.816	1.886	2.920	4.303	6.965	9.925	31.598
3	0.765	1.638	2.353	3.182	4.541	5.841	12.941
4	0.741	1.533	2.132	2.776	3.747	4.604	8.610
5	0.727	1.476	2.015	2.571	3.365	4.032	6.859
6	0.718	1.440	1.943	2.447	3.143	3.707	5.959
7	0.711	1.415	1.895	2.365	2.998	3.499	5.405
8	0.706	1.397	1.860	2.306	2.896	3.355	5.041
9	0.703	1.383	1.833	2.262	2.821	3.250	4.781
10	0.700	1.372	1.812	2.228	2.764	3.169	4.587
11	0.697	1.363	1.796	2.201	2.718	3.106	4.437
12	0.695	1.356	1.782	2.179	2.681	3.055	4.318
13	0.694	1.350	1.771	2.160	2.650	3.012	4.221
14	0.692	1.345	1.761	2.145	2.624	2.977	4.140
15	0.691	1.341	1.753	2.131	2.602	2.947	4.073
16	0.690	1.337	1.746	2.120	2.583	2.921	4.015
17	0.689	1.333	1.740	10	2.567	2.898	3.965
18	0.688	1.330	1.734	2.101	2.552	2.878	3.922
19	0.688	1.328	1.729	2.093	2.539	2.861	3.883
20	0.687	1.325	1.725	2.086	2.528	2.845	3.850
21	0.686	1.323	1.721	2.080	2.518	2.831	3.819
22	0.686	1.321	1.717	2.074	2.508	2.819	3.792
23	0.685	1.319	1.714	2.069	2.500	2.807	3.767
24	0.685	1.318	1.711	2.064	2.492	2.797	3.745
25	0.684	1.316	1.708	2.060	2.485	2.787	3.725
26	0.684	1.315	1.706	2.056	2.479	2.779	3.707
27	0.684	1.314	1.703	2.052	2.473	2.771	3.690
28	0.683	1.313	1.701	2.048	2.467	2.763	3.674
29	0.683	1.311	1.699	2.045	2.462	2.756	3.659
30	0.683	1.310	1.697	2.042	2.457	2.750	3.646
40	0.681	1.303	1.684	2.021	2.423	2.704	3.551
60	0.679	1.296	1.671	2.000	2.390	2.660	3.460
120	0.677	1.289	1.658	1.980	2.358	2.617	3.373
∞	0.674	1.282	1.645	1.960	2.326	2.576	3.291

Adapted from Table III of R. A. Fisher and F. Yates, *Statistical Tables for Biological, Agricultural, and Medical Research*, by Oliver & Boyd Ltd., Edinburgh.

TABLE B.3
Cumulative Normal Distribution

z	0.00	0.01	0.02	0.03	0.04	0.05	0.06	0.07	0.08	0.09
0.0	0.5000	0.5040	0.5080	0.5120	0.5160	0.5199	0.5239	0.5279	0.5319	0.5359
0.1	0.5398	0.5438	0.5478	0.5517	0.5557	0.5596	0.5636	0.5675	0.5714	0.5753
0.2	0.5793	0.5832	0.5871	0.5910	0.5948	0.5987	0.6026	0.6064	0.6103	0.6141
0.3	0.6179	0.6217	0.6255	0.6293	0.6331	0.6368	0.6406	0.6443	0.6480	0.6517
0.4	0.6554	0.6591	0.6628	0.6664	0.6700	0.6736	0.6772	0.6808	0.6844	0.6879
0.5	0.6915	0.6950	0.6985	0.7019	0.7054	0.7088	0.7123	0.7157	0.7190	0.7224
0.6	0.7257	0.7291	0.7324	0.7357	0.7389	0.7422	0.7454	0.7486	0.7517	0.7549
0.7	0.7580	0.7611	0.7642	0.7673	0.7704	0.7734	0.7764	0.7794	0.7823	0.7852
0.8	0.7881	0.7910	0.7939	0.7967	0.7995	0.8023	0.8051	0.8078	0.8106	0.8133
0.9	0.8159	0.8186	0.8212	0.8238	0.8264	0.8289	0.8315	0.8340	0.8365	0.8389
1.0	0.8413	0.8438	0.8461	0.8485	0.8508	0.8531	0.8554	0.8577	0.8599	0.8621
1.1	0.8643	0.8665	0.8686	0.8708	0.8729	0.8749	0.8770	0.8790	0.8810	0.8830
1.2	0.8849	0.8869	0.8888	0.8907	0.8925	0.8944	0.8962	0.8980	0.8997	0.9015
1.3	0.9032	0.9049	0.9066	0.9082	0.9099	0.9115	0.9131	0.9147	0.9162	0.9177
1.4	0.9192	0.9207	0.9222	0.9236	0.9251	0.9265	0.9279	0.9292	0.9306	0.9319
1.5	0.9332	0.9345	0.9357	0.9370	0.9382	0.9394	0.9406	0.9418	0.9429	0.9441
1.6	0.9452	0.9463	0.9474	0.9484	0.9495	0.9505	0.9515	0.9525	0.9535	0.9545
1.7	0.9554	0.9564	0.9573	0.9582	0.9591	0.9599	0.9608	0.9616	0.9625	0.9633
1.8	0.9641	0.9649	0.9656	0.9664	0.9671	0.9678	0.9686	0.9693	0.9699	0.9706
1.9	0.9713	0.9719	0.9726	0.9732	0.9738	0.9744	0.9750	0.9756	0.9761	0.9767
2.0	0.9772	0.9778	0.9783	0.9788	0.9793	0.9798	0.9803	0.9808	0.9812	0.9817
2.1	0.9821	0.9826	0.9830	0.9834	0.9838	0.9842	0.9846	0.9850	0.9854	0.9857
2.2	0.9861	0.9864	0.9868	0.9871	0.9875	0.9878	0.9881	0.9884	0.9887	0.9890
2.3	0.9893	0.9896	0.9898	0.9901	0.9904	0.9906	0.9909	0.9911	0.9913	0.9916
2.4	0.9918	0.9920	0.9922	0.9925	0.9927	0.9929	0.9931	0.9932	0.9934	0.9936
2.5	0.9938	0.9940	0.9941	0.9943	0.9945	0.9946	0.9948	0.9949	0.9951	0.9952
2.6	0.9953	0.9955	0.9956	0.9957	0.9959	0.9960	0.9961	0.9962	0.9963	0.9964
2.7	0.9965	0.9966	0.9967	0.9968	0.9969	0.9970	0.9971	0.9972	0.9973	0.9974
2.8	0.9974	0.9975	0.9976	0.9977	0.9977	0.9978	0.9979	0.9979	0.9980	0.9981
2.9	0.9981	0.9982	0.9982	0.9983	0.9984	0.9984	0.9985	0.9985	0.9986	0.9986
3.0	0.9987	0.9987	0.9987	0.9988	0.9988	0.9989	0.9989	0.9989	0.9990	0.9990
3.1	0.9990	0.9991	0.9991	0.9991	0.9992	0.9992	0.9992	0.9992	0.9993	0.9993
3.2	0.9993	0.9993	0.9994	0.9994	0.9994	0.9994	0.9994	0.9995	0.9995	0.9995
3.3	0.9995	0.9995	0.9995	0.9996	0.9996	0.9996	0.9996	0.9996	0.9996	0.9997
3.4	0.9997	0.9997	0.9997	0.9997	0.9997	0.9997	0.9997	0.9997	0.9997	0.9998

TABLE B.4
Critical Values of the F Distribution $\alpha = .05$ and $.01$

df_1 degrees of freedom (for greater mean square)

df_2	1	2	3	4	5	6	7	8	9	10	11	12
1	161	200	216	225	230	234	237	239	241	242	243	244
	4,052	**4,999**	**5,403**	**5,625**	**5,764**	**5,859**	**5,928**	**5,981**	**6,022**	**6,056**	**6,082**	**6,106**
2	18.51	19.00	19.16	19.25	19.30	19.33	19.36	19.37	19.38	19.39	19.40	19.41
	98.49	**99.00**	**99.17**	**99.25**	**99.30**	**99.33**	**99.34**	**99.36**	**99.38**	**99.40**	**99.41**	**99.42**
3	10.13	9.55	9.28	9.12	9.01	8.94	8.88	8.84	8.81	8.78	8.76	8.74
	34.12	**30.82**	**29.46**	**28.71**	**28.24**	**27.91**	**27.67**	**27.49**	**27.34**	**27.23**	**27.13**	**27.05**
4	7.71	6.94	6.59	6.39	6.26	6.16	6.09	6.04	6.00	5.96	5.93	5.91
	21.20	**18.00**	**16.69**	**15.98**	**15.52**	**15.21**	**14.98**	**14.80**	**14.66**	**14.54**	**14.45**	**14.37**
5	6.61	5.79	5.41	5.19	5.05	4.95	4.88	4.82	4.78	4.74	4.70	4.68
	16.26	**13.27**	**12.06**	**11.39**	**10.97**	**10.67**	**10.45**	**10.27**	**10.15**	**10.05**	**9.96**	**9.89**
6	5.99	5.14	4.76	4.53	4.39	4.28	4.21	4.15	4.10	4.06	4.03	4.00
	13.74	**10.92**	**9.78**	**9.15**	**8.75**	**8.47**	**8.26**	**8.10**	**7.98**	**7.87**	**7.79**	**7.72**
7	5.59	4.74	4.35	4.12	3.97	3.87	3.79	3.73	3.68	3.63	3.60	3.57
	12.25	**9.55**	**8.45**	**7.85**	**7.46**	**7.19**	**7.00**	**6.84**	**6.71**	**6.62**	**6.54**	**6.47**
8	5.32	4.46	4.07	3.84	3.69	3.58	3.50	3.44	3.39	3.34	3.31	3.28
	11.26	**8.65**	**7.59**	**7.01**	**6.63**	**6.37**	**6.19**	**6.03**	**5.91**	**5.82**	**5.74**	**5.67**
9	5.12	4.26	3.86	3.63	3.48	3.37	3.29	3.23	3.18	3.13	3.10	3.07
	10.56	**8.02**	**6.99**	**6.42**	**6.06**	**5.80**	**5.62**	**5.47**	**5.35**	**5.26**	**5.18**	**5.11**
10	4.96	4.10	3.71	3.48	3.33	3.22	3.14	3.07	3.02	2.97	2.94	2.91
	10.04	**7.56**	**6.55**	**5.99**	**5.64**	**5.39**	**5.21**	**5.06**	**4.95**	**4.85**	**4.78**	**4.71**
11	4.84	3.98	3.59	3.36	3.20	3.09	3.01	2.95	2.90	2.86	2.82	2.79
	9.65	**7.20**	**6.22**	**5.67**	**5.32**	**5.07**	**4.88**	**4.74**	**4.63**	**4.54**	**4.46**	**4.40**

(Continued)

TABLE B.4
(Continued)

	df₁ degrees of freedom (for greater mean square)											
df_2	1	2	3	4	5	6	7	8	9	10	11	12
12	4.75	3.88	3.49	3.26	3.11	3.00	2.92	2.85	2.80	2.76	2.72	2.69
	9.33	**6.93**	**5.95**	**5.41**	**5.06**	**4.82**	**4.65**	**4.50**	**4.39**	**4.30**	**4.22**	**4.16**
13	4.67	3.80	3.41	3.18	3.02	2.92	2.84	2.77	2.72	2.67	2.63	2.60
	9.07	**6.70**	**5.74**	**5.20**	**4.86**	**4.62**	**4.44**	**4.30**	**4.19**	**4.10**	**4.02**	**3.96**
14	4.60	3.74	3.34	3.11	2.96	2.85	2.77	2.70	2.65	2.60	2.56	2.53
	8.86	**6.51**	**5.56**	**5.03**	**4.69**	**4.46**	**4.28**	**4.14**	**4.03**	**3.94**	**3.86**	**3.80**
15	4.54	3.68	3.29	3.06	2.90	2.79	2.70	2.64	2.59	2.55	2.51	2.48
	8.68	**6.36**	**5.42**	**4.89**	**4.56**	**4.32**	**4.14**	**4.00**	**3.89**	**3.80**	**3.73**	**3.67**
16	4.49	3.63	3.24	3.01	2.85	2.74	2.66	2.59	2.54	2.49	2.45	2.42
	8.53	**6.23**	**5.29**	**4.77**	**4.44**	**4.20**	**4.03**	**3.89**	**3.78**	**3.69**	**3.61**	**3.55**
17	4.45	3.59	3.20	2.96	2.81	2.70	2.62	2.55	2.50	2.45	2.41	2.38
	8.40	**6.11**	**5.18**	**4.67**	**4.34**	**4.10**	**3.93**	**3.79**	**3.68**	**3.59**	**3.52**	**3.45**
18	4.41	3.55	3.16	2.93	2.77	2.66	2.58	2.51	2.46	2.41	2.37	2.34
	8.28	**6.01**	**5.09**	**4.58**	**4.25**	**4.01**	**3.85**	**3.71**	**3.60**	**3.51**	**3.44**	**3.37**
19	4.38	3.52	3.13	2.90	2.74	2.63	2.55	2.48	2.43	2.38	2.34	2.31
	8.18	**5.93**	**5.01**	**4.50**	**4.17**	**3.94**	**3.77**	**3.63**	**3.52**	**3.43**	**3.36**	**3.30**
20	4.35	3.49	3.10	2.87	2.71	2.60	2.52	2.45	2.40	2.35	2.31	2.28
	8.10	**5.85**	**4.94**	**4.43**	**4.10**	**3.87**	**3.71**	**3.56**	**3.45**	**3.37**	**3.30**	**3.23**
21	4.32	3.47	3.07	2.84	2.68	2.57	2.49	2.42	2.37	2.32	2.28	2.25
	8.02	**5.78**	**4.87**	**4.37**	**4.04**	**3.81**	**3.65**	**3.51**	**3.40**	**3.31**	**3.24**	**3.17**
22	4.30	3.44	3.05	2.82	2.66	2.55	2.47	2.40	2.35	2.30	2.26	2.23
	7.94	**5.72**	**4.82**	**4.31**	**3.99**	**3.76**	**3.59**	**3.45**	**3.35**	**3.26**	**3.18**	**3.12**

df												
23	4.28 / **7.88**	3.42 / **5.66**	3.03 / **4.76**	2.80 / **4.26**	2.64 / **3.94**	2.53 / **3.71**	2.45 / **3.54**	2.38 / **3.41**	2.32 / **3.30**	2.28 / **3.21**	2.24 / **3.14**	2.20 / **3.07**
24	4.26 / **7.82**	3.40 / **5.61**	3.01 / **4.72**	2.78 / **4.22**	2.62 / **3.90**	2.51 / **3.67**	2.43 / **3.50**	2.36 / **3.36**	2.30 / **3.25**	2.26 / **3.17**	2.22 / **3.09**	2.18 / **3.03**
25	4.24 / **7.77**	3.38 / **5.57**	2.99 / **4.68**	2.76 / **4.18**	2.60 / **3.86**	2.49 / **3.63**	2.41 / **3.46**	2.34 / **3.32**	2.28 / **3.21**	2.24 / **3.13**	2.20 / **3.05**	2.16 / **2.99**
26	4.22 / **7.72**	3.37 / **5.53**	2.98 / **4.64**	2.74 / **4.14**	2.59 / **3.82**	2.47 / **3.59**	2.39 / **3.42**	2.32 / **3.29**	2.27 / **3.17**	2.22 / **3.09**	2.18 / **3.02**	2.15 / **2.96**
27	4.21 / **7.68**	3.35 / **5.49**	2.95 / **4.60**	2.73 / **4.11**	2.57 / **3.79**	2.46 / **3.56**	2.37 / **3.39**	2.30 / **3.26**	2.25 / **3.14**	2.20 / **3.06**	2.16 / **2.98**	2.13 / **2.93**
28	4.20 / **7.64**	3.34 / **5.45**	2.95 / **4.57**	2.71 / **4.07**	2.56 / **3.76**	2.44 / **3.53**	2.36 / **3.36**	2.29 / **3.23**	2.24 / **3.11**	2.19 / **3.03**	2.15 / **2.95**	2.12 / **2.90**
29	4.18 / **7.60**	3.33 / **5.42**	2.93 / **4.54**	2.70 / **4.04**	2.54 / **3.73**	2.43 / **3.50**	2.35 / **3.33**	2.28 / **3.20**	2.22 / **3.08**	2.18 / **3.00**	2.14 / **2.92**	2.10 / **2.87**
30	4.17 / **7.56**	3.32 / **5.39**	2.92 / **4.51**	2.69 / **4.02**	2.53 / **3.70**	2.42 / **3.47**	2.34 / **3.30**	2.27 / **3.17**	2.21 / **3.06**	2.16 / **2.98**	2.12 / **2.90**	2.09 / **2.84**
32	4.15 / **7.50**	3.30 / **5.34**	2.90 / **4.46**	2.67 / **3.97**	2.51 / **3.66**	2.40 / **3.42**	2.32 / **3.25**	2.25 / **3.12**	2.19 / **3.01**	2.14 / **2.94**	2.10 / **2.86**	2.07 / **2.80**
34	4.13 / **7.44**	3.28 / **5.29**	2.88 / **4.42**	2.65 / **3.93**	2.49 / **3.61**	2.38 / **3.38**	2.30 / **3.21**	2.23 / **3.08**	2.17 / **2.97**	2.12 / **2.89**	2.08 / **2.82**	2.05 / **2.76**
36	4.11 / **7.39**	3.26 / **5.25**	2.86 / **4.38**	2.63 / **3.89**	2.48 / **3.58**	2.36 / **3.35**	2.28 / **3.18**	2.21 / **3.04**	2.15 / **2.94**	2.10 / **2.86**	2.06 / **2.78**	2.03 / **2.72**
38	4.10 / **7.35**	3.25 / **5.21**	2.85 / **4.34**	2.62 / **3.86**	2.46 / **3.54**	2.35 / **3.32**	2.26 / **3.15**	2.19 / **3.02**	2.14 / **2.91**	2.09 / **2.82**	2.05 / **2.75**	2.02 / **2.69**
40	4.08 / **7.31**	3.23 / **5.18**	2.84 / **4.31**	2.61 / **3.83**	2.45 / **3.51**	2.34 / **3.29**	2.25 / **3.12**	2.18 / **2.99**	2.12 / **2.88**	2.07 / **2.80**	2.04 / **2.73**	2.00 / **2.66**
42	4.07 / **7.27**	3.22 / **5.15**	2.83 / **4.29**	2.59 / **3.80**	2.44 / **3.49**	2.32 / **3.26**	2.24 / **3.10**	2.17 / **2.96**	2.11 / **2.86**	2.06 / **2.77**	2.02 / **2.70**	1.99 / **2.64**

(Continued)

TABLE B.4
(Continued)

					df_1 degrees of freedom (for greater mean square)							
df_2	1	2	3	4	5	6	7	8	9	10	11	12
44	4.06	3.21	2.82	2.58	2.43	2.31	2.23	2.16	2.10	2.05	2.01	1.98
	7.24	**5.12**	**4.26**	**3.78**	**3.46**	**3.24**	**3.07**	**2.94**	**2.84**	**2.75**	**2.68**	**2.62**
46	4.05	3.20	2.81	2.57	2.42	2.30	2.22	2.14	2.09	2.04	2.00	1.97
	7.21	**5.10**	**4.24**	**3.76**	**3.44**	**3.22**	**3.05**	**2.92**	**2.82**	**2.73**	**2.66**	**2.60**
48	4.04	3.19	2.80	2.56	2.41	2.30	2.21	2.14	2.08	2.03	1.99	1.96
	7.19	**5.08**	**4.22**	**3.74**	**3.42**	**3.20**	**3.04**	**2.90**	**2.80**	**2.71**	**2.64**	**2.58**
50	4.03	3.18	2.79	2.56	2.40	2.29	2.20	2.13	2.07	2.02	1.98	1.95
	7.17	**5.06**	**4.20**	**3.72**	**3.41**	**3.18**	**3.02**	**2.88**	**2.78**	**2.70**	**2.62**	**2.56**
55	4.02	3.17	2.78	2.54	2.38	2.27	2.18	2.11	2.05	2.00	1.97	1.93
	7.12	**5.01**	**4.16**	**3.68**	**3.37**	**3.15**	**2.98**	**2.85**	**2.75**	**2.66**	**2.59**	**2.53**
60	4.00	3.15	2.76	2.52	2.37	2.25	2.17	2.10	2.04	1.99	1.95	1.92
	7.08	**4.98**	**4.13**	**3.65**	**3.34**	**3.12**	**2.95**	**2.82**	**2.72**	**2.63**	**2.56**	**2.50**
65	3.99	3.14	2.75	2.51	2.36	2.24	2.15	2.08	2.02	1.98	1.94	1.90
	7.04	**4.95**	**4.10**	**3.62**	**3.31**	**3.09**	**2.93**	**2.79**	**2.70**	**2.61**	**2.54**	**2.47**

210

70	3.98	3.13	2.74	2.50	2.35	2.23	2.14	2.07	2.01	1.97	1.93	1.89
	7.01	**4.92**	**4.08**	**3.60**	**3.29**	**3.07**	**2.91**	**2.77**	**2.67**	**2.59**	**2.51**	**2.45**
80	3.96	3.11	2.72	2.48	2.33	2.21	2.12	2.05	1.99	1.95	1.91	1.88
	6.96	**4.88**	**4.04**	**3.56**	**3.25**	**3.04**	**2.87**	**2.74**	**2.64**	**2.55**	**2.48**	**2.41**
100	3.94	3.09	2.70	2.46	2.30	2.19	2.10	2.03	1.97	1.92	1.88	1.85
	6.90	**4.82**	**3.98**	**3.51**	**3.20**	**2.99**	**2.82**	**2.69**	**2.59**	**2.51**	**2.43**	**2.36**
125	3.92	3.07	2.68	2.44	2.29	2.17	2.08	2.01	1.95	1.90	1.86	1.83
	6.84	**4.78**	**3.94**	**3.47**	**3.17**	**2.95**	**2.79**	**2.65**	**2.56**	**2.47**	**2.40**	**2.33**
150	3.91	3.06	2.67	2.43	2.27	2.16	2.07	2.00	1.94	1.89	1.85	1.82
	6.81	**4.75**	**3.91**	**3.44**	**3.14**	**2.92**	**2.76**	**2.62**	**2.53**	**2.44**	**2.37**	**2.30**
200	3.89	3.04	2.65	2.41	2.26	2.14	2.05	1.98	1.92	1.87	1.83	1.80
	6.76	**4.71**	**3.88**	**3.41**	**3.11**	**2.90**	**2.73**	**2.60**	**2.50**	**2.41**	**2.34**	**2.28**
400	3.86	3.02	2.62	2.39	2.23	2.12	2.03	1.96	1.90	1.85	1.81	1.78
	6.70	**4.66**	**3.83**	**3.36**	**3.06**	**2.85**	**2.69**	**2.55**	**2.46**	**2.37**	**2.29**	**2.23**
1000	3.85	3.00	2.61	2.38	2.22	2.10	2.02	1.95	1.89	1.84	1.80	1.76
	6.66	**4.62**	**3.80**	**3.34**	**3.04**	**2.82**	**2.66**	**2.53**	**2.43**	**2.34**	**2.26**	**2.20**
∞	3.84	2.59	2.60	2.37	2.21	2.09	2.01	1.94	1.88	1.83	1.79	1.75
	6.64	**4.60**	**3.78**	**3.32**	**3.02**	**2.80**	**2.64**	**2.51**	**2.41**	**2.32**	**2.24**	**2.18**

The function, $F = \alpha$ with exponent 2, is computed in part from Fisher's table VI (7). Additional entries are by interpolation, mostly graphical.

Source: Adapted from George W. Snedecor, *Statistical Methods* (Ames, Iowa: Iowa State College Press, 1946), pp. 222–225.

References

Allport, G. W., Vernon, P. E., & Lindzey, G. (1951). *Study of values* (rev. ed.). Test booklets with manual. Boston: Houghton Mifflin.

Anderson, N. H. (1962). Application of an additive model to impression formation. *Science, 138,* 817–818.

Andrich, D. A. (1978). A rating formulation for ordered response categories. *Psychometrika, 43,* 561–573.

Bennett, J. F., & Hays, W. L. (1960). Multidimensional unfolding: Determining the dimensionality of ranked preference data. *Psychometrika, 25,* 27–43.

Bergman, G., & Spence, K. W. (1944). The logic of psychphysical measurement. *Psychological Review, 51,* 1–24.

Binet, A., & Simon, T. (1916). *The development of intelligence in children* (E. S. Kite, trans.). Vineland, NJ: Publications of the Training School, Number 11, 336.

Bontempo, R. (1993). Translation fidelity of psychological scales. *Journal of Cross-cultural Psychology, 24,* 149–166.

Boring, E. G. (1945). The use of operational definitions in science. *Psychological Review, 52,* 243–255.

Brownless, V. T., & Keats, J. A. (1958). A re-test method of studying partial knowledge and other factors influencing item response. *Psychometrika.*

Buros, O. K. (1977). *The Tenth Mental Measurement Yearbook.* Highland Park, NJ: Mental Measurement Yearbook.

Campbell, N. R. (1957). *Foundations of science* (formerly Physics: The elements, 1917). New York: Dover.

Carroll, J. B. (1994). Factor analysis since Spearman. In R. Kanter, P. L. Ackerman, & R. Kreck (Eds.), *The Minnesota Symposium on Learning and Individual Differences: Abilities, Motivation, and Methodology.* Hillsdale, NJ: Lawrence Erlbaum Associates.

Cattell, J. McK (1890). Mental tests and measurements. *Mind, 15,* 373–381.

Cliff, N. (1972). Consistencies among judgments of adjective combinations. In A. K. Romney, R. N. Shepard, & S. B. Nerlove (Eds.), *Multidimensional scaling: Theory and applications in the behavioral sciences,* Vol. II. New York: Seminar Press.

Cliff, N. (1975). Complete orders from incomplete data: Interactive ordering and tailored testing. *Psychological Bulletin, 82*, 289–302.

Cliff, N. (1977). A theory of consistency of ordering generalizable to tailored testing. *Psychometrika, 42*, 375–399.

Cliff, N. (1979). Test theory without true scores? *Psychometrika, 44*(4), 373–393.

Cliff, N. (1983). Evaluating Guttman scales: Some old and new thoughts. In H. Wainer & S. Messick (Eds.), *Principals of modern psychological measurement: A festschrift for Frederic M. Lord* (pp. 283–301). Hillsdale, NJ: Lawrence Erlbaum Associates.

Cliff, N. (1989). Ordinal consistency and ordinal true scores. *Psychometrika, 54*, 75–91.

Cliff, N. (1991). Ordinal methods in the assessment of change. In L. M. Collins & J. L. Horn (Eds.), *Best methods for the analysis of change* (pp. 34–46). Washington, DC: American Psychological Association.

Cliff, N. (1992). Abstract measurement theory and the revolution that never happened. *Psychological Science, 3*, 186–190.

Cliff, N. (1993). What is and isn't measurement. In G. Keren & C. Lewis (Eds.), *A handbook for data analysis in the social and behavioral sciences: Methodological issues* (pp. 59–93). Hillsdale, NJ: Lawrence Erlbaum Associates.

Cliff, N. (1994). Predicting ordinal relations. *British Journal of Mathematical and Statistical Psychology, 47*, 127–150.

Cliff, N. (1996). *Ordinal methods for behavioral data analysis.* Mahwah, NJ: Lawrence Erlbaum Associates.

Cliff, N., Collins, L. M., Zatkin, J., Gallipeau, D., & McCormick, D. J. (1988). An ordinal scaling method for questionnaire and other ordinal data. *Applied Psychological Measurement, 12*, 83–97.

Cliff, N., & Donoghue, J. R. (1992). Ordinal test theory estimated by an item-sampling model. *Psychometrika, 57*, 217–236.

Cliff, N., & Keats, J. A. (2000). *Validity of score differences from simple assumptions.* Unpublished manuscript.

Cliff, N., & Young, F. W. (1968). On the relations between unidimensional judgments and multidimensional scaling. *Organizational Behavior and Human Performance, 3*, 269–285.

Collins, L. M., & Cliff, N. (1985). Axiomatic foundations of a three-set Guttman simplex model with applicability to longitudinal data. *Psychometrika, 50*, 147–158.

Cook, W. D., & Kress, M. (1990). An *m*th generation model for weak ranking of players in a tournament. *Journal of the Operations Research Society, 41*, 1111–1119.

Coombs, C. H. (1951). *A theory of psychological scaling.* University of Michigan Engineering Research Institute Bulletin, *34*(6), 94.

Coombs, C. H. (1964). *A theory of data.* New York: Wiley.

Cronbach, L. J. (1951). Coefficient alpha and the internal structure of tests. *Psychometrika, 16*, 297–334.

Cronbach, L. J., Gleser, G. C., Nanda, H., & Rajaratnam, N. (1973). *The dependability of behavioral measurements: Theory of generalizability of scores and profiles.* New York: Wiley.

Cronbach, L. J., Rajaratnam, N., & Gleser, G. C. (1963). Theory of generalizability: A liberalization of reliability theory. *British Journal of Statistical Psychology, 16*, 137–163.

David, H. A. (1987). Ranking from unbalanced paired comparisons data. *Biometrika, 74*, 432–436.

Davidson, J. A. (1972). A geometrical analysis of the unfolding model: Nondegenerative solutions. *Psychometrika, 37*, 193–216.

Davidson, J. A. (1973). A geometrical analysis of the unfolding model: general solutions. *Psychometrika, 38*, 305–336.

de Gruijter, D. N. M., & van der Kamp, L. J. Th. (1984). *Statistical models in psychological and educational testing.* Lisse: Swets & Zeitlinger.

Ducamp, A., & Falmagne, J.-C. (1968). Composite measurement. *Journal of Mathematical Psychology, 6,* 359–390.

Embretson, S. E. (1999). Issues in the measurement of cognitive abilities. In S. E. Embretson & S. L. Hershberger (Eds.), *The new rules of measurement* (pp. 1–15). Mahwah, NJ: Lawrence Erlbaum Associates.

Embretson, S. E., & Hershberger, S. (1999). *New rules of measurement.* Mahwah, NJ: Lawrence Erlbaum Associates.

Fechner, G. T. (1860). *Elemente der psychophysik.* Leipzig: Breitkopf & Hartel.

Frederiksen, N. (1966). In-basket tests and factors in administrative performance. In A. Anastasi (Ed.), *Testing problems in perspective* (pp. 208–221). Washington, DC: American Council on Education.

Green, B. F. (1956). A method of scalagram analysis using summary statistics. *Psychometrika,* 79–88.

Green, P. E., & Carmone, F. J. (1972). Marketing research applications of nonmetric multidimensional scaling methods. In A. K. Romney, R. N. Shepard, & S. B. Nerlove (Eds.), *Multidimensional scaling: Theory and Applications* (Vol. II, pp. –). New York: Seminar Press.

Gulliksen, H. (1946). Paired comparisons and the logic of measurement. *Psychological Review, 53,* 199–213.

Gulliksen, H. (1950). *Theory of mental tests.* New York: Wiley.

Gulliksen, H., & Tucker, L. R. (1961). A general procedure for obtaining paired comparisons from multiple rank orders. *Psychometrika, 26,* 173–183.

Guilford, J. P. (1954). *Psychometric methods.* New York: McGraw-Hill.

Guttman, L. (1947). The Cornell method for scale and intensity analysis. *Educational and Psychological Measurement, 7,* 247–279.

Guttman, L. (1971). Measurement as structural theory. *Psychometrika, 36,* 329–347.

Hambleton, R. K., Yu, J.-Y., & Slater, S. C. (1999). Fieldtest of the ITC guidelines for adapting educational and psychological tests. *European Journal of Psychological Assessment, 15,* 270–276.

Harrington, G. M. (1985). Developmental perspectives, behavior-genetic analysis, and models of the individual. In C. J. Brainerd & V. F. Reyna (Eds.), *Developmental psychology.* Amsterdam: North Holland Press.

Ho, S. W. (1998). *Validation of the "kiasu" typology—A five-nation comparison.* Unpublished masters thesis, University of Newcastle, Australia.

Ho, S. W., Munro, D., & Carr, S. C. (1999). Kiasuism across cultures: Singapore and Australia. In J.-C. Lasry, J. Adair, & K. Dion (Eds.), *Latest contributions to cross-cultural psychology* (pp. 212–227). Lisse: Swets & Zeitlinger.

Holland, P. W., & Thayer, D. T. (1988). Differential item performance and the Mantel-Haenszel procedure. In H. Wainer & H. I. Braun (Eds.), *Test validity.* Hillsdale, NJ: Lawrence Erlbaum Associates.

Hotelling, H. (1933). Analysis of a complex of statistical variables into principal components. *Journal of Educational Psychology, 24,* 417–441, 498–520.

Jackson, D. N., & Messick, S. (1962). Response styles in the MMPI: Comparison of clinical and normal samples. *Journal of Abnormal and Social Psychology, 65,* 285–299.

Jackson, D. N., & Messick, S. (1967). Response styles and the assessment of psychopathology. In D. N. Jackson & S. Messick (Eds.), *Problems in human assessment* (pp. 541–558). New York: McGraw-Hill.

Jeanrie, C., & Bertrand, R. (1999). Translating tests with the ITC Guidelines: Keeping validity in mind. *European Journal of Psychological Assessment, 15,* 277–283.

Jensen, A. R. (1980). *Bias in mental testing.* New York: Free Press.

Keats, J. A. (1957). Estimation of error variances of test scores. *Psychometrika, 22,* 29–41.

Keats, J. A. (1962). Attitudes towards idealized types in Australia and Malaya. *Journal of Social Psychology,* 353–362.

Keats, J. A. (1964a). A method of treating individual differences in multidimensional scaling. *British Journal of Statistical Psychology*, 37–50.

Keats, J. A. (1964b). Some generalizations of a theoretical distribution of mental test scores. *Psychometrika, 29*, 215–231.

Keats, J. A. (1967). Test theory. In O. Farnsworth & Q. McNemar (Eds.), *Annual Review of Psychology, 18*, 217–238.

Keats, J. A. (1972). *An introduction to quantitative psychology.* Sydney, Australia: Wiley.

Keats, J. A. (1985). Operational and psychometric approaches to the study of intellectual abilities. In C. J. Brainerd & V. F. Reyna (Eds.), *Developmental psychology* (pp. 189–200). Amsterdam: North Holland.

Keats, J. A. (1995). Justification of the scoring procedures for dichotomous and other polytomous items. *Australian Psychologist.*

Keats, J. A. (1997). The use of ordinal test theory in cross-cultural research in behavioural science. *South Pacific Journal of Psychology*, 20–30.

Keats, J. A., Biddle, B. J., Keats, D. M., Bank, B. J., Hauge, R., Wan, R., & Valantin, S. (1983). Parents, friends, siblings and adults: Unfolding referent other importance data for adolescents. *International Journal of Psychology*, 239–262.

Keats, J. A., & Lord, F. M. (1962). A theoretical distribution of mental test scores. *Psychometrika, 27*, 59–72.

Keats, J. A., & Munro, D. (1992). The use of the test-retest method to study guessing, partial knowledge, learning and memory in performance on multiple choice tests. *Bulletin of the International Test Commission, 19*, 85–98.

Kehoe, J. F., & Cliff, N. (1975). INTERORD: A computer-interactive Fortran program for developing simple orders. *Educational and Psychological Measurement, 35*, 676–678.

Kelley, T. L. (1914). Comparable measures. *Journal of Educational Psychology, 5*, 589–595.

Kelley, T. L. (1947). *Fundamentals of statistics.* Cambridge, MA: Harvard University Press.

Kelly, R. L. (1903). Studies from the psychological laboratoriy of the University of Chicago. Psychophysical tests of normal and abnormal children. *Psychological Review, 10*, 345–372.

Kendall, M. G. (1955). Further contributions to the theory of paired comparisons. *Biometrics, 11*, 43–62.

Kendall, M. G. (1975). *Rank correlation methods.* London: C. Griffin.

Kirkpatrick, E. A. (1900). Individual tests of school children. *Psychological Review, 7*, 274–280.

Krantz, D. H., Luce, R. D., Suppes, P., & Tversky, A. (1971). *Foundations of measurement: Vol. 1.* New York: Academic Press.

Kuder, G. F., & Richardson, M. W. (1937). The theory of the estimation of test reliability. *Psychometrika, 2*, 151–160.

Lee, S. Y., Poon, W. Y., & Bentler, P. M. (1990). A three-stage estimation procedure for structural equation models with polytomous variables. *Psychometrika*, 45–51.

Likert, R. A. (1932). A technique for the measurement of attitudes. *Archives of Psychology, 140*, 52.

Loevinger, J. (1948). The technique of homogeneous tests compared with some aspects of "scale analysis" and factor analysis. *Psychological Bulletin, 45*, 507–529.

Loevinger, J. (1954). The attenuation paradox in test theory. *Psychological Bulletin, 51*, 493–504.

Lord, F. M. (1962). Cutting scores and errors of measurement. *Psychometrika, 27*, 19–30.

Lord, F. M. (1965). A strong true score theory, with applications. *Psychometrika, 30*, 239–270.

Lord, F. M., & Novick, M. R. (1968). *Statistical theories of mental test scores.* Reading, MA: Addison-Wesley.

Luce, R. D., & Tukey, J. W. (1964). Simultaneous conjoint measurement: A new type of fundamental measurement. *Journal of Mathematical Psychology, 1*, 1–27.

McDonald, R. P. (1985). *Factor analysis and related methods.* Hillsdale, NJ: Lawrence Erlbaum Associates.

McDonald, R. P. (1999). *Test theory: A unified treatment.* Mahwah, NJ: Lawrence Erlbaum Associates.

McElwain, D. W., & Keats, J. A. (1961). Multidimensional unfolding: Some geometrical solutions. *Psychometrika, 26,* 325–332.

Mellenbergh, G. J. (1982). Contingency table models for assessing item bias. *Journal of Educational Statistics, 7,* 105–107.

Miccieri, T. (1989). The unicorn, the normal curve and other improbable creatures. *Psychological Bulletin, 105,* 156–166.

Michell, J. (1990). *An introduction to the logic of measurement.* Hillsdale, NJ: Lawrence Erlbaum Associates.

Mokken, R. J. (1971). *A theory and procedure of scale analysis.* Den Haag: Mouton.

Mollenkopf, W. (1950). Variation of the standard error of measurement. *Psychometrika, 15,* 189–229.

Muniz, J., Cuesta, M., Paz, D., Navas, M. J., & Barbero, I. (1992). Dimensionality invariance. *Bulletin of the International Test Commission,* 181–190.

Narens, L., & Luce, R. D. (1993). Further comments on the 'nonrevolution' arising from axiomatic measurement theory. *Psychological Science, 4,* 127–130.

Otis, A. S. (1917). A criticism of the Yerkes-Bridges point scale, with alternative suggestions. *Journal of Educational Psychology, 8,* 129–150.

Pfister, H. P. (1995). New techology for administering group tests. *Australian Psychologist, 30,* 24–26.

Piaget, J. (1947). *The psychology of intelligence.* London: Routledge and Kegan Paul.

Porteus, S. D. (1915). Mental tests for the feebleminded. A new series. *Journal of Psycho-Asthenics, 19,* 200–213.

Rasch, G. (1960). *Probabilistic models for some intelligence and attainment tests.* Copenhagen: Danish Institute for Educational Research.

Reynolds, T. J., & Cliff, N. (1975). IRIS: A computer-interactive APL program for recovering simple orders. *Educational and Psychological Measurement, 35,* 671–675.

Reynolds, T. J., & Cliff, N. (1984). An interactive preference ordering model and its Monte Carlo evaluation. *Psychometrika, 49,* 247–256.

Roberts, F. S. (1970). On nontransitive indifference. *Journal of Mathematical Psychology, 7,* 243–258.

Roberts, F. S. (1971). Homogeneous families of semiorders and the theory of probabilistic consistency. *Journal of Mathematical Psychology, 8,* 248–263.

Rokeach, M. (1973). *The nature of human values.* New York: The Free Press.

Rosenzweig, S. (1960). The Rosenzweig picture frustation study, children's form. In A. I. Rohm & M. R. Haworth (Eds.), *Projective techniques with children.* New York: Grune & Stratton.

Rothwell, J. W., & Miller, K. M. (1988). *Rothwell-Miller Interest Blank.* Melbourne: A.C.E.R.

Shaw, M. E., & Wright, J. M. (1967). *Scales for the measurement of attitudes.* New York: McGraw-Hill.

Spearman, C. (1904). The proof and measurement of association between two things. *American Journal of Psychology, 15,* 72–101.

Stern, W. (1914). *The psychological method of testing intelligence* (G. M. Whipple, Trans.). Baltimore: Warwick & York.

Stevens, S. S. (1951). Mathematics, measurement and psychophysics. In S. S. Stevens (Ed.), *Handbook of experimental psychology* (pp. 1–49). New York: Wiley.

Tanzer, N. K., & Sim, C. Q. E. (1999). Adapting instruments for use in multiple languages and cultures: A review of the ITC guidelines for test adaptations. *European Journal of Psychological Assessment,* 258–269.

Tomkins, S. S. (1952). A discussion of "Personality structure and personality measurement" of R. B. Cattell. In H. S. Dyer (Ed.), *Proceedings of the 1951 Invitational Conference on Testing Problems* (pp. 97–107). Princeton: ETS.

Torgerson, W. (1952). Multidimensional scaling: I. Theory and method. *Psychometrika, 17,* 401–418.

Torgerson, W. (1958). *Theory and methods of scaling.* New York: Wiley.

Thorndike, R. M., & Lohman, D. F. (1990). *A century of ability testing.* Chicago: The Riverside Publishing Company.

Van der Vijver, F., & Hambleton, R. (1996). Translating tests: Some practical guidelines. *European Psychologist, 1,* 89–99.

Verweij, A. C. (1994). *Scaling transitivity inference in 7–12 year old children.* Amsterdam: Free University.

Wechsler, D. (1939). *The measurement of adult intelligence.* Baltimore: Williams and Wilkins.

Wechsler, D. (1997). *Wechsler Adult Intelligence Scale—Third Edition.* San Antonio, TX: Psychological Corp.

Woodworth, R. S. (1938). *Experimental psychology.* New York: Holt.

Wundt, W. (1896/1907). *Outline of psychology* (C. H. Judd, Trans.). Leipzig: Engelmann.

Zhang, H.-C. (1992). Problems in using foreign tests in China. *Bulletin of the International Test Commission, 19,* 173–180.

Author Index

Subject Index